AMERICAN LITERATURE
In Nineteenth-Century
ENGLAND

AMERICAN LITERATURE
In Nineteenth-Century
ENGLAND

By CLARENCE GOHDES

New York : Morningside Heights
COLUMBIA UNIVERSITY PRESS
1944

To Celestine

PREFACE

THE PRESENT VOLUME is the first ever written with the purpose of proving the wide interest in American literature displayed by the English people. It is meant primarily for specialists in American literary history, for students of the Victorian Age, and for political historians who are particularly interested in Anglo-American relations.

While the study is confined to the nineteenth century, it will be apparent that most of the illustrations come from the period following the Reform Bill of 1832. There are two reasons for the limitation. First, the consumption of American books in England before 1833 was insignificant compared with that which followed later; and, secondly, the late William B. Cairns has already provided a number of able studies concerned especially with British criticisms of American writings prior to 1833. There are many aspects of the reception of American literature among the British which are either neglected altogether or merely mentioned incidentally in this volume, for example, the record of the enormous quantity of American plays which were produced in London. The failure to cover more terrain in my studies is a natural consequence of the hugeness of my topic. *Ubi ingenium par materiae?* It will be found, also, that a large share of my attention has been claimed by the history of the English book-trade. This is due to my belief that literary history, especially that of the nineteenth century, which merely records critical opinions and forgets that publishing was a business conducted for profit is as flimsy as the study of psychology without reference to the nervous system.

The method of this book probably needs initial elucidation, for it may seem to be merely a collection of essays. In the Introduction I have retraced the general view of the United States held by the British during the century and have offered the suggestion that the literature of the United States has a "great tradition" of its own, a tradition which, it is hoped, will enhance interest in the record of its impact upon the English. In the following chapter, by presenting certain particulars in the history of the booktrade I have undertaken to show how and why so many books by our authors came to the attention of British readers. I have next illustrated the importance of American magazines to our transmarine cousins and of American writers for their periodicals. After these very broad surveys I have narrowed the field to one type of literary production, namely, humor, a type which was very cordially received in the British Isles despite the "vulgar error" that an Englishman cannot understand a joke. Then, in the next chapter, I have restricted the point of view still further by concentrating upon just one author, Longfellow. I should have preferred to use instead Emerson or Whitman, but my choice was determined not only by the very great popularity of Longfellow but by my desire to break virgin soil in my researches. The final chapter attempts a cursory review of the critical reaction to American literature during the entire century and ends with a brief indication that it was not altogether without influence. It should be remembered that an entire monograph could easily be written on each of my chapter-topics. I have intended to present in simple exposition the broadest features of the topics along with a variety of particulars which serve as concrete illustrations. By using the index a reader especially interested in the British reputation of only one of our major authors may find it possible to reconstruct from the scattered illustrations a "partial portrait," to use the apt phrase of Henry James.

During the years which have been devoted to the preparation of this work I have often profited by the kindness of others. Librarians have been especially helpful, and I wish to express my gratitude to the staffs of the following institutions: the Library of Congress, the New York Public Library, the Huntington Library, the Harvard College Library, the Columbia University Library, and, last but not least, the Library of Duke University. To Mr. F. L. Kent, Assistant-Keeper of Books in the British Museum, I am obligated for bibliographical information assembled by himself or by Mrs. Kent. To Mr. Frederick B. Tolles, Mr. Ellis Raesly, Miss Ellen Frey, Miss Amy Cruse, and Professor Richard H. Heindel, I am grateful for various types of information. Professor Emery E. Neff, Professor Paull F. Baum, Professor Howard F. Lowry, Professor Lewis Leary, and Mr.

J. Lee Harlan have read the entire first draft of this book; and Professor Walter Blair, Professor Walter Graham, Mr. Henry W. L. Dana, Mr. David K. Jackson, Mr. Alfred Knopf, and Mr. Frederic G. Melcher have gone over various of the individual chapters. To each of these gentlemen my thanks for valuable suggestions and criticisms. The Research Council of Duke University has in its kindness seen fit to supply funds for the employment of research assistants and typists.

Miss Mildred Howells has generously allowed me to quote from various books by her father, William Dean Howells; and permissions have been obtained from the following publishers for quotations from the works specified: Houghton Mifflin Company (Charles E. Stowe, *Life of Harriet Beecher Stowe*); Harper & Brothers (*The Correspondence of John Lothrop Motley*, ed. G. W. Curtis, and *Mark Twain's Letters*, ed. Albert Bigelow Paine); The Macmillan Company (Frederic Harrison, *Autobiographic Memories*, and Alfred Austin, "A Voice from the West"); Longmans, Green and Co. (Charles H. E. Brookfield, *Random Reminiscences*, and *Letters to William Allingham*, ed. H. Allingham and E. B. Williams); Ernest Benn, Ltd. (*Mary Russell Mitford: Correspondence with Charles Boner & John Ruskin*, ed. Elizabeth Lee).

CONTENTS

INTRODUCTION 1

I. THE BOOKTRADE 14

II. THE PERIODICALS 47

III. HUMOR 71

IV. LONGFELLOW 99

V. OF CRITICS AND INFLUENCE 127

APPENDIX 151

INDEX 181

INTRODUCTION: THE BRITISH ATTITUDE

ᵔ

"Cultured persons complain that the society there is vulgar, less agreeable to the delicate tastes of delicately trained minds. But it is infinitely preferable to the ordinary worker"—JOSEPH CHAMBERLAIN.

THE ATTITUDE of one nation toward another represents a congeries of contradictions based largely on ignorance and prejudice, with a constant succession of storm centers of high emotional intensity provoked by political events. As a result, one who wishes to map the course of international feeling must speak as Sir Oracle—and pray that no dogs bark.

There was much in the nineteenth century to draw the United States and its mother country together. Despite the confusion of races seething in our melting pot the English element was at all times dominant. As late as 1920, even after the tremendous influx of the "new" immigration, it was decided that 51 percent of the population of our country was of Colonial extraction. As important as the quantitative dominance of British blood was the cultural dominance of British literature, law, and speech, the community of language being the most significant of all. Then, too, there was trade, next to language the most universal solvent, as well as creator, of international ill feeling. Countless millions of English pounds sought, and found, an increase in the Magna Graecia of the West. Even Carlyle, who objected to democracy on the ground that it gave Jesus Christ and Judas Iscariot the same vote, had investments in America, which, unlike those of Sydney Smith, were profitable to a high degree. All through the century Englishmen with money to sow reaped a harvest in the nation acting its epic of finance in the rounding out of a continent. At the opposite end of the economic scale were the hosts of the poor whose relatives and friends had followed the course of empire in such amazing numbers—three millions of them before Victoria had ruled for thirty years. Such people must have provided the largest mass of British friends of America.

On the other hand, there was much to keep the apple of discord rolling in the center. The animosities engendered by the Revolution and the War of 1812, the Anglophobia of the Jacksonian democrats and the Irish-Americans, the conflicts of opinion over the boundaries of Maine, Oregon, and Alaska, the Trent Affair, the Alabama Claims, quarrels over fish, fur, and tariff, word battles involving Cuba and Venezuela—all these are reminders that during the century the United States squabbled more with England than with any nation of Europe. More consequential than the gusts of emotion in provoking international bad feeling was the sensitivity of the average American to European opinion of himself and the concomitant supercilious, disdainful, and condescending, if not always directly hostile, air of the British ruling classes, whose opinions as expressed in speeches, in sermons, in books of travel, or in the London *Times* were received as the gruff voice of John Bull himself. For most of the nineteenth century an established church viewed the United States as a strange confusion of dissenting sects; West End society pronounced Americans to be vulgar; the leisured class which was comfortably settled in the "gilded bondage of the country house" looked in vain for a kindred set across the ocean; a political hierarchy, whether Whig or Tory, feared democracy as it feared the plague. British officials marvelled at the lack of diplomacy displayed by the American government and its drably dressed ministers; army officers had scant respect for Indian fighters and admired the tactics of the rebel Lee; their naval brethren found little to learn of us until the heyday of Captain Mahan. Oxford and Cambridge men were almost totally ignorant of the nature of American colleges and scarcely felt a need for the study of American history—the United States was so recent a foundation it hardly had a past worth considering. Sportsmen were indeed interested in American hunting, but it was the wild turkey or the buffalo rather than the hunter about whom they sought to learn. Until late in the century these "classes" were the voice of England: the friends or relatives of émigrés, the tradesmen, or the minor journalists had little part in expressing the official attitude toward the younger nation.[1] Washington Irving's essay "English Writers on America"

[1] An Englishman has described Parliament as "relatively aristocratic" up to 1906 (R. C. K. Ensor, *England 1870–1914,* Oxford, 1936, p. 496).

(1820) dwelt on the "eagerness and unhesitating faith" with which the aristocracy received the gross misrepresentations of even the coarsest writers who dealt with the United States; and James Russell Lowell provided the classic denunciation of their attitude in 1869 with his article "On a Certain Condescension in Foreigners." Even after 1870 when the onslaughts against the United States were fewer and more discreetly guised, the cat was sometimes loosed from the bag. In 1874, for example, a reviewer observed in passing: "We are apt to look on Yankees in the mass as vulgar, sectarian, swaggering, democratic, money-worshipping folk, who have degraded the English language to a colonial level"; and Ruskin added to the picture a missing element:

England taught the Americans all they have of speech or thought, hitherto. What thoughts they have not learned from England are foolish thoughts; what words they have not learned from England, unseemly words; the vile among them not being able even to be humorous parrots, but only obscene mocking-birds.[2]

No event exhibited the fundamental cleavage between the English upper classes and the American people better than the Civil War, when even a mind like Charles Darwin's was converted to the official British view. John Bright, in a letter to the historian Motley, provided an acute analysis:

Coming down from the War of Independence and from the war of 1815, there has also been in this country a certain jealousy of yours. It has been felt by the ruling class that your escape from George III and our Aristocratic Government had been followed by a success and a progress of which England could offer no example. The argument could not be avoided, if Englishmen west of the Atlantic can prosper without Crown, without Lords, without Church, without a great territorial class with feudal privileges, and without all this or these can become great and happy, how long will Englishmen in England continue to think these things necessary for them? Any argument in favour of freedom here, drawn from your example, was hateful to the ruling class; and therefore it is not to be wondered at that a great disaster happening to your country and to its constitution should not be regarded as a great calamity by certain influential classes here.[3]

---

[2] *Dublin Review,* XXIII (July, 1874), 68; *Fors Clavigera* for June 1, 1874.

[3] March 9, 1863, *The Correspondence of John Lothrop Motley,* ed. G. W. Curtis, New York, 1889, II, 120. Cf. George Ticknor's similar diagnosis in a letter to B. R.

At Cambridge, the more "liberal" of the universities, Leslie Stephen, who was an exception to the rule, found that his friends would hardly speak to him after a Northern victory; but he had the dubious pleasure of inciting elderly Tories to declare that they would "rather have heard of the British Guards being annihilated by the French" than learn of a defeat of the Southern army.[4] Even when the English in general were profoundly shocked at the assassination of Abraham Lincoln there were those staunch churchmen who felt that he perhaps deserved his fate because he had attended the theatre on Good Friday.[5] In 1866 a Liverpool gentleman offered to endow a Cambridge lectureship on American "history, literature, and institutions," with the stipulation that the President and Fellows of Harvard nominate the lecturer. Knowing the grave fears of democracy regnant in academic minds, the sponsors of the measure merely offered a motion to the Senate that "by way of experiment" one of the rooms of the university be put at the disposal of the contemplated instructor "for a single course of lectures." Charles Kingsley, who in 1862 as Regius Professor of Modern History had worked up a course on American history without any knowledge of the subject, issued a broadside in favor of the motion in which he argued, incidentally, that a study of the United States would be an effective method of combating any attempts to "Americanize" England. When the Senate met they began by "bemoaning themselves about democracy" until one of them "luckily discovered for the first time" that Harvard had a connection with the Unitarian church. The charge of Socinianism did the business, and the motion was lost by one hundred and ten votes to eighty-two.[6]

Curtis, May 12, 1857 (*Life, Letters and Journals of George Ticknor*, Boston, 1877, II, 402). J. S. Mill's views were akin to those of Bright. See also Leslie Stephen, *Some Early Impressions*, London, 1924, pp. 87–88.

[4] F. W. Maitland, *The Life and Letters of Leslie Stephen*, New York and London, 1906, pp. 148, 158. For a history of the British reaction during our Civil War, see Donaldson Jordan and Edwin J. Pratt, *Europe and the American Civil War*, Boston and New York, 1931, Part I.

[5] *The Hardman Papers: a Further Selection (1865–1868) from the Letters and Memoirs of Sir William Hardman*, ed. S. M. Ellis, London, 1930, pp. 12 ff., 18–19.

[6] Maitland, *op. cit.*, pp. 175–177; and *Charles Kingsley: His Letters and Memories of His Life*, ed. his wife, London, 1877, II, 134, 228–229. In 1879–1880 the lectures on the United States delivered by John Fiske at London University and the Royal Institution were notably successful (*The Letters of John Fiske*, ed. Ethel F. Fisk, New York, 1940, pp. 391 ff., 441 ff.).

But the Civil War and the perfervid discussions of the "American question," which alone had prompted Kingsley to attempt lectures on the United States at Cambridge, undoubtedly served to dispel a bit of British ignorance concerning the new country across the sea; and the eventual victory of the Northern forces set at nought the proclamations of the upper classes that such a government could not endure. Traditional political conservatism was rocked to its foundations; the *Times* "sacked" its chief American correspondent who had been so wrong in telling its readers what they wanted to believe; and the radicals, for years merely a kind of tail on the Whig party, were to have their inning. Young Henry Adams, rejoicing in the turn of events, in 1865 boldly claimed that America now wielded "a prodigious influence on European politics," and with the election to Parliament of such friends of America as J. S. Mill and Tom Hughes, prophesied: "Our influence on England will be strong enough to carry a new reform through within ten years. . . . Piece by piece the only feudal and middle-age harness will drop off, that remains." [7] The harness did drop off, with astonishing speed, and the experience and example of the United States may not have been without influence. Disraeli's Act of 1867 opened the first notable breach in the narrow franchise of 1832, a breach widened with the Ballot Act of 1872 and the extension of the voting privilege in 1884. The British government, which in the forties had spent less on public education than the city of Boston, laid the groundwork for national elementary schools in the summer of 1870; and the next year a University Tests Act robbed the Church of England of another medieval trapping by throwing open for the first time all lay posts in the colleges to men of all creeds on equal terms.

In the *Pickwick Papers* the elder Weller concocted a plan for the escape of the hero by concealing him in a piano, and then suggested: "Have a passage ready taken for 'Merriker. . . . Let the gov'ner stop there, till Mrs. Bardell's dead . . . and then let him come back and write a book about the 'Merrikins as'll pay all his expenses and more,

[7] *Letters of Henry Adams (1858–1891)*, ed. W. C. Ford, Boston and New York [1930], pp. 120–122. Matthew Arnold in 1865 admitted that "American example is perhaps likely to make most impression on England . . ." but he doubted its immediate effect (*Letters of Matthew Arnold 1848–1888*, ed. George W. E. Russell, London, 1895, I, 245).

if he blows 'em up enough." Dickens, himself, like many another, found that there was truth in the suggestion. But by the time the new reforms had reshaped British political life the English travellers to America who wrote books needed to be on the lookout lest they blow up something which they might find also at home.[8] Even Matthew Arnold in commenting on the shortcomings of American civilization reminded himself that he could find in his own country "an upper class materialized, a middle class vulgarized, and a lower class brutalized." [9] Late in the century there was an increase in the tribe of travel-book writers who, like William Archer, were inclined to praise almost everything American, from a Columbia seminar to George Ade, and to acknowledge the prevalence of "journalese" in English vocabularies as well as American.[10]

A new era in Anglo-American relations begins about 1870, when the ruling classes of England were convinced that the "republican experiment" was not doomed to failure and when the British government really began to shape itself into a democracy. One may attribute something of the more favorable attitude of the upper classes toward the United States to a variety of factors, such as the frequent Anglo-American marriages, the rise in immigration to America from the United Kingdom, the furtherance of trade back and forth between the two countries, the amazing increase in the population and wealth of the United States,[11] the growth of an imperialism which forced Britain to look for a friend, and, more specifically, the threatening ascendancy of Germany in Continental Europe. But perhaps the most potent force of all was the fact that life in England came to be more and more like life in the United States, with the spread of middle-class capitalism and the rise to power of the common man, a rise which was accompanied by an ever-increasing diffusion of intellectual

---

[8] Cf. Allan Nevins, *American Social History as Recorded by British Travellers,* New York [1931], pp. 425 ff.

[9] *Civilization in the United States,* 1888, Part IV. In 1885 he had written his American daughter that England would come "more and more" to the social conditions of the United States (*Letters,* II, 289).

[10] *America To-Day,* London, 1900, p. 179.

[11] United Kingdom in millions: (1821) 20.8, (1871) 31.8, (1881) 35.2, (1891) 38.1, (1901) 41.9; United States: (1820) 9.6, (1870) 38.5, (1880) 50.1, (1890) 62.6, (1900) 75.9.

mediocrity. But the "classes" were still not without influence; *flecti—non frangi* was their motto, and the cause of their strength.

At the same time that the condescension or hostility toward the United States on the part of the British classes became less overt and in many cases disappeared, in America the "society" of the Atlantic Seaboard, the colleges in the same region, and the intellectuals in general became increasingly Anglophile, in part perhaps as a means of escape from the swarms of new immigrants babbling in unknown tongues. The similar folk of the West followed suit; there was many a Charles Eliot Norton *in parvo* in the new universities on the prairie. Long before the Civil War Lowell had warned his literary countrymen in *A Fable for Critics:*

> Though you brag of your New World, you don't half believe in it;
> And as much of the Old as is possible weave in it;
> Your goddess of freedom, a tight, buxom girl,
> With lips like a cherry and teeth like a pearl,
> With eyes bold as Herë's, and hair floating free,
> And full of the sun as the spray of the sea,
> Who can sing at a husking or romp at a shearing,
> Who can trip through the forests alone without fearing,
> Who can drive home the cows with a song through the grass,
> Keeps glancing aside into Europe's cracked glass,
> Hides her red hands in gloves, pinches up her lithe waist,
> And makes herself wretched with transmarine taste.

Emerson had also observed: "The object of education in the United States seems to be to fit persons to travel in Europe," and after 1870 there was yet more than a half-truth in the utterance, as any reader of Henry James or even Mark Twain can see.

One of the evidences of a decline in the antagonism of the upper classes of England toward the United States after the Civil War was the appearance of attempts to better Anglo-American relations through the establishment of English-speaking Unions and similar organizations. Early in 1871 an Anglo-American Association was formed, with Thomas Hughes as chairman. A chief difficulty in the way of its progress, he thought, was "the lamentable ignorance of contemporary American history," an ignorance which James Bryce was soon to try to dispel with his *American Commonwealth* (1888).

Conan Doyle in 1891 dedicated his *White Company* "to the Hope of the Future, the Reunion of English-speaking Races," and, in the exciting days of our war with Spain, Anglo-American Leagues and Alliances sprang up like magic. Even a Bishop of London wrote in 1898: "The question of the future of the world is the existence of the Anglo-Saxon civilization on a religious basis"; and a prominent dissenting clergyman, Hugh Price Hughes, conceived an Imperial Anglo-Saxon Federation in which Methodism would lead the way to harmony. As the century ended, Walter Besant sponsored an Atlantic Union to unite the professional classes of the Colonies and the States with the corresponding elements in the United Kingdom. The year 1898 was an Annus Mirabilis in the history of Anglo-American relations, with the Laureate Alfred Austin voicing the sentiment of accord:

> Yes, this is the Voice on the bluff March gale,
> We severed have been too long.
> But now we have done with a worn-out tale,
> The tale of an ancient wrong,
> And our friendship shall last as long as Love doth last,
> And be stronger than death is strong.[12]

Henry Adams, who visited London in 1898, found the shift of attitude rather melodramatic to the last survivor of the American Legation of 1861, and concluded that "Germany as the grizzly terror" had effected in twenty years what his ancestors had tried in vain for two hundred to accomplish.[13]

A little later another Adams, impressed by the British reaction to the death of McKinley, wrote an essay on "A National Change of Heart," in which he commented on "an extremely noticeable recent something" which appeared to him to mark a "change in demeanor" on the part of England.[14] Curious to know whether a sympathetic

---

[12] "A Voice from the West." Information concerning the Anglo-American Unions, etc., comes from Richard H. Heindel, *The American Impact on Great Britain 1898–1914*, Philadelphia, 1940, chaps. iii, iv, and vi, and especially pp. 38 ff. and 127 ff.

[13] *The Education of Henry Adams*, chap. xxiv.

[14] Charles Francis Adams, *Lee at Appomattox and Other Papers*, Boston and New York, 1902, pp. 256–273. The list of town councils, etc., in England which passed resolutions on the death of Garfield in 1881 is indicative of a "change of heart" also. For the list see Lowell's communication No. 261 to the Secretary of State, dated October 6, 1881 (MS, Department of State).

Englishman had any opinion on the subject, in 1901 Adams wrote to Leslie Stephen, who had begun his literary career with a blast against the London *Times* and its hostility to America during the Civil War. In reply he received these modest words:

I have probably seen more of your countrymen than the great majority of Englishmen in my own class—far more than ninety-nine out of one hundred in the less educated classes, and I may claim average intelligence. Yet I feel utterly disqualified by sheer ignorance from pronouncing any general judgment on your seventy millions. I have not the materials. . . . We feel a little better able to understand people who talk English than the barbarians who gabble French or German, and we have a vague idea that we are cousins. If we come into opposition, that makes our jealousy rather keener, and if we happen to be on the same side, makes us more friendly. The antipathy to the U.S. in 1861, &c., meant the hatred of the upper class to Bright and Cobden, who were taken to be unpatriotic as well as democratic. At present that sentiment is pretty well dead—we have "Shot Niagara"—and the "imperialist" sentiment opposes us to Germany and France and Russia, and makes us look for friends.[15]

So far as even the intellectuals of England were concerned, Leslie Stephen was probably right in his reference to "sheer ignorance" about the United States. Nothing is more revelatory than the fact that the Unions and Leagues flickered on feebly or sputtered out and that from 1888 to 1914 only about nine thousand copies of Bryce's study of the United States were sold in the land which produced it.[16]

The foregoing remarks lead to the general conclusion that the ruling classes of England passed from an open hostility to a tranquil indifference to the United States, and that after the time of our Civil War the rapid democratization of the tight little island led to an era of comparative good feeling reaching a climax in cousinly affection in the nineties. It is natural, nevertheless, to assume that one would find elements in the British population at odds with the ruling classes and more or less favorably disposed toward the nation rising with raw but tremendous energy in the West. Thus, political and religious radicals, thwarted elements in the middle or lower classes, and a variety of dissenters might be expected to be exceptions to the rule. The best evidence of the favorable disposition of the more plebeian strata of the British population is afforded by the large number of

[15] Maitland, *op. cit.*, pp. 467–468.   [16] Heindel, *op. cit.*, p. 312.

emigrants who preferred the United States to Canada or Australia; and the succession of liberals who were friends of America supplies a brilliant thread for the fabric of English political history, from the days of Price and Priestley, through the season of Bright, Cobden, and Mill, to the era of Morley and Joseph Chamberlain. Democratic zealots of all sorts, as well as Quakers, Unitarians, Methodists, and others opposed to the dominance of the established church, from time to time found an interest in America; and they were many.[17]

So much for the outline of the history of the British attitude toward the United States. At a time when the two nations are engaged in the closest diplomatic, economic, and military coöperation which the world has ever witnessed it may seem ungrateful to dig up the buried past and remind readers of the animosities of yesteryear. But the reception of American literature among the British during the nineteenth century was conditioned by political and social views, especially in the higher critical circles, as one may see by glancing at the final chapter of the present volume. Moreover, without a reminder of the general atmosphere of English opinion concerning America, the important, but hitherto neglected, role played by our literary men in promoting cordial feelings between the two countries cannot be properly appreciated. The following chapters, it is hoped, will demonstrate a very important fact in the history of Anglo-American relations, namely, that of all the products of American intellect our literature was the most widely and most favorably received among the citizens of the British Isles. Students of diplomatic history have often wondered at the supposed stupidity of our government in choosing so many literary men as ambassadors, ministers, and consuls—all of them amateurs in the affairs of state. But when it is realized that Motley, Lowell, Hawthorne, and Bret Harte were much better known to the English people, high and low, than all but a few of our most eminent political figures the supposed stupidity turns out to have been very good sense indeed.

Literature as an effective instrument in winning sympathy and friendship beyond the confines of a nation has only recently been adequately recognized, and the recognition has been largely on the part of propagandists, not historians. That Americans are, and for

[17] For a good illustration see Jordan and Pratt, *op. cit.*, especially chaps. iii and iv.

many a year have been, readier to believe in the cause of the British rather than in that of any other European people is partially due to the fact that they regard Shakespeare and Milton, Dickens and Hardy as a valued portion of their intellectual heritage. To a less extent, there is a counterpart; and Hawthorne and Emerson, Longfellow and Mark Twain may be said to have played a similar role in promoting more cordial relations with English readers. For many a decade of the nineteenth century one out of every dozen new titles displayed on the counters of bookstores in London and Edinburgh was of American origin, and, as will be seen, there was a special economic advantage in purchasing the reprints of works by authors of the United States.

But what especially peculiar quality marked these American books, it may be asked. Were they not merely reflections of British literature, and nothing more? If the literary products of the entire first century of our republic were not tinged by the conditions of a democratic society we should behold in our literature the most unusual phenomenon known to man. Earlier than any other nation in the world the United States produced a literature which was entirely the product of the great middle class. American literature was directed at the people, not at the salons,[18] and the levelling of taste against the *aristoi,* which is the chief aesthetic phenomenon of recent history, received an impetus from the outset merely because of the nature of American society. Of our older authors now esteemed eminent, a far larger percentage were journalists, at least for a time, than was the case in England.

Long before Wordsworth, Philip Freneau, the chief poet of the American Revolution, argued for a democratic simplicity in style; and the first important theorist in our poetical history, William Cullen Bryant, considered the needs of the common man in his "Lectures on Poetry." [19] Whitman in avoiding the stock conventions of verse, which he dubbed "feudal," undoubtedly hoped to spread the message of his Bible of Democracy among the lowly, and Lowell's notion

---

[18] S. Foster Damon is the only recent critic who has properly appreciated this fact. See his volume, *Thomas Holley Chivers Friend of Poe,* New York and London, 1930, pp. 4–5.

[19] Lewis Leary, *That Rascal Freneau,* New Brunswick, N.J. [1941], p. 105. See especially the third of Bryant's lectures, "On Poetry in Its Relation to Our Age and Country."

of a true lyric was that its "meaning should float steadfast in the centre of every stanza," so that all could understand.[20] Hawthorne was not apologetic for his interest in writing down to the minds of children, and Emerson tried out his essays first as lectures to the people. There is a fundamental difference in the social point of view suggested by Emerson's title *Representative Men* and Carlyle's, *Heroes and Hero Worship*. George Ticknor wrote to Lyell in 1848: "You know our reading public in the United States, how large it is, as well as how craving and increasing; so that you will be less surprised than others, that I have prepared my book as much for *general* readers as for scholars." [21] Poe, who was more the practical journalist than the drugged dreamer, argued for the short story in terms of its democratic appeal. If not so elevated as the poem, he observed, the short story "is a table-land of far vaster extent. . . . Its products are never so rich, but infinitely more numerous, and *more appreciable by the mass of mankind*." [22]

The respect for the intellectual and emotional satisfaction of "the mass of mankind," inherent in the democratic tradition, can well be seen also in the works of the most resolutely American author of the latter half of the nineteenth century—William Dean Howells, whose volume on *Criticism and Fiction* proves conclusively his awareness of the pragmatic importance of adjudging literary values according to their effect upon the humbler readers. And, finally, hear Mark Twain in his literary apologia:

I have never tried in even one single instance, to help cultivate the cultivated classes. I was not equipped for it, either by native gifts or training. And I never had any ambition in that direction, but always hunted for bigger game—the masses.[23]

[20] *Letters of James Russell Lowell*, ed. Charles E. Norton, New York, 1893, I, 281–282.

[21] *Life, Letters, and Journals of George Ticknor*, Boston, 1877, II, 253. His book was the *History of Spanish Literature*.

[22] The essay on Hawthorne's *Twice Told Tales* (1842); italics mine.

[23] *Mark Twain's Letters*, ed. Albert Bigelow Paine, New York and London [1917], II, 527. Very early in the nineteenth century William Hazlitt compared Washington Irving and Charles Lamb and remarked that while Elia had "exhibited curious specimens" for the benefit of "the more inquisitive and discerning part of the public," Geoffrey Crayon had "culled and transplanted the flowers of modern literature" for the delectation of "the general reader" (*The Complete Works of William Hazlitt*, ed. P. P. Howe, London and Toronto, XI, 1932, 178).

Demos, to our nineteenth-century authors, was not the fatuous old man depicted by Aristophanes but a young giant in the American earth. And to many an English reader he must have come to appear the same, if one may judge by the perusal of books from the United States.

I. THE BOOKTRADE

⌁

"In the four quarters of the globe, who reads an American Book?"
—SYDNEY SMITH in the *Edinburgh Review* for January, 1820.

LONG BEFORE the Revolutionary War the American book was a well-known, albeit minor, feature of the English and Scottish book-trade, and a few authors—like Jonathan Edwards—had laid the groundwork for a European reputation which is now theirs. A Colonial writer who had produced a manuscript which seemed to be of more than local interest often arranged for first publication in Europe, then as now a sure means of securing respect at home. Increase Mather may be taken as an example. Of the nonfragmentary separates which he published during the years 1663 to 1726, one hundred and two in number, thirteen were first brought out in London, one in Amsterdam, and one in Edinburgh.[1] But more numerous by far than such first editions were the British reprints of works previously published in America. The very first book of which the historian of printing in the United States may boast, *The Bay Psalm Book* of 1640, went through at least eighteen editions in England and twenty-two in Scotland before 1759.[2] Then, too, many books manufactured in the Colonies were exported and offered for sale in certain British bookstores, especially those owned by the men engaged in the fairly lucrative business of dispatching reading matter to the tradesmen of Boston, New York, and Philadelphia.

The struggles of the Revolution and the War of 1812 served to quicken European interest in the new States, and British trade in American books was probably enhanced,[3] although, for a time, first

---

[1] Thomas J. Holmes, *Increase Mather: a Bibliography of His Works*, Cleveland, 1931, I, xxviii–xxxii.

[2] Henry W. Boynton, *Annals of American Bookselling 1838–1850*, New York, 1932, p. 28; *The Bay Psalm Book*, New York [1903], Introduction, pp. viii–ix.

[3] For interest in the United States and in its early writings see the following: William B. Cairns, *British Criticisms of American Writings 1783–1815*, Madison, Wis., 1918; W. B. Cairns, *British Criticisms of American Writings 1815–1833*, Madison, Wis., 1922; R. B. Heilman, *America in English Fiction 1760–1800: the Influence of*

publication in London on the part of transatlantic authors declined. But in the confusion of the wars and the birth pangs of the republic American production lagged, and recovery was very difficult. The economic misfortunes of the Tories or their emigration took a toll of potential authors and especially of potential patrons of works of learning or art. But more significant was the traditional dependence of the new nation upon England for most of its supply of intellectual pabulum and the consequent discouragement of native authorship— a situation aggravated by the fact that publishers in the United States found more profit in pirating the books of well-established English writers than in gambling upon the success of new American authors and paying them royalty to boot.[4] But such writers as reared their heads in the midst of British reprints soon found their way across the Atlantic, and as early as 1803 one finds an American periodical commenting on the "elegant editions" of novels by Royall Tyler and Charles Brockden Brown brought out in London—and even asserting that "more attention" was paid to such productions abroad than at home.[5] During the first thirty-eight years of the nineteenth century no less than six hundred works of all sorts first produced in the United States are said to have been reprinted in England,[6] and au-

the American Revolution, Baton Rouge, La., 1937, chaps. i and ix; Jane L. Mesick, *The English Traveller in America 1785–1835*, New York, 1922; R. E. Spiller, *The American in England during the First Half Century of Independence*, New York, 1926; Dora M. Clark, *British Opinion and the American Revolution*, New Haven, 1930; Leon Fraser, *English Opinion of the American Constitution and Government 1783–1798*, New York, 1915; Edgar F. Smith, *Priestley in America 1794–1804*, Philadelphia, 1920; Roland Thomas, *Richard Price, Philosopher and Apostle of Liberty*, London, 1924; Crane Brinton, *The Political Ideas of the English Romanticists*, Oxford, 1926; Joseph J. Jones, "British Literary Men's Opinions about America, 1750–1832," MS, Stanford University Dissertation, 1934; J. J. Espey, "English Criticisms of American Literature during the Period 1800 to 1850 as Reflected in the Periodicals," MS, B. Litt. Thesis, Oxford University, 1938; Paul M. Wheeler, *America through British Eyes*, Rock Hill, S.C., 1935; Louise H. Johnson, "America in the Thought of Leading British Men of Letters: 1830–1890," MS, Wisconsin University Dissertation, 1943.

[4] For a variety of other factors militating against the development of a literary class see the present writer's essay, "The Theme-Song of American Criticism," *University of Toronto Quarterly*, VI (October, 1936), 49–65.

[5] *Port Folio*, III (June 4, 1803), 181. Cf. *ibid.*, IV (September 1, 1804), 277.

[6] George H. Putnam, *International Copyright Considered in Some of Its Relations to Ethics and Political Economy*, New York, 1879, p. 17. See also W. B. Cairns, "British Republication of American Writings, 1783–1833," *PMLA*, XLIII (March, 1928), 303–310.

thors like Washington Irving, James Fenimore Cooper, and William
Ellery Channing were as well known during the eighteen twenties
and thirties as most of their British contemporaries.

But however great the European interest in our first important
authors and however numerous the British reprints of their books,
the quantity of American works sold in the United Kingdom up to
1839 was a mere trickle to that which was to come. The constant
increase in the demand of British readers throughout the nineteenth
century is partially responsible, as well as the steady rise of the supply
of American authors, especially after 1840; but just as important is
the history of international copyright, a topic which during the century elicited more discussion involving Anglo-American literary relations than any other.

In the general copyright statutes of Great Britain, Parliament seems
to have made no positive distinction between native and foreign
writers, and as a result the interpretation of the rights of American
authors to British copyright was for most of the century not at all
clear.[7] The general assumption was that first publication in Great
Britain assured an American author of copyright, especially if he
were resident in the British Isles at the time his book appeared. But
in 1838 a law was enacted which provided for reciprocal international
copyright; and since the Congress of the United States failed to re-
spond, it was argued that no American book could be protected in
Great Britain. Immediately there was an outbreak of piracy more
virulent than ever before.[8] But, in the course of a few years, prior or
"simultaneous" publication in the United Kingdom seems to have

[7] For a practical view of the British law as affecting American books earlier in
the nineteenth century see George T. Curtis, *A Treatise on the Law of Copyright,*
Boston, 1847, chap. iii; and Robert E. Spiller and Philip C. Blackburn, *A Descriptive
Bibliography of the Writings of James Fenimore Cooper,* New York, 1934, Intro-
duction. For the situation in 1878, as digested by James Stephen, see Richard R.
Bowker, *Copyright: Its Law and Its Literature,* New York, 1886, pp. 43 and 45. For
an interpretation of the law in 1881 see Sidney Jerrold, *A Handbook of English and
Foreign Copyright,* London, 1881. Richard R. Bowker, *Copyright: Its History and
Its Law,* Boston and New York, 1912, provides a history of legislation looking toward
an international copyright act in the United States, as does also Walter L. Pforzheimer
in "Copyright and Scholarship," *English Institute Annual 1940,* New York, 1941,
pp. 164–199. Various works by George H. Putnam, especially the one cited in foot-
note 6 of this chapter, are of great value.

[8] The *Publishers' Circular* for October 15, 1839, contains an announcement of
Bentley's action in connection with the piracies of Cooper's works. See also Spiller
and Blackburn, *op. cit.,* Introduction and Appendix D.

been regarded as sufficient to establish a copyright. In 1854, however, after much discussion and dissension, it was decided that the foreign author who published his book first in England was *not* entitled to British copyright unless he was actually resident in the United Kingdom at the time of publication. In May, 1868, the House of Lords concluded that an alien became entitled to copyright by first publishing in the United Kingdom provided he were at the time of publication anywhere in the British dominions. As a consequence of this ruling a number of American authors—Mark Twain and Bayard Taylor, for example—were led to make trips to Canada at such times as their London publishers brought out their new books. But the validity of this practice was soon questioned, and many a British bookman doubted the legality of a so-called "Canadian copyright." Not until after July, 1891, when the first American law providing for international copyright went into effect, was it possible for the troublous problems of American rights in Great Britain to be viewed from any very firm legal position—and even then there were still difficulties.

One may assume therefore that, with the exception of such American works as had been first published in England at a time when their authors were in residence there, up to 1868 the best way for an English firm to obtain an American book was simply to reprint it and take a chance. After 1868 the chances were slighter; but they were still there, for most works by Americans were, naturally, first published in the United States. While a large percentage of the English imprints were piracies pure and simple—as was the case with a still larger percentage of British books published in the United States— an author was sometimes given a sum of money as a "courtesy" payment; and the most popular writers or their publishers or agents were paid for proof sheets or early copies of their books, the purpose of acquiring the sheets or early copies being, of course, to beat competition by forestalling the market. Such payments increased in frequency after the middle of the century, when "simultaneous" publication in both the United States and England became standard practice for certain authors.[9] The best means of securing a valid British copy-

[9] Illustrations of various practices indulged in by British publishers in connection with the printing of American authors may be found in the present writer's "Longfellow and His Authorized British Publishers," *PMLA*, LV (December, 1940), 1165–1179.

right was, of course, to be in England when one's book appeared. This fact may help to explain the prolonged foreign residence of such American authors as Washington Irving, Bret Harte, and even Henry James.

The copyright problem, moreover, had certain effects upon the critical appreciation of American literature in England. Since so many American books were reprints, often unauthorized, most of the British critical journals were not inclined to review them; and as a result only the bookseller's periodicals, like the *Publishers' Circular,* provide the proper perspective for evaluating the quantitative importance of the American book to the British trade, although weeklies like the *Athenæum,* with considerable space for short notices, devoted much attention to reprints, including those of transatlantic origin. Moreover, from the heyday in England of Washington Irving to that of young Gertrude Atherton and Stephen Crane in the nineties, an American author resident abroad and possessed of a "regular" British copyright was likely to be more respectfully dealt with—and more frequently reviewed—by critics than if his work were a direct import, an authorized reprint, or a piracy. For example, Hawthorne's *Transformation (The Marble Faun),* which was brought out in 1860 by Smith and Elder while the novelist was living in Europe, and issued in orthodox three-decker style at 31s. 6d., elicited many more reviews in important journals than had any of his previous romances, though all were known in England and most of them had been widely read.

But to return to the survey of American books in the British trade. Reprints, legitimate or otherwise, made up the bulk of such works so far as the number of copies sold is concerned; and it may be said that in general their history is that of the so-called "cheap" book in the United Kingdom, with such variations as changes in the interpretation of international copyright effected from time to time, and, of course, with such variations as are always induced in the graph of book production by the phenomenon of a "best-seller." If there were a simple outline of the history of the "cheap" book in England throughout the century one might very easily point to it and say, "So went the course of the American reprint." But before any such simplification can be made a variety of monographs must be forthcoming—

a series which might well be *followed* by a special study of the very important role played by the American reprint in supplying literature for the English masses. Accordingly, one may ask forgiveness for venturing where scholars should fear to tread and hope that the immediately following generalizations and illustrations may not be too far removed from reality.

While the efforts of Constable, Chambers, Knight, and the Society for the Diffusion of Useful Knowledge enjoyed a success for a time and undoubtedly provided reading for the masses, these efforts were met by the indifference of most of the publishers who enjoyed a respectable standing, for the latter found that profits were best maintained by publishing new books in small editions at fairly high prices.[10] Gladstone, speaking in Parliament on May 12, 1852, expressed the belief that the number of new books published in England which surpassed a sale of five hundred copies was "not more than something like five per cent, or, at any rate, not more than from one-twentieth to one-tenth of the whole number that has been produced." [11] When it is remembered that from 1801 to 1851 the population of Great Britain had almost doubled, that wages had been considerably increased, that the number of illiterates had declined, and that the average price of books, especially reprints, had fallen somewhat,[12] one suspects not only the effect of the tax on paper, which Knight and others blamed for their failure to succeed with mass production, but a controlled market.[13] An effective combination of publishers with an eye on the circulating library and the well-to-do trade

[10] Among the various books which offer material on the history of the "cheap" book in England the following are the most important: Charles Knight, *Passages from the Life of Charles Knight,* New York, 1874; the following three works by Frank A. Mumby: *The Romance of Bookselling,* London, 1910; *Publishing and Bookselling,* London [1930]; and *The House of Routledge,* London, 1934; Herbert Maxwell, *Life and Times of the Right Honourable William Henry Smith, M.P.,* Edinburgh and London, 1893; Marjorie Plant, *The English Book Trade,* London [1939], chap. xx; A. S. Collins, *The Profession of Letters . . . , 1780–1832,* London, 1928. Especially important is the period following the education acts of the 1870s, on which very little information seems to be available.

[11] *Hansard's Parliamentary Debates,* 3d Ser., CXXI, 587 ff.

[12] Marjorie Plant, *op. cit.,* p. 446. Mr. J. Lee Harlan has expressed to me his doubts as to a decline in the prices of *new* books.

[13] Knight, *op. cit.,* pp. 345–346. The tax on paper (repealed in 1861) was in 1850 a little more than 1½d. per pound, "a fifth of the selling price of most papers used for printing" (John Chapman, *Cheap Books and How to Get Them,* London, 1852, p. 2).

had long been in existence, and, with intermittent periods of free trade, continued as late as the 1870s to limit the size of the editions of new books and to keep up prices by coercive methods.[14] Indeed, it was not until the nineties that *new* books (not reprints) almost universally were produced with the purpose of selling large editions at a comparatively low price. The decline of the three-volume novel in the 1890s may serve as a reminder of the long-delayed triumph of the cheap book. But in the middle of the century not only was the price of new books controlled, but the Bookseller's Association was powerful enough to ruin the business of a dealer who undertook to retail works imported from America on a cost-plus-small-commission basis.[15]

With the prices of new works controlled and with the supply of readers constantly increasing, it is small wonder that the history of books for the masses in nineteenth-century England is largely a history of the reprints, very frequently issued in series or "libraries," brought out at lower prices by respectable firms as well as by the at-first disreputable "remainder" men like Henry G. Bohn, Thomas Tegg, and George Routledge. The contribution of these men to the growth of democracy in the British booktrade is quite as important as that of Knight or Constable. If it is remembered that an English publisher was limited to his own list of authors for his reprint "library" or to authors whose copyright he could secure at a relatively low price, it is easy to conclude that when Americans were in the offing with their specialty of appealing to the masses, nothing would be simpler than to make a small payment for advance sheets, agree to half profits, or merely pirate their works, and thus add to the number of volumes in the series or "library." The American book in the cheap series of reprints appears early, is stimulated by the varying interpretations of the copyright laws, shows a rise in quantity about 1840, another astonishing increase in the 1850s, a slight decline during the Civil War, a remarkable revival thereafter, and a climax in the last two decades of the century, when the education acts of the 1870s demonstrated their effects in spreading literacy.[16]

14 Chapman, *op. cit.;* Gladstone, *op. cit.;* Marjorie Plant, *op. cit.,* p. 416.

15 Gordon S. Haight, *George Eliot & John Chapman: with Chapman's Diaries,* New Haven, 1940, pp. 50–54.

16 Mr. Lee Harlan has drawn my attention to the following passage from Charles

Bentley's "Standard Novels and Romances," published at six shillings, and eminently respectable in every way, had by August, 1833, run to twenty-nine volumes, six of which were by Fenimore Cooper and one by Charles Brockden Brown. Early in 1840 John Green announced a series of "Standard American Literature," which included such works as Mrs. Eliza Follen's *Sketches of Married Life;* and the next year J. Clements projected a "Romancist and Novelists' Library" —largely composed of transatlantic fiction—issued in weekly numbers at 2*d*. each.[17] These are merely a few samples.

In the late forties the establishment by W. H. Smith of bookstalls in the railway stations added considerably to the interest in the cheap series; and publishers like George Routledge, who had begun as a "remainder" man, formed "Railway Libraries" to meet the demand. By the end of 1869 this one series of Routledge included about four hundred titles, a large portion of them by Americans. Before many years had passed W. H. Smith & Son gave a standing order for 1,040 copies of each new volume which his firm issued in this series.[18] By the middle of the century Routledge was recognized as the chief purveyor of American books to English readers, so far as quantity is concerned; and one could find his products not only at the railway stations but also in the shops of numerous dealers, of whom he seems to have had a weblike network. For some of his American authors he had copyright; for others he had none; and he kept a close connection with the source of supply of advance sheets through a branch house which was opened in New York in 1854.[19] To the end of the century his lists of writers for his various series were heavily weighted with transatlantic authors. Choosing only one series from the list given in Appendix B of *The English Catalogue* covering the years 1835-

---

Knight, *The Case of the Authors as Regards the Paper Duty,* 2d ed., London, 1851, p. 16: "The Publishers of 'The Parlour Library' include many original works in their series. . . . But with these, and a few other exceptions, these new libraries are mostly reprints of American works, or of novels of which the copyright has expired." For a partial survey of the cheap series in the United States, see Raymond H. Shove, *Cheap Book Production in the United States, 1870 to 1891,* Urbana, Ill., 1937.

[17] *Bent's Monthly Literary Advertiser* for August, 1833; *Publishers' Circular* for February 15, 1840; "Pirated Editions of American Novels," *Times Literary Supplement* for November 27, 1924, p. 804.

[18] F. A. Mumby, *The House of Routledge 1834-1934,* pp. 39, 90, 140. See also Herbert Maxwell, *op. cit.,* Vol. I, chap. ii.

[19] F. A. Mumby, *The House of Routledge 1834-1934,* p. 63.

1863, one finds that in 1862 Routledge's so-called "Cheap Series," issued to sell at from one shilling to two and six per volume, included several works by Hawthorne, Irving, Longfellow, Emerson, Prescott, and Susan Warner, as well as Melville's *Israel Potter,* Richard Hildreth's *The White Slave,* Poe's *Tales,* and specimens of the work of Maria Cummins, Mrs. Stowe, George Bancroft, and others. In "one week," we are told, he disposed of twenty thousand copies of *Queechy,* a novel by Susan Warner.[20] One may guess that the sales of his series of transatlantic dime novels called "Beadle's American Sixpenny Library" were also remunerative.

But Routledge was by no means alone in his interest in the American author. Listed for 1862, for example, is also Bohn's "Cheap Series," with two works by Emerson, four by Hawthorne, eighteen by Irving, six by Nathaniel P. Willis, along with *Uncle Tom's Cabin* and Richard Hildreth's *The White Slave,* a novel which had a tremendous sale in the wake of Mrs. Stowe's sentimental classic, although first published as early as 1836 under the title *The Slave; or Memoirs of Archy Moore.* Another illustration is offered by the "Parlour Library," started in 1847 by Simms and later taken over by Hodgson, which listed, as did many another series, various works by Irving and Cooper, *Zenobia* by William Ware, Brown's *Edgar Huntly,* Holmes's *Elsie Venner,* and, of course, books by Mrs. Stowe and Susan Warner. There was a "Library of Old Authors," published by J. R. Smith, in which two works by the Mathers were listed, along with volumes by John Aubrey, John Webster, and Thomas Malory. And a "Miniature Classical Library," first published by Bogue, advertised Channing's essays, sketches by Irving, and *Gems from the American Poets.*

Going on to 1871 and viewing the increasing number of "Collections, Libraries, Series, etc." listed in *The English Catalogue* for the years 1863–1872, one finds, of course, that Routledge has added more American books as his various collections flourished, and "Beadle's American Library," for example, has added about fifty new titles of dime novels. As previously, a number of different publishers have an American or two on their lists, but now another "specialist" in transatlantic books is successfully competing, the firm of Sampson Low, whose "Copyright Editions of American Authors" consisted of twenty

20 Henry Curwen, *A History of Booksellers,* London, n.d., p. 439.

volumes by Mrs. Cummins, Mrs. Stowe, Mrs. Dodge, Miss Phelps, Louisa Alcott, Charles D. Warner, and O. W. Holmes. The triumph of the sentimental school is further indicated by a "Golden Ladder Series" of nineteen different works, dominated by the author of *The Wide Wide World* and her sister. A third firm, Bell and Daldy, is represented by the "Elzevir Series of Standard Authors," which included Burns, Coleridge, Cowper, Irving, Longfellow, Milton, Shakespeare, and Southey—a conjunction of English and American names which is by no means rare, for Poe, Longfellow, and others from across the sea frequently appear in lists otherwise wholly English, even in "libraries" entitled "British Poets."

Turning to the appendix of the volume of *The English Catalogue* next in order, that covering the years 1872–1880, one finds the offerings again greatly increased. Sampson Low, for example, has since 1871 added twelve works to his "American Copyright Series"—chiefly by Charles D. Warner, Mrs. Stowe, Will Carleton, and Louisa Alcott. The firm of Ward and Lock announces a "Lily Series" at one and six per volume, filled with American sentimentalists, from Fanny Fern to J. G. Holland and Elizabeth Stuart Phelps. The same company has also a library of "Favourite Authors," which included works by Charles D. Warner, Josh Billings, Major Jack Downing, James Russell Lowell, and others; and another series issued by the same publisher under the name of "People's Standard Library" contains about twenty American titles among a total of eighty-four. Still another series by Ward and Lock, this one called a "Select Library of Fiction," places Hawthorne, Max Adeler, Mark Twain, Henry James, E. P. Roe, Artemus Ward, Cooper, Bret Harte, and others side by side. Such a double-barreled title as *Funny Stories and Humourous Poems,* by Mark Twain and O. W. Holmes, and the number of humorists competing with the sentimentalists and the old guard of more stable authors indicate that during the seventies Great Britain as well as the United States enjoyed the vogue of the American "funny fellow." In addition to the house of Sampson Low and that of Ward and Lock, one should remember, the firm of George Routledge continued to specialize in American reprints. Its several collections, with many American authors, may be illustrated by the "Excelsior Series of Standard Authors," which ran the gamut from Susan and Elizabeth

Warner, Maria Cummins, and Mrs. Stowe to Longfellow, Poe, and Bret Harte.

A fourth publisher soon to become prominent as a source of supply of American books at a cheap price was the firm of Chatto and Windus, who, having taken over many Americans on the list of the piratical John C. Hotten, continued to exploit the transatlantic favorites along with their British rivals. Their "Golden Library," consisting in 1879 of twenty-three books, represents six by Americans—Bayard Taylor, Emerson, Holmes, and Irving—all of the older school. But their more important "Popular Novels," sold for two shillings each, lists five volumes by Bret Harte, three by Julian Hawthorne, three by Mark Twain, as well as Poe's *Tales* and Henry James's *Confidence*.

Going on to the last two decades of the century, one may behold in the vastly increased number of "libraries" and series the fullest flowering of the cheap book. As earlier, with the general increase in the number of titles presented in collections there is a general increase in the number of American books; and a few more publishers, like Cassell and Walter Scott, join the list of those already prominently identified with the printing of transatlantic authors in cheap format. It is not without interest, perhaps, to note that Scott's inclusion of a volume of Whitman in his "Canterbury Poets," edited by William Sharp, and priced at one shilling, probably gave the Good Gray Poet more British readers than all the efforts of the critics.

In the eighties, after becoming angered at the very justifiable charges of certain Englishmen that American publishers were pirating hosts of British books, Brander Matthews delivered himself of a thundering reply and gave many examples of the reverse practice.[21] In his statistical analysis he charged that in 1885, for example, Warne's "Star Series" contained ninety-one numbers, of which thirty-six were American; and the same company's "Select Books" embraced nineteen works, all but two of which were from the United States. Again in the same year Ward, Lock & Tyler announced a "Home Treasury Library" of thirty-eight volumes, thirty of which were transatlantic; and "Beeton's Humorous Books" included between sixty and seventy American titles in its total of about eighty. Further illustration of the

---

[21] *American Authors and British Piracies,* New York, 1889, a reprint from the *Princeton Review,* IV (September, 1887), 201–212.

importance of the American author to the cheap series is perhaps unnecessary. One may look in the appendix of *The English Catalogue* and find sufficient enlightenment.

What proportion of the American books in the British cheap "libraries" consisted of piracies it is impossible to say, but it was large. Already in the early fifties certain British journalists were of the opinion that "the whole race of English booksellers, with few exceptions worth mentioning," were "greater literary pirates than the Americans." [22] It is possible that during the middle of the century the facts justified this opinion, but over the course of the decades it may be assumed that the British booktrade was less guilty than the American. One should note, in addition, that the quantity of unauthorized reproduction of books from the United States reached its highest point in the eighties.[23]

One notices that with the increased consumption of the "series" book in the eighties and nineties the number of the *newer* American authors does not increase in direct proportion—rather the names of the *older* writers are repeated. Of course there are numerous exceptions, and the "libraries" of the eighties list, for example, works by Frank Stockton, Constance Woolson, Lew Wallace, George W. Cable, Joel C. Harris, and Bill Nye; but the fact is that from the 1870s on more effective arrangements were made between American authors and British publishers whereby more respectable formats were forthcoming along with, presumably, greater royalties. The so-called "Canadian copyright" cannot explain the situation altogether, although doubtless it had its effect, too. Mark Twain's arrangements with Chatto and Windus, soon after his earliest efforts had been pirated in huge quantities and spurious works had been attributed to his pen, made impossible the widespread use of his newer books; and Howells

---

[22] *Illustrated London News,* XXII (February 12, 1853), 121–122.

[23] The statistics presented by Edward Marston indicate a decline of about 10 percent in the offerings of new books and reprints after 1891 (*After Work,* London and New York, n.d., p. 39), but his figures do not agree with those of the *Publishers' Circular.* According to the *Circular,* the total number of new books and new editions in England for the year 1891 was 5,706, a slight decrease from the figure for 1890, a larger decrease from that for 1889, and a very considerable falling off from the grand total for 1888—6,591. The English were inclined to ignore the fact that their own publishers were pirates on a large scale, but occasionally one may find evidences of an awareness of the situation. See, for example, "Threepence, Sixpence, and a Shilling," *Saturday Review,* LX (November 21, 1885), 683.

enjoyed late in the century a "regular" copyright with an Edinburgh publisher, David Douglas, who issued a considerable number of American books in better style. Yet Howells's novel *The Undiscovered Country,* with the popular interest in spiritism, appeared in the eighties in Low's "Rose Library" at one shilling. But the closer connection existing between certain American and British houses in the last quarter of the century tended to protect the new author, *if he had the right publisher;* and, of course, the passage of the American International Copyright Act in 1891 cut considerably the financial inducements to reprint a transatlantic author in a volume selling for a shilling or two. But there were plenty of the older American authors to bolster up the transmarine element in the cheap series after 1891.

So far as the number of copies of American books (or English books) actually sold is concerned, the "libraries" or series of cheap reprints, authorized or pirated, were the most important. In viewing their contents in general one finds that they included all the old group of standard American writers: Irving, Cooper, Emerson, Longfellow, Holmes, Hawthorne, Lowell, Poe—to a less extent Franklin, Channing, Whittier, Melville, Bryant, and in the eighties and nineties Thoreau and Whitman. The earliest works of Bret Harte and Mark Twain appeared regularly in the cheap series, but those of Howells and James sporadically or rarely. As in the United States, the first rank in popularity belongs to a variety of sentimentalists of lesser consequence and to the writers of books for children. Peter Parley, Mrs. Stowe, and Susan Warner head this list, with hosts of others like Jacob Abbott, Maria Cummins, J. H. Ingraham, Louisa Alcott, E. P. Roe, Frank Stockton, and Elizabeth Stuart Phelps following.[24]

With the early prominence of public education in the United States it was natural that the country which has been given credit for Mother Goose should have led the nation which produced *Alice in Wonderland* in the special field of literature for children.[25] There is no reason

[24] I have merely chosen a few examples. For the importance of the sentimentalists and writers for children to the American booktrade see, for example, J. C. Derby, *Fifty Years among Authors, Books and Publishers,* New York, 1884, pp. 122, 305, 572. For the authorized publisher of E. P. Roe in England see Mary A. Roe, *E. P. Roe: Reminiscences of His Life,* New York, 1899, p. 220. Ednah D. Cheney mentions English editions in *Louisa May Alcott,* Boston, 1928, pp. 136, 150, 165, 175, 222, 338.

[25] Algernon Tassin, "Books for Children," *CHAL,* Vol. II, chap. vii. It seems to have been forgotten that Mrs. Dodge's *Hans Brinker* (1865) was awarded a prize

to wonder, then, that Jacob Abbott, of "Rollo" fame, was a prominent author reprinted in cheap form in England. Indeed, many an English child first learned of the old monarchs of Britain in Abbott's juveniles. It is amusing to note that with the tremendous interest in his works for children certain of his heretical views also were circulated in England so that one of the *Tracts for the Times* was devoted to the extirpation of his radicalism and that of one of his fellow heretics.[26] But more important for the English child was Samuel Goodrich, who in instituting the "Peter Parley" Series appears to have been the pioneer in the field of the children's book as included in a "library" with a name—like Elsie, Rollo, or Daisie. Up to the middle of the century more different works bearing the pseudonym "Peter Parley" appear in the lists of English reprints of American books than those of any other single author.[27] Indeed, it is almost impossible to identify many of the numberless "Peter Parley" reprints in England because the enthusiastic demand for the originals exceeded the supply, and at least six different Englishmen stole the name and wrote more "Peter Parley's." [28] In 1841 a trusted adviser of Prince Albert named Henry Cole announced a new series of books for children and asserted: "The character of most Children's Books published during the last quarter of a century, is fairly typified in the name of Peter Parley, which the writers of some hundreds of them have assumed. . . . The conductor of this series purposes to produce a series of Works, the character of which may be briefly described as anti-Peter Parleyism." [29] Apparently, only a head-on attack against Peter Parley enabled Jack the Giantkiller, Cinderella, and Little Red Ridinghood to come into English cottages, and the victory was for years in doubt.

---

by the French Academy (*ibid.,* pp. 408, 402). Some of Hans Andersen's stories were published in English in the United States before appearing even in their original language (Jean Hersholt, "Hans Andersen Fairy Tales Published First in America," *Colophon,* New Graphic Series, No. IV., Vol. I, 1940). For prominent English contributors to the *Youth's Companion* in 1896, see M. A. DeWolfe Howe, "You Used to Read It, Too," *Saturday Review of Literature,* XXI (March 23, 1940), 4.

[26] Tract Number 73. The new catalogue of the British Museum lists a large number of the British editions of Abbott but by no means all of them.

[27] See the catalogue of American books published in Great Britain appearing in a memorial to Congress in 1848 (H.R., 1st Sess., 30th Cong.: *Miscellaneous No. 76,* pp. 16 ff.).

[28] F. J. Harvey Darton, *Children's Books in England,* Cambridge, 1932, chap. xiii. Cf. also a letter on Peter Parley in the *Athenæum* for January 4, 1896, p. 18.

[29] Darton, *op. cit.,* pp. 240–241.

Later in the century, when Mark Twain, Frank Stockton, Louisa Alcott, and others were active, the tradition of English interest in American books for children was, of course, maintained; and the enthusiasm for Uncle Remus was high, even though the Negro dialect was occasionally deleted and the illustrations sometimes presented Brer Fox walking down a lane at the end of which stood a Dutch windmill.[30]

During the first half of the nineteenth century it is doubtful whether many British writers of children's books were more popular in England than Goodrich and Abbott; and during the last fifty years the consumption of copies of *St. Nicholas* and of the works of Susan Warner, Frank Stockton, Thomas Bailey Aldrich, and many another American beloved of children can be described as nothing short of enormous. In the middle of the 1880s, a period when the reprinting of American books in the British Isles reached a high peak, a questionnaire was concocted to ascertain which authors were regarded as the favorites of English schoolgirls between the ages of eleven and nineteen. The analysis of the thousand replies showed Dickens and Scott at the top. But Susan Warner stood next to Shakespeare, Louisa Alcott surpassed Bunyan and Tennyson in favor, and Mrs. Stowe was equal with the author of *Pilgrim's Progress*. Mark Twain was on a par with Defoe—and far ahead of Lewis Carroll, who trailed Susan Warner at the rate of five to fifty-four. Even Louisa Alcott was mentioned twice as often as the creator of *Alice in Wonderland*. Longfellow appeared thirty-one times to Tennyson's nine. The author of an article embodying the results of the questionnaire pointed out that the girls who replied to it had a natural tendency to mention an author with a good name rather than one actually read, and expressed his own belief not only that two novels by Susan Warner gave place "to no books in the English language for popularity among girls old and young," but that one of her characters in *Queechy* was, "as a literary study," second only to Little Nell in Dickens's *The Old Curiosity Shop*.[31] One can readily understand why a London pub-

[30] Julia Collier Harris, "Uncle Remus at Home and Abroad," *Southern Literary Messenger*, II (February, 1940), 84–86. The *English Catalogue* lists for the 1890s alone about forty issues or editions of Stockton, twenty-three of Louisa Alcott, and twenty-two of Harris.

[31] Edward G. Salmon, "What Girls Read," *Nineteenth Century*, XX (October, 1886), 515–529.

lisher named a whole series of books "The Wide-Wide World Library."

Of all the American works reprinted in Great Britain during the century by all odds *Uncle Tom's Cabin* had the largest *immediate* or *relatively immediate* sale. Indeed, this work supplied the English booktrade with its first example of "best sellerism" in the modern sense, far surpassing anything by Scott or Dickens in its initial success. One version of the early history of the tale in England comes from the pen of Sampson Low, whose firm found the publication of Mrs. Stowe's works to be a "leading feature" during the 1850s: [32]

The first edition printed in London was in April, 1852, by Henry Vizetelly, in a neat volume at ten and sixpence, of which he issued 7,000 copies. He received the first copy imported, through a friend who had bought it in Boston the day the steamer sailed, for his own reading. He gave it to Mr. V., who took it to the late Mr. David Bogue [a prominent publisher of American books, often piracies], well known for his general shrewdness and enterprise. He had the book to read and consider over night, and in the morning returned it, declining to take it at the very moderate price of five pounds.

Vizetelly at once put the volume into the hands of a friendly printer and brought it out on his own account, through the nominal agency of Clarke & Co. [also well-known for American reprints]. The 7,000 copies sold, other editions followed, and Mr. Vizetelly disposed of his interest in the book to the printer and agent, who joined with Mr. [Samuel O.] Beeton [another trader in American books] and at once began to issue monster editions. The demand called for fresh supplies, and these created an increased demand. The discovery was soon made that any one was at liberty to reprint the book, and the initiative was thus given to a new era in cheap literature, founded on American reprints. A shilling edition followed the one-and-sixpence, and this in turn became the precursor of one "complete for sixpence." From April to December, 1852, twelve different editions (not reissues) were published, and within the twelve months of its first appearance eighteen different London publishing houses were engaged in supplying the great demand that had set in, the total number of editions being forty. . . .

After carefully analyzing these editions and weighing probabilities with ascertained facts, I am able pretty confidently to say that the aggregate number of copies circulated in Great Britain and the colonies exceeds one and a half millions.[33]

[32] Marston, *op. cit.*, p. 61.
[33] Charles E. Stowe, *Life of Harriet Beecher Stowe*, Boston and New York, 1889, pp. 189–190. For other versions of the history of the first printing see *ibid.*, pp. 190–

The London *Times* for September 3, 1852, in a review three and a half columns long, began its discussion with the announcement that the book was "at every railway book-stall in England, and in every third traveller's hand," praised the "skill in the delineation of character," displayed by Mrs. Stowe, but attacked the reality of the conditions depicted and the nobility of Uncle Tom. "If Uncle Tom is a type of a class," the critic went on, "we deliberately assert that we have nothing more to communicate to the negro, but everything to learn from his profession and practice." Four days later a "constant reader" corroborated the latter opinion and remarked, "As to Uncle Tom, no Archbishop of Canterbury ever came near him in morality." But such reactions were of minor consequence. Far more typical was the review in the *Illustrated London News,* which devoted two and a half columns to unmitigated enthusiasm and concluded that Mrs. Stowe's portrayal of life and conditions in the South bore the "stamp of truth." [34] Susceptible young men at Oxford, like Frederic Harrison, could write:

I have lately been employed on that great dialogue on slavery, *Uncle Tom's Cabin.* It is a crushing piece of logic, and takes the right point of view. . . . The religious element, so offensive in fiction, is natural and consistent. . . . The value of the book is that its tone is so elevated and its truth so great that it is equally directed against any institution which represses man's moral development.[35]

The *Publishers' Circular* for October 15, 1852, announced ten different editions of the novel in one fortnight but soon ceased trying to

---

192; *Times Literary Supplement* for July 8, 1926, p. 468; *International Bookseller,* I (June 25, 1892), 236; and *Publishers' Weekly,* CXXXVII (May 18, 1940), 1933, bibliographical item by John T. Winterich. An incomplete list of British editions appears in "The Harriet Beecher Stowe Collection," chap. v of Kate B. Knight, *History of the Work of Connecticut Women at the World's Columbian Exposition Chicago, 1893,* Hartford, Conn., 1898. The best account of Mrs. Stowe's reception in England appears in Forrest Wilson, *Crusader in Crinoline,* Philadelphia [1941], pp. 325 ff.

[34] XXI (October 2, 1852), 290–291.

[35] *Autobiographic Memories,* London, 1911, I, 125. For the concrete effects of the novel in England see Forrest Wilson, *op. cit.,* and F. S. Klingberg, "Harriet Beecher Stowe and Social Reform in England," *American Historical Review,* XLIII (April, 1938), 542–552. As late as 1883 people were still publishing works like *Uncle Pat's Cabin; or Life among the Agricultural Labourers of Ireland* (Dublin: Gill), by W. C. Upton.

list all the other editions and was content to note merely the issues from a few of the major firms and add the words "And Others." As a number of the earlier reviews acknowledged, this anti-slavery classic supplied the greatest sensation in book sales which the British trade had ever witnessed.

Of the forty publishers who printed Mrs. Stowe's novel in Great Britain during the middle of the century the house of George Routledge, chief specialist in cheap American books, was of course one of the most active; and he is said to have sent out to his agents as many as ten thousand copies per day, the total number in his various "libraries" and editions being estimated at "more than a half million copies." [36] Of the chief American rival of *Uncle Tom's Cabin* in the fifties—Susan Warner's *The Wide Wide World*—his company (again merely one of many) is said to have sold in all eighty thousand copies.[37] Such figures assume additional significance perhaps when it is recalled that Bulwer himself maintained that the largest sale of any one of his works was of a political pamphlet entitled *The Crisis* (1834), of which thirty thousand copies were distributed in six weeks and about double that number in a later reprint at a reduced price.[38]

In the nineties these works were still in great demand: a hasty count in *The English Catalogue* reveals eleven different editions or issues of *The Wide Wide World* and about twenty of *Uncle Tom's Cabin* during the decade. Indeed, more impressive evidence of the diffusion of these books long after their first appearance is at hand. In 1891 "a careful investigator" determined to find out just what books were read by the English peasants. Four works, he concluded, were to be discovered in "most English well-to-do labourers' cottages": *Pilgrim's*

---

[36] F. A. Mumby, *The House of Routledge 1834–1934*, pp. 52–54.

[37] *Ibid.*, p. 56. Routledge was not the chief publisher of Susan Warner.

[38] *The Life of Edward Bulwer First Lord Lytton*, by his grandson, London, 1913, I, 474 n. (Bulwer refers of course to an earlier period.) Cf. also G. H. Lewes to one of his children, March 17, 1860 (Arthur Paterson, *George Eliot's Family Life and Letters*, London [1928], p. 80). (For indications of Lewes's interest in American authors and in the American reputation of George Eliot see *ibid.*, pp. 136–137 and 163.) In 1872 the sales of Trollope's works in both the expensive editions and the cheaper reprints were estimated at not more than thirty thousand copies ("On the Forms of Publishing Fiction," *Tinsley's Magazine*, X, May, 1872, 412). *Adam Bede* was considered remarkably successful in 1859, with a sale of sixteen thousand copies in a year (Blanche C. Williams, *George Eliot: a Biography*, New York, 1936, p. 162).

Progress, Foxe's *Book of Martyrs, Uncle Tom's Cabin,* and *The Wide Wide World.*[39]

But to return to the cheap book in general. It should not be assumed that all of the works issued at a shilling or two were disseminated in "libraries" or series. Many reprints of *Uncle Tom's Cabin* and *The Wide Wide World,* for example, were brought out without the advertising value of being included in a series, for they needed no advertising. But almost every very popular American book not protected by copyright found its way into one or more of the series. Thus, of the twelve different London publishers who brought out such volumes by Poe as were issued in the 1880s and are now in the British Museum, five included his work in one or more series. Routledge offered the poems in both a "Pocket Library" and an "Excelsior Series," F. Warne and Company in the "Chandos Classics," Walter Scott in the "Canterbury Poets," and Ward, Lock, and Company in "Moxon's Popular Poets." Selections from his tales were to be had in the "World Library" and in a "Sixpenny Novels" series, both issued by Routledge, as well as in Scott's "Camelot Classics." Cassell and Company combined both the prose and verse of Poe in their popular "Red Library."

Such American works as were first published in Great Britain were often brought out at the fairly high price which in general characterized the new book in the English market until the 1890s, although, if popular in appeal, like some of their British rivals, they were shortly afterwards issued in one or more series. Patrons of Mudie's circulating library and the high-class country trade were, of course, not averse to popular works but apparently preferred them in an expensive format. De luxe editions were especially popular as Christmas gifts, and prominent American authors were frequently brought out in sumptuous style to satisfy the demand. Thus, *Uncle Tom's Cabin* could be bought in a fifteen-shilling edition as well as a yellowback, and for some years an oversplendid volume of Longfellow's poems, with one hundred and eighty drawings by John Gilbert, was one of the leaders

[39] *Illustrated London News,* XCIX (September 12, 1891), 342. Occasionally an old edition of *Pamela* or *Clarissa* was also found, but "Scott and Dickens are almost unknown; none of the modern men have penetrated below a certain genteel stratum, if we except religious writers and preachers, whose written sermons command a certain sale in the country districts. Shakspere is read in Warwickshire, but nowhere else, 'Robinson Crusoe' in all the seacoast villages, and Burns in Scotland."

in the Christmas trade. Its publisher, Routledge again, is said to have paid a thousand pounds for the art work of the first edition.

The "legitimate" editions of American authors for which the British publisher held a respectable copyright are also important even though their history for most of the century is the record of the publications in England by such transatlantic authors as lived in Europe. But later when there were "Canadian copyrights" and closer coöperation across the sea on the part of the publishers—especially after 1891 —the control of advance copy, proofs, plates, and so on made possible more numerous "orthodox" editions. With the varying interpretations of the copyright laws, a publisher would scarcely risk the regular limited edition at a high price—for fear of the rival sales of cheaper piracies—unless the author at the time of publication was resident in England. But Washington Irving, James Fenimore Cooper, John Neal, Nathaniel P. Willis, Moncure D. Conway, Bayard Taylor, Charles G. Leland, Bret Harte, James Russell Lowell, Henry James, Francis Marion Crawford, Harold Frederic, Nathaniel and Julian Hawthorne, Joaquin Miller—all these and many more—profited by residing in Europe at a time when certain of their works were first published in London, and thus enjoyed, along with royalties presumably greater than the average for Americans, publication in a more dignified and expensive format and so, often received, through the business connections of their publishers, more favorable attention in the review columns of newspapers and magazines.[40] Some other American authors took advantage of shorter visits to Europe, as well as the services of friends resident abroad, to arrange for a type of production more respectable than that of the series or "library," Holmes with *Our Old Home* and Longfellow with *The New England Tragedies,* for example. The number of books by Americans published in England before their appearance in the United States is rather large, although it does not compare in quantity with their English counterparts which first appeared in this country.[41] This circumstance illus-

[40] The influence of publishers upon reviews may be taken for granted throughout the century as, of course, today. For early illustrations see Matthew W. Rosa, *The Silver-Fork School: Novels of Fashion Preceding Vanity Fair,* New York, 1936, chap. ix.

[41] Examples of a number of works first published in transatlantic editions are to be found in two volumes compiled by I. R. Brussel: *Anglo-American First Editions 1826–1900: East to West,* London and New York, 1935; and *Anglo-American First Editions: Part Two: West to East 1786–1930,* London and New York, 1936.

trates from another point of view the obvious fact that throughout the century American readers were more interested in the works of English authors than were the British in the products of American pens.

Already by the middle of the century almost all of the most important firms in England, as well as a number of the minor ones, had issued in regular fashion works by one or more American authors. The house of Murray, for example, was the first to publish Melville's *Typee* and *Omoo,* in 1846 and 1847 respectively, but apparently did not succeed very well in selling them even at the low price of six shillings.[42] Murray undoubtedly fared better with Motley's *History of the United Netherlands,* for the first two volumes in 1860 led all the other new works issued by the firm in the demand manifested at its annual trade sale.[43] *The Rise of the Dutch Republic,* issued by John Chapman in 1856, had previously enjoyed a phenomenal success, with a sale of seventeen thousand copies in its first year in England— a result as spectacular as the lionizing of its author by West End society.[44] But the earliest of Murray's stars from America had been Washington Irving, to whom in 1824 he paid fifteen hundred guineas for *Tales of a Traveller.* For *The Conquest of Granada,* published when the enthusiasm for Irving, engendered by *The Sketch Book,* was on the wane and when the work could not legally be secured from piracy, the firm gave two thousand guineas, a price which compares favorably with the £1,575 paid Byron for the first two cantos of *Don Juan.*[45] But because of constant piracies Murray sold his rights

[42] Some months after *Omoo* had appeared Murray wrote: "Of Typee, I printed 5,000 copies and have sold 4,104. Of Omoo, 4,000 and have sold 2,512. Thus I have gained by the former £51. 2s. 0d. and by the latter I am a loser of £57. 16s. 10d." Murray offered one hundred pounds for the English copyright of *Typee* and agreed to publish *Omoo* on half profits but demanded proof that Melville had really gone to the South Seas (George Paston [E. M. Symonds], *At John Murray's: Records of a Literary Circle 1849–1892,* London [1932], pp. 51–52). (See *ibid.,* p. 53, for objections to these books on moral grounds.) Some of the earlier critical notices of Melville's books have been analyzed by Charles Anderson in "Melville's English Debut," *American Literature,* XI (March, 1939), 23–38.

[43] *The Correspondence of John Lothrop Motley,* ed. G. W. Curtis, New York, 1889, I, 355.

[44] *Ibid.,* I, 190 n.

[45] Samuel Smiles, *A Publisher and His Friends: Memoir and Correspondence of the Late John Murray,* London and New York, 1891, II, 133–134, 258; I, 403.

in Irving's works to Bohn, from whom eventually they went far and wide in cheap reprints by various publishers.[46]

Another of the giants of the early nineteenth-century booktrade—Bentley—apparently paid well for the earlier novels of Fenimore Cooper, and issued most of them in orthodox three-decker style with a price of 31*s.* 6*d.*; but he was unable to hold the copyright long in spite of occasional law suits.[47] His firm was the first to publish Melville's *Mardi, Redburn, White-Jacket,* and *The Whale; or Moby Dick,* in expensive editions at 21*s.* or 31*s.* 6*d.*; but the house of Longman, which bought the rights to *The Confidence Man,* issued it in 1857 at five shillings.

One of the minor publishers who brought out a number of transatlantic works in authorized editions not included in cheap series was John Chapman, who printed books by Ralph Waldo Emerson, Theodore Parker, and other Americans, but rarely, it seems, made payments.[48] Probably through Emerson's instrumentality, he sponsored in 1849 Thoreau's *A Week on the Concord and Merrimack Rivers.*

In the middle of the century—and for some years following—the outstanding publisher of American books in more orthodox format was Nicholas Trübner, who set up in business in 1851 and specialized in importing American and Oriental works, and frequently brought out authorized editions of books by transatlantic authors, especially those of a more intellectual character. For example, while W. D. Howells was in Italy Trübner agreed, through Moncure D. Conway as mediator, to publish *Venetian Life* at half profits, under the condition that an American firm should take five hundred copies.[49] Trübner is of interest also as a publisher of American humor, for it

---

[46] *Ibid.,* II, 262. For the popularity of Irving's biography of Goldsmith see Knight, *The Case of the Authors as Regards the Paper Duty,* p. 19.

[47] For Cooper's later tales, "as fast as they were written," Bentley paid three hundred pounds each, presumably for advance copy of proofs or sheets (Thomas R. Lounsbury, *James Fenimore Cooper,* Boston, 1883, p. 262). See also Spiller and Blackburn, *op. cit.,* Introduction.

[48] *The Letters of Ralph Waldo Emerson,* ed. Ralph L. Rusk, New York, 1939, III, 351; IV, 14.

[49] *Life in Letters of William Dean Howells,* ed. Mildred Howells, Garden City, N.Y., 1928, I, 95.

was he who first gave the British reader the Breitmann poems, although they were soon pirated by John C. Hotten.[50]

The firm of Sampson Low, which in 1847 became Harpers' agents in England, soon achieved prominence not only as importers and, as we have seen, as publishers of American books in cheap series but also as sponsors of transatlantic authors in more expensive editions, for example, Melville's *Clarel* (1876). After the 1870s the number of British publishers who brought out "simultaneous" editions of American works increased consequentially; and, of course, with the passage of the Copyright Act of 1891 such coöperation became standard practice. In the last two decades of the century Macmillan, Chatto and Windus, and David Douglas were among the firms most prominently identified with authorized editions of works by American writers. Between the years 1883 and 1885, both dates inclusive, the last-mentioned publisher brought out volumes by John Burroughs, George W. Cable, W. D. Howells, Frank Stockton, George W. Curtis, O. W. Holmes, Henry Thoreau, Joel Chandler Harris, and Thomas Bailey Aldrich. In the nineties, very possibly the outstanding specialist in new American books of a literary sort was William Heinemann, whose connections with cosmopolitan intellectual currents of the period made it very natural that he should have a good many Americans on his list. Then, too, he had been trained in the booktrade by Trübner.[51] Among the writers whose books he published were James M. Whistler, Harold Frederic, Gertrude Atherton, Edward Bellamy, Charles G. Leland, the Pennells, Henry James, and Stephen Crane. Crane's war classic, *The Red Badge of Courage,* was one of Heinemann's marked successes in 1895 and 1896.

The increase in coöperation between certain American and British publishers in the latter half of the century, especially after 1870, is to be ascribed in large part to the establishment of branch houses; and a few illustrations may be introduced properly at this point. It is natural to find that the chief British publisher of American books during

[50] Elizabeth R. Pennell, *Charles Godfrey Leland: a Biography,* Boston and New York, 1906, I, 356–357, *et passim.* See also William E. A. Axon, "In Memoriam: Nicholas Trübner," *Library Chronicle,* I (1884), 42 ff.

[51] A work on Heinemann is available: Frederic Whyte, *William Heinemann,* London [1928].

the middle of the century and for some time following, namely, the house of Routledge, was the first to invade the United States by establishing a branch. The date, as stated earlier in this chapter, is 1854. By 1881 Cassell and T. Nelson also had established active branches across the Atlantic; by 1890 Longmans, Macmillan, and Warne had followed suit; and at the end of the century John Lane and the Oxford University Press were added to the list.[52] Of course these branch houses were established primarily to sell English books in the United States, but the necessary coöperation with American firms resulted in an increased number of authorized British editions of books written by citizens of the United States.

More important, though less numerous, were the branches of American publishing houses in England. Daniel Appleton seems to have been the pioneer, for in 1839 he decided to establish a branch in London, although he appears not to have issued in Great Britain any literary works bearing his own imprint until late in the century.[53] Two years earlier an agency of Wiley and Putnam seems to have been established in London for the stimulation of the export trade; and by 1841, we are to believe, this agency had become a branch of the New York office.[54] The house of Putnam, however, does not become important in the use of a British imprint until later in the century, for its branch was closed in 1847 and not reopened until after the Civil War.[55] During the forties, however, it issued authors like Poe, Hawthorne, Margaret Fuller, and William Gilmore Simms in a "Library of American Books," but its chief European function for most of the century was exporting and importing, not publishing.

Like many an American firm, Harpers early had an agent in Eng-

---

[52] See *The Trade Circular Annual* for the years in question. The idea of a "great international publishing house" seems to have struck Alexander Macmillan on a trip to the States in 1867 (Charles L. Graves, *Life and Letters of Alexander Macmillan*, London, 1910, p. 275). Longmans had had an agent in New York since 1875 (Harold Cox and John E. Chandler, *The House of Longman*, London, 1925, pp. 35–36). It is to be remembered that the illustrations provided here are not intended to form a complete history of the Anglo-American booktrade.

[53] Grant Overton, *Portrait of a Publisher*, New York and London, 1925, p. 32.

[54] George H. Putnam, *A Memoir of George Palmer Putnam*, New York and London, 1903, I, 49–50, 161–162.

[55] George H. Putnam, *Memories of a Publisher 1865–1915*, New York and London, 1916, pp. 58–59.

land. As has been pointed out, Sampson Low represented that house from 1847 until the 1880s.[56] But since the New York establishment for years had made its income through English reprints, at first often piracies, one would hardly expect a Harper branch in Great Britain very early in the century. But when the American copyright law of 1891 went into effect the situation was very different, for the firm had a long list of American authors many of whom were of great value in the English trade. In order to secure its share of profits from the demands of British readers the house abandoned its connection with the firm of Sampson Low and backed the establishment in London of James R. Osgood, McIlvaine & Co., whose name appears on numerous works brought out in England early in the 1890s; but upon the death of Osgood, Harpers took over the company and made it a branch of the New York house.[57] So far as the world of books is concerned the mightiest American invader of English business in the nineties was the house of Harper.

Such are a few examples of the reciprocal operation of the Anglo-American booktrade during the century. As the number of transatlantic agencies and branches increased the likelihood of a mutual respecting of rights was enhanced, even though the legal basis for it was flimsy. But there were too many new firms arising and too many companies without transatlantic branches to insure orthodox publication for the foreign author, and the true picture after 1870 is probably one of an increased number of regularly authorized editions in regular format along with an increased number of cheap reprints often piratical in nature. Of the increase there can be no doubt, for bookmen sometimes guessed that the number of readers in the British Isles trebled during the final quarter of the century. Since the passage of the Copyright Act of 1891 tended to force the prices of American books upward the natural effect of a diminution in sales may be taken for granted. Since 1890 many American authors have appeared in

[56] J. Henry Harper, *The House of Harper,* New York and London, 1912, p. 131.
[57] *Ibid.,* pp. 519 ff. J. M. Dent tells us that in the late nineties Macmillan accepted nearly all of his publications for America, and that he himself bought American editions to sell in Britain, from Little, Brown, from Scribners', and others (*The House of Dent 1888–1938,* London, 1938, p. 99). An examination of the various opinions in Carroll D. Wright, *A Report on the Effect of the International Copyright Law in the United States,* Washington, 1901, leads to the conclusion that the chief American publishers exported more plates to England after 1891 than before.

England in a more respectable format, but the number who have been read by the hundreds of thousands has declined from the days when the latest American book could be read in a shilling yellowback purchased at any railway station. So far as the mutual interest in the literature of the two countries is concerned the most favorable season for the agitation for an English-speaking Union must have been the last two decades of the century.

Thus far I have illustrated the reproduction in England of American books in cheap format—especially in series or "libraries"—and also the printing in more orthodox form of authorized editions, sometimes "simultaneous"; and the second topic has led to a brief description of the establishment of branch houses, a feature of the booktrade which serves to show why an increasing number of "legitimate" issues of books by Americans made their appearance in England even before 1891. While accounting for a good many titles, especially of works by newer authors, the "legitimate" publications rarely achieved a sale which compared favorably with that of the cheap series. There were exceptions, of course, like Mrs. Stowe's *Dred,* which was brought out in an authorized edition by Sampson Low in 1856 and sold 165,000 copies within a year; but more typical, no doubt, were smaller editions such as the nine thousand copies of *Among My Books,* for which Lowell was paid twenty pounds by Low in 1875.[58] Of the third type of American book in the British trade, namely, the direct import, something remains to be said. We may assume that the sales of an individual title directly imported were, speaking by and large, relatively small, since any important demand for such a book would immediately have led to a reprint. But the number of titles represented by the imported books is very large, and chiefly on that account some illustration of their history in the century must be given.

It may be taken for granted that practically every English publisher who issued any considerable number of books ventured at least once or twice to print or reprint an American work. Just so, it may be taken for granted that it was a rare bookseller who did not display on his shelves an occasional book from across the sea. Many of the publishers—in fact, most of them—operated retail bookstores, often with a

[58] Forrest Wilson, *op. cit.,* p. 419; *New Letters of James Russell Lowell,* ed. M. A. DeWolfe Howe, New York and London, 1932, p. 213. Mrs. Stowe was paid ten thousand dollars for the English rights to *Dred.*

circulating library, and a large number of them had made their first ventures in the publishing business because of the interest in and familiarity with the trade engendered thereby. As previously, we may confine our illustrations to such dealers as seem to be important because of a special or unusual interest in the American trade.

In the 1820s, according to the recollections of John Neal, "Miller of Black Friars" was known as the "American bookseller" [59] in London, but concerning his activities little information appears to be available. Toward the end of the decade Obadiah Rich, American consul in Spain and elsewhere, returned from Valencia and immediately opened a bookstore in London which was soon advertised as a "Depôt for American Publications." The business was continued by Rich or his son for a number of years, but its specialty seems to have been the collecting of rare works dealing with North and South America, a fact which has made Rich's book lists of considerable interest to bibliographers.[60] There is no reason to suppose, however, that at his shop American books of all sorts were not for sale. In the thirties a certain Richard J. Kennett was also a specialist in the importation of volumes from the United States, and in 1836 or 1837 the firm of Wiley and Putnam became very active in the field.[61]

After the abandonment by Putnam of his London branch—in 1847 —one of his former employees, Thomas Delf, undertook to continue as an importer, and he was in 1851 joined in partnership with Nicholas Trübner.[62] Shortly afterward the partnership was broken up, and Trübner, forming another company with David Nutt, continued to specialize in importing American books. As has been seen, he soon became one of the recognized publishers of transmarine authors. But for years the chief part of his business was the import-and-export trade, in the course of which he came to be the London agent for a number of American publishers of books and periodicals. With the

---

[59] *Wandering Recollections of a Somewhat Busy Life*, Boston, 1869, p. 251.

[60] See the sketch of Rich in the *D.A.B.* and Adolph Growell, *Book-Trade Bibliography in the United States in the XIXth Century*, New York: The Dibdin Club, 1898, pp. xlv–xlviii. Rich's firm acted also as publishers on occasion, bringing out, for example, the first part of Longfellow's *Outre-Mer* in 1832, and Holmes's *Poems* in 1846, in both cases the very first English imprints of these authors known to exist.

[61] Advertisements in *Bent's Monthly Literary Advertiser.*

[62] Axon, *op. cit.;* and Mumby, *The House of Routledge 1834–1934.* Trübner's firm was eventually united with that of Routledge.

encouragement to the importation of American works consequent upon the success of *Uncle Tom's Cabin,* Trübner in 1852 began running in one of the outstanding trade journals, *Bent's Monthly Literary Advertiser,* a regular list of American books to be had for sale through his auspices [63]—a list of considerable length and inclusiveness, for few of the important books brought out in the United States were omitted. In 1865, with the renewed quickening of British interest in American books stimulated by the Civil War, Trübner started a periodical of his own, designed to advertise the works in which he specialized—namely, American books first, and secondly, Oriental works. The title given the new journal was *Trübner's American and Oriental Literary Record,* but from time to time this was slightly changed.[64] While best known today by students of the Orient, up to March, 1889, the periodical was primarily identified with the import trade in American books.

Between the time of his listing his American imports in *Bent's Advertiser* and the establishment of his own journal, Trübner made another important contribution to the bibliography of American publications, for in 1855, he issued a volume entitled *Trübner's Bibliographical Guide to American Literature Being a Classified List of Books, in All Departments of Literature and Science Published in the United States of America during the Last Forty Years.* The preface to this work asserted that the majority of the books listed in the guide were in stock, and a thirty-seven-page introduction on the history of publishing and of intellectual progress in America undertook to defend the United States from conventional British misconceptions.[65] With the interest of the English trade in American books

---

[63] The list begins to appear in the number for November 11, 1852.

[64] Announcements of forthcoming books, literary chitchat, occasional obituaries of Americans, and, above all, lists of new periodicals and books for sale made up the contents at first. Contemporary publications in South American countries were also listed. Beginning with the issue for January, 1880, a new series was started; and a third series was inaugurated in March, 1889. The periodical lasted until April, 1891.

[65] Poe's "The Raven" Trübner considered "the most remarkable poem written in the last thirty years" (p. xvii). In the United States in 1853, he announced, there were 733 books published, 278 being reprints of English books and 35 being translations. English reprints of American books in 1853, exclusive of such as appeared under disguised titles, were estimated at 119. In 1854 no less than 185 American productions were reprinted in England (p. xxiv). Trübner seems to have been following his predecessor Putnam in defending the cause of American literature (see George P. Putnam, *American Facts,* London, 1845).

stimulated by a recent decision in the House of Lords that nonresident foreigners were not entitled to copyright, Trübner's manual was quickly sold out; and four years later, in 1859, he issued a second and larger work of a similar nature. The title reads: *Trübner's Bibliographical Guide to American Literature: a Classed List of Books Published in the United States of America during the Last Forty Years.* A sixty-seven-page introduction, "Contributions towards a History of American Literature," was supplied by Benjamin Moran, an assistant secretary of the American legation. Such efforts indicate full well the importance of the American book to the English trade, as well as the systematic nature of their German compiler.

But Trübner had a powerful rival who also listed American books in a periodical and even undertook the compilation of a bibliography. He was Sampson Low, who as Harpers' agent from 1847 on to the middle of the eighties was one of the chief importers of American books as well as a publisher of them. As editor, and later owner, of the chief trade journal of the century, the *Publishers' Circular,* Low soon took advantage of his position to list in the periodical the chief American works imported into England, and this practice was of considerable importance in enabling the London trade to keep its eye on the latest transatlantic offerings. In 1856 he brought out a bibliography of American books as a rival to Trübner's *Guide* with the title: *The American Catalogue of Books: or, English Guide to American Literature Giving the Full Title of Original Works Published in the United States since the Year 1800, with Especial Reference to Works of Interest to Great Britain, with the Prices at Which They May Be Obtained in London.* Few, however, if any, of the works in the list were published before 1840. Like the compilations of Trübner, this bibliography also contains prefatory matter calculated to convince the British reader that no longer could American books be considered as for the most part merely reprints of English titles.[66]

Various minor dealers and publishers with special interests were also prominently identified with the importation of American books, for example, John Chapman—editor of the *Westminster Review*—

---

[66] Low asserted that in the United States during the year 1853 there were 879 new books or new editions, including 298 reprints of English works and 37 translations. In 1854, of 765 new books or editions, 277 were of English origin and 41 were translations. For 1855 his figures ran: 1,092; 250; and 38 (p. vi).

who favored works by the Unitarians and other liberals; [67] and of course agents at branch houses continued to provide markets for the American import in ever-increasing numbers. After the Civil War, with Low and Trübner as centers, books made in America must have been available throughout the United Kingdom; and sometimes they cropped up in very strange places indeed. For example, it was a wandering bookseller, a Civil War veteran, who sold Ruskin's cork-cutter, Thomas Dixon, a first edition of *Leaves of Grass* in Sunderland. From him the book went via William Bell Scott to the Rossetti circle, with the eventual result of the first English appearance of Whitman, edited in 1868 by William M. Rossetti and published by John Camden Hotten—notorious as the publisher who took over Swinburne after Moxon had dropped him because of the "immorality" of *Poems and Ballads*.[68] Hotten, it may be added, was known not only for the broadness of his views but also for his interest in slang.[69]

These imported American books were not always ultimately of American origin, since a number of translations from the German or the French came to England via the United States; George Ripley's "Specimens" of foreign literature are examples. Then, too, either because of inclusiveness, editorial material, or price, English works sometimes came back to England in the shape of books manufactured in the United States. As early as 1845, it is claimed, American publishers were ahead of their British rivals in first collecting and first printing relatively complete editions of such writers as Cudworth, Bolingbroke, Burke, Paley, Dugald Stewart, Macaulay, and others.[70] The collections of Macaulay's essays brought out in 1840 and 1841 in the United States were imported into England in such quantities that their author was forced to prepare his own substitute. As he himself described the situation in 1843, "The question is now merely this, whether Longman and I, or Carey and Hart of Philadelphia, shall have the supplying of the English market with these papers. The

---

[67] Haight, *op. cit., passim.* Edward Marston in his list of bookmen known to him in 1846 mentions Wiley and Putnam, Delf, and a certain D. Kimpton as specialists in American books (*After Work,* Appendix).

[68] *Autobiographical Notes of the Life of William Bell Scott,* ed. W. Minto, London, 1892, II, 32–33, 267–269. See also Harold Blodgett, *Walt Whitman in England,* Ithaca, N.Y., 1934, chap. ii.

[69] *D.N.B.* See chap. iii of the present volume.

[70] Putnam, *American Facts,* p. 80.

American copies are coming over by scores, and measures are being taken for bringing them over by hundreds." [71] Forty years later W. Clark Russell was, likewise, to complain of the return to England of American reprints of his books.[72]

Of course, like the reprint, the imported book was of every imaginable type. Trübner's list compiled for his 1855 *Guide* may be analyzed according to his own criteria: theology, 13 pages of titles; jurisprudence, 2½ pages; medicine and surgery, 9 pages; natural history and science, 6 pages; philosophy and mathematics, 1 page; education, 5 pages, with one and a half of these five devoted to "juvenile books"; philology, linguistics, and antiquities, 5 pages; modern languages, 1 page; history, 8 pages; geography, 4 pages; military and naval science, 2 pages; politics, 3 pages; belles-lettres, 8 pages. But it must be said that the number of titles per page varies somewhat, and that the works catalogued as belles-lettres were actually more numerous than any excepting those listed under theology and history.

In the twelfth number of his *American and Oriental Literary Record,* that for February 26, 1866, Trübner made mention of the fact that, in addition to the contents of various periodicals, he had for the preceding twelve months listed 1,775 titles which he had imported from the United States. Of these, he said, 222 were theology; 165, history; 129, poetry; 113, novels; 117, works for the young; 99, biography; 77, medicine; 67, law; 66, geography and travel; 53, commerce and business; 45, politics; 38, philology; 35, natural history; and 43, general and practical science.

Lest one should forget that American books often educated as well as entertained British readers even early in the nineteenth century, the fact should be noted that hosts of American textbooks were not only imported but reprinted in the United Kingdom—even those

[71] George O. Trevelyan, *The Life and Letters of Lord Macaulay,* London, 1876, II, 124 n. Carey and Hart were the publishers of the 1841 edition. In the middle of the century the British imposed the maximum tax on imports of American books, and the United States retaliated with a 10 percent tax on English publications, or 20 percent if the works in question had already been printed in the country (Marjorie Plant, *op. cit.,* p. 424). John Chapman, in 1852, observed that at that time the English tax on books imported from the United States was about sixpence per pound. He further stated that the American tariff of July 30, 1846, levied a duty of 10 percent on English books—and 20 percent if they were in the course of republication (*Cheap Books and How to Get Them,* pp. 15, 16).

[72] *Athenæum,* November 1, 1884, p. 562.

which dealt with Latin and Greek, such as the various productions of Charles Anthon. To thousands of British students the name Webster meant *dictionary*. And, of course, religious books, which in the number of titles led all the others until late in the century the novel usurped first place, were of great concern in the history of British reprints of transatlantic authors.[73] In 1845 a practical analysis of reprints—not importations—of American books covering the preceding ten years was reported as follows: theology, 68; fiction, 66; juvenile, 56; travel, 52; education, 41; biography, 26; history, 22; poetry, 12; ethics, 11; philology, 10; science, 9; law, 9 — a total of 382 reprints in about a decade.[74]

But to return to the imported book—and with two illustrations to dispose of the problem of "How many titles?" As has been earlier recorded, Sampson Low, one of the two chief specialists in the importation of American works in and after the middle of the century, for many years owned and edited the *Publishers' Circular,* leading organ of the trade, and in this journal he listed regularly the titles of the "chief books" brought over from the United States and offered for sale by himself—and presumably by Trübner and others. *The English Catalogue,* moreover, which is based upon the entries in the *Publishers' Circular,* records a total of 75,493 new books offered for sale in England during the period 1856 to, but not including, 1876. Of these the total number of American imports—not reprints—is 5,779, a proportion of more than 7.5 percent. These statistics, it should be remembered, cover the period of the Civil War.[75] For the period 1881–1889,

---

[73] The great indebtedness of the British to American theological writers deserves a special study. In 1853 when Newman became Rector of the Catholic University of Ireland the first person to whom he applied to deliver lectures in Dublin was an American, Orestes Brownson (Arthur M. Schlesinger, Jr., *Orestes A. Brownson: a Pilgrim's Progress,* Boston, 1939, pp. 216–217).

[74] Putnam, *American Facts,* p. 87. Putnam did not include disguised titles, etc., in the above. In regard to British plagiarisms of American works of intellectual consequence, he wrote: "The Londoners take a Natural History from Dr. Harris, a translation of Heeren from Mr. Bancroft, a Greek Grammar from Mr. Everett, and a Law of Bailments from Judge Story, not only with no 'by your leave,' but with a false assumption of paternal honours. And more recently a bulky Greek Lexicon of high standing, by an Edinburgh professor, has copied page after page from the American work of Mr. Pickering, without so much as alluding to the existence of such a work in its list of authorities" (*ibid.,* pp. 85–86).

[75] These figures are based on the *Index to the English Catalogue of Books,* London, 1876.

of a total of 45,493 titles, American imports accounted for 5,164, an average of almost 9 percent.[76]

From 1840, and perhaps earlier, on to the end of the century the English people read more books by American authors than by all the writers of the European continent combined. In the number of reprints, authorized or pirated, in the number of first editions, and in the number of titles imported from the United States the American portion was larger than all of the other non-British elements in the English booktrade. Especially important to the student of the Victorian literary background appear to be the last two decades of the century, when the consumption of books by Americans reached its highest point. During these *twenty years* publishing houses in the British Isles brought out at least thirty-five editions or issues of one or more volumes by Poe, twenty by Whitman, nine by Melville, twenty by Thoreau, fifty by Lowell, sixty by Irving, fifty by Cooper, seventy by Holmes, ninety by Hawthorne, twenty-five by Emerson, fifteen by Bryant, twenty-five by Whittier, forty-five by Howells, and sixty by Mark Twain.[77] But long before the eighties, if Sydney Smith had reappeared to ask, "Who reads an American book?" his reputation as a jokester would have been enhanced by the irony of recognized fact.

[76] Based on the *Index to the English Catalogue of Books,* London, 1889.

[77] Figures based on entries in *The English Catalogue.* (For the earlier period the listing of American reprints is not very reliable.) For the tremendous increase in the reading of transatlantic literature by the subscribers to Mudie's see an article, by the present writer, entitled "British Interest in American Literature during the Latter Part of the Nineteenth Century as Reflected by Mudie's Select Library," *American Literature,* XIII (January, 1942), 356–362.

II. THE PERIODICALS

"We have many things to learn from America. The maintenance of the honour and the reputation and the authority of the critical columns of our journals is one of these"—WALTER BESANT.

EARLY in the nineteenth century British travellers and critics acknowledged American superiority in one aspect of intellectual culture, namely, the diffusion of the reading habit among the less cultivated classes. The quantity of newspapers and magazines consumed in the United States was, like Niagara Falls, a wonder of the New World. Of course there were complaints about the low and vulgar tone of the public press, and the vast store of English material reprinted in American magazines was eyed with little satisfaction; but already in the 1830s there was no denying the fact that the United States had surpassed England in its devotion to the newspaper and the magazine.[1] With no taxes on paper, on advertisements, or on periodicals issuing news—and with a much more extensive system of elementary schools—it was only natural that the production of newspapers in the United States should have surpassed that in the United Kingdom. So far as quality is concerned, no one could compare the London *Times* and the New York *Herald* in the middle of the century without admitting that the former was far more genteel.[2] And

[1] Jane L. Mesick, *The English Traveller in America 1785–1835*, New York, 1922, pp. 207, 227 ff. Parliamentary discussions of the taxes on knowledge frequently led the liberals to comment on American superiority in newspaper reading. For example, Edward Lytton Bulwer, speaking in the House of Commons on June 14, 1832, is reported as saying: ". . . in America a newspaper sells on the average for 1½d. What is the result? Why, that there is not a town in America with 10,000 inhabitants, that has not its daily paper. Compare Boston and Liverpool: Liverpool has 165,175 inhabitants; Boston had, in 1829, 70,000 inhabitants. Liverpool puts forth eight weekly publications, and Boston, with less than half the population, and with about a fourth part of the trade of Liverpool, puts forth eighty weekly publications. In 1829, the number of newspapers published in the British Isles was 33,050,000, or 630,000 weekly, which is one copy for every thirty-sixth inhabitant. In Pennsylvania, which had only in that year 1,200,000 inhabitants, the newspapers amounted to 300,000 copies weekly, or a newspaper to every fourth inhabitant" (*Hansard's Parliamentary Debates*, 3d Ser., XIII, 626).

[2] Note Emerson's enthusiasm over the *Times* in *English Traits* (1856).

the debt of the American magazine to its British counterpart was for most of the century as great as was the indebtedness of the American booktrade to the British book.

By way of illustration one need only recall that in 1838 when N. P. Willis and T. O. Porter were planning the *Corsair* they thought first of naming the new journal the *Pirate* and contemplated a frank announcement of their purpose "to take advantage . . . of the privilege assured to us by our piratical law of copyright . . . . and take what we can get for nothing (that is good), holding, as the publishers do, that while we can get Boz and Bulwer for a thank-ye or less, it is not pocketwise to pay much for Halleck and Irving." [3] *Harper's* during its early years was likewise filled with foreign material; and the numerous "eclectic" magazines were parasites thriving on the British periodical press, two examples coupled with the name of Littell being the *Museum of Foreign Literature and Science,* which began publication in 1822, and the *Living Age,* which first appeared in 1844. Of the role of British author as contributor to the later American magazines, a glance at *Scribner's,* the *Century,* and their like in the eighties or nineties is sufficient demonstration. Charles Reade stated the case for many an English novelist when, in demanding more money from the firm of Harpers, he wrote: "Now this [sum] might be just in England; but hardly just in America, where as you know very well, I rank at least three times higher than I do in this country." [4]

The great respect paid by the intellectuals in the United States to the standard British reviews is, of course, a noted feature of the general dependence of American literature upon English criticism. It was furthered by the extensive circulation of the so-called American editions which were published at a very low price. [5] A Boston merchant, writing to his son-in-law in Iowa, in 1851 could observe: "I subscribed the other day for the *Westminster*—the *North British*—the *London Quarterly*—the *Edinburgh Review*—and *Blackwood's Monthly Maga-*

---

[3] Henry A. Beers, *Nathaniel Parker Willis,* Boston, 1896, p. 240.

[4] July 30, 1859 (J. Henry Harper, *The House of Harper,* New York and London, 1912, p. 161).

[5] By 1882, when Houghton Mifflin took over American editions of the *Quarterly Review* and the *Edinburgh Review,* the pirating of British critical journals in their entirety had practically ceased.

zine—all for 10 dollars." [6] Of the effect of such journals one may judge not only from the plans of Emerson and others for their own periodicals but also from the recollections of William Dean Howells, who wrote of his youth in Ohio:

I fancy it was well for me at this period to have got at the four great English reviews, the Edinburgh, the Westminster, the London Quarterly and the North British, which I read regularly, as well as Blackwood's Magazine. We got them in the American editions in payment for printing the publishers' prospectus, and their arrival was an excitement, a joy and a satisfaction. . . . I do not think I left any paper upon a literary topic unread, and I did read enough politics, especially in Blackwood's, to be of Tory opinions. [7]

But the reverse of the picture, namely, the effect of American periodicals in Britain, is also not without interest. As for the newspapers, for present purposes they may be dismissed with the general statement that the English product was often indebted to the American press not only for materials but for policies, the most notable influence appearing at the end of the century when the commercialized newspaper pioneered by Alfred Harmsworth, afterwards Lord North-cliffe, forged into the lead. The *Daily Mail,* launched in May, 1896, in three years reached a circulation of 543,000, twice the figure of any of its rivals, and proved the success of the methods which Harmsworth and his coadjutor Kennedy Jones had previously studied in the United States. W. T. Stead, whom Matthew Arnold considered to be one of the apostles of the "new journalism," likewise profited by his knowledge of the press of New York. [8] In his inaugural address delivered before the Institute of Journalists in 1900, Sir James Henderson, with some degree of truth, lamented the "American sensationalism" of the British press. The methods of the New York *Herald* and its successors were far more influential on popular journalism in Great Britain in the closing years of the century than those of the old London *Times.*

As for the magazines, we may begin with a few illustrations of the

[6] *Letters of Eliab Parker Mackintire of Boston* . . . , ed. Philip D. Jordan, New York, 1936, p. 72.

[7] *My Literary Passions,* New York, 1895, pp. 121, 123.

[8] R. C. K. Ensor, *England 1870–1914,* Oxford, 1936, pp. 310–312; and Richard H. Heindel, *The American Impact on Great Britain 1898–1914,* Philadelphia, 1940, chap. ii.

use of American material in the more democratic journals. With the taxes on paper and advertisements it would be natural to expect that the producers of cheap periodicals should often have looked for material for which payment was unnecessary. Nothing was more available than American books and periodicals. Vast quantities of such selections are hidden beneath the anonymity which for so long dominated the journalistic practices of the century; but occasionally sources are indicated. Turning to the most famous of the earlier British periodicals for the masses, the *Penny Magazine,* published by Charles Knight and sponsored by the Society for the Diffusion of Useful Knowledge, one finds in the very first volume—that for 1832—selections from an American almanac; from a "useful little book" called *The Frugal Housewife* by Lydia M. Child; from an old set of Virginia laws; and from the *North American Review;* as well as copious extracts from Franklin's autobiography, bits of Irving, and two poems by Bryant.[9] In introducing "To a Waterfowl," the editor observed that "while written in a style elegant enough to please the most fastidious" the verses were yet "simple and intelligible enough for the commonest reader."[10] As a publication designed especially for the lower classes the *Penny Magazine* could well praise Bryant's pellucid simplicity as a virtue—just as it could well demonstrate a generally favorable attitude toward all things American. A fair percentage of the two hundred thousand subscribers whom it acquired during its first year, we may be sure, were people of the sort who might be interested in emigrating to the new land in the West.[11]

---

[9] *Penny Magazine,* I, 34, 38, 126–127, 288, 71–72, 331, 120, 134–135. For the use of American material in British magazines prior to 1832, see William B. Cairns, *British Criticisms of American Writings, 1815–1833,* Madison, Wis., 1922, pp. 58–60, 71, 81–82, 225, 258. A very interesting example of the reprinting of the works of a Colonial poet is to be had in C. Lennart Carlson, "Richard Lewis and the Reception of His Work in England," *American Literature,* IX (November, 1937), 301–316.

[10] I (June 30, 1832), 134. The poem was reproduced from the edition of Bryant sponsored by Irving and published in London by Andrews in 1832. Selections from Bryant had appeared much earlier, in *Specimens of the American Poets; with Critical Notices, and a Preface,* London, 1822. The editor observed of the lines entitled "Thanatopsis": "There are few pieces in the works of even the first of our living poets, which exceed them" (p. 190).

[11] Note the disapproval of Mrs. Trollope's *Domestic Manners of the Americans* in the issue for May 31, 1832 (I, 83). Mrs. Trollope's book was in general more severely dealt with in England than the sensitive Americans supposed; and she herself became somewhat of an advocate of the United States after her return to her home.

One of the leading rivals of the *Penny Magazine* in its appeal to the "poor man" was *Chambers' Edinburgh Journal.* This also began publication in 1832 and its first volume likewise reveals the use of American material: Audubon, the *Token,* the New York *Mirror,* Lydia M. Child, and Bryant were drawn upon for selections.[12] Two Irish counterparts of these magazines, the *Irish Penny Magazine* (started January 5, 1833) and the *Irish Penny Journal* (started July 4, 1840) are less indebted to American sources, but a selection from Cooper shows up in the fourth number of the former, and the early issues of the latter include material from S. G. Goodrich, Dr. Channing, Prescott, and the *Knickerbocker.*[13]

Charles Knight, after the suspension of his own *Penny Magazine,* looked back on the wildfire spread of the cheap periodical and remarked:

In 1846, fourteen penny and penny-halfpenny Magazines, twelve Economical and Social Journals, and thirty-seven weekly sheets, forming separate books, were to be found in the shops of many regular booksellers, and on the counters of all the small dealers in periodicals that had started up throughout the country. The cheapness was accomplished in some by pilfering from every copyright work that came in their way.[14]

What was more probable than that they, like their predecessors, should reprint huge quantities of transatlantic offerings? A few further illustrations may suffice to prove that they did. *Hogg's Instructor,* which began with an issue for March 1, 1845, priced at a penny and a half, used bits from Irving in its first and third numbers; and sandwiched in between, one finds a poem by N. P. Willis, later followed by essays from the New York *Baptist Advocate* and the *American Biblical Repository.* As the journal grew older, fiction, filler, and travel articles from America appear more frequently, better authors sometimes being reprinted, for instance, Poe, whose story "The Gold Beetle" adorns the pages of two numbers brought out in 1853.[15] An-

[12] I, 48, 77, 191–192, 374, 262, 303–304, 181, 391–392, 160.

[13] *Irish Penny Magazine,* I, 36; *Irish Penny Journal,* I, 40, 109–110, 104, 136, 147–148, 168.

[14] *Passages from the Life of Charles Knight,* New York, 1874, p. 411.

[15] *Hogg's Instructor,* New Ser., X, 616–622, 634–638. An editorial note is not without the usual suggestion of American lack of originality: "This exceedingly interesting tale is taken from the American edition of the writings of Edgar A. Poe. Of the genius and errors of that ill-starred man, our readers must have heard generally ere now;

other cheap journal of the mid-century, the *Home Circle,* boldly announced Hawthorne, Longfellow, and Bryant on its list of contributors, although it merely pirated their work as it saw fit.[16] The *Family Friend* during the fifties likewise reprinted American authors at will, Phoebe Cary, Fanny Fern, James Gates Percival, and Longfellow being favorites; [17] and the *Home Magazine* was adequately described in 1859 as "almost entirely filled with stories . . . transplanted chiefly from American sources." [18]

Proceeding to the 1880s, one finds as a ready illustration a journal inspired by the deep conviction that nothing was needed in England more than "the spread of pure and lofty ideas." *Great Thoughts from Master Minds* is its full title, and it began publication as a penny weekly on January 5, 1884. The very first number indicates that America, too, could supply "great thoughts," for selections from Bryant, Emerson, Channing, Lowell, Longfellow, Bushnell—and even Henry Ward Beecher—find a place beside those from Shakespeare and Milton, Shelley and Plato. Turning at random to the issue for March 22, 1884, the reader discovers selections by W. R. Alger, brother of the more famous Horatio, Whittier, Parker, Channing, Bushnell, and J. G. Holland along with Tennyson, Ruskin, and St. Anselm.[19] It may be taken for granted that, up to the time of the passage of the International Copyright Act in the United States, the cheap periodical press of London and Edinburgh found support in the use of transatlantic material just as the cheap series of books thrived on the same source of supply.[20]

---

and few, above all, can have failed to meet with and admire his exquisite poem of 'The Raven.' In the case of the present story he is not quite original, Alexandre Dumas having introduced an episode of much the same bearing into his 'Monte Cristo'; but Mr. Poe has placed the subject in a comparatively novel light, and has handled it with a skill altogether masterly."

[16] For example, VI (1852), iv.

[17] The volume for 1854 (IX) has page after page taken from Fanny Fern's *Fern Leaves.*

[18] *British Quarterly Review,* XXIX (April 1, 1859), 339. For other periodicals which "borrowed" heavily from American sources see "Reading Raids: The Cheap Press," *Tait's Edinburgh Magazine,* XXII (April, 1855), 222–229.

[19] For the place of this journal in the cheap press of the 1880s see Edward G. Salmon, "What the Working Classes Read," *Nineteenth Century,* XX (July, 1886), 113.

[20] For American fiction in the cheap periodicals late in the century see "Penny Fiction," *Quarterly Review,* CLXXI (July, 1890), 150–171.

Of course there were early in the century a number of journals which were more especially concerned with the reprinting of American works than were the periodicals which have thus far been mentioned in the present chapter. The "Novel Newspaper," published by Elliott and Cunningham in weekly numbers at two pence each, included in 1839 seven works by Fenimore Cooper, three by Robert M. Bird, as well as others by Daniel P. Thompson, Timothy Flint, and William Gilmore Simms.[21] In the same year one could purchase in London the *American Miscellany,* a weekly of sixteen pages filled with tales, essays, and verse from abroad; and from time to time thereafter similar pirating miscellanies were brought out, such as the *American Magazine* (1851–1852), the *American Scrap-Book and Magazine of United States Literature* (1861–1863),[22] and the *Transatlantic* (1872).

Journals of a more intellectual character sometimes imitated their humbler rivals in culling material from American sources. As early as 1845 G. P. Putnam had affirmed:

Two or three articles from the North American Review, at different times, have been appropriated entire, as *original,* in the pages of a London Review, whose age and respectability should have discountenanced such an act. The transplanting of American magazine articles into English periodicals, frequently in so disguised a shape that the exotic loses its identity, has become an ordinary occurrence.[23]

He further illustrated the practice of piracy on the part of more intellectual periodicals by citing the case of the English *Quarterly Journal of Education,* which had "the habit of extracting entire articles from the 'American Annals of Education,' and other works, and publishing them as original communications." [24]

In addition to selections from American books and periodicals, readers of English magazines early and late in the nineteenth century sometimes found original material written by transatlantic authors, usually those who were living in Europe. In spite of the long-prevail-

---

[21] "Pirated Editions of American Novels," *Times Literary Supplement* for November 27, 1924, p. 804.

[22] *Ibid.,* and Frank L. Mott, *A History of American Magazines,* Cambridge, Mass., 1938, II, 130.

[23] *American Facts,* London, 1845, p. 85.

[24] *Ibid.,* p. 247. The annuals, of course, like the periodicals, frequently did the same thing with American originals.

ing practice of anonymity a large body of such material has been identified, and a few illustrations may be advanced to make clear the point. Irving, it will be recalled, early in the period of his European sojourn was offered the editorship of a British magazine at the hands of Sir Walter Scott, but this he refused. Later, he contributed to the *Quarterly Review*,[25] but probably because of his youthful experiments in journalism he was a very indifferent and reluctant magazinist—a rare specimen in the museum of American authors. A better illustration is the swashbuckling John Neal, who invaded England in 1824 and eventually penetrated to the most intimate circle of Jeremy Bentham. During the years 1824 to 1827, which embrace his stay abroad, he managed to place articles on American and other subjects in *Blackwood's,* the *European Magazine,* the *London Magazine,* the *European Review,* the *Monthly Magazine, or British Register,* the *New Monthly Magazine,* the *Oriental Herald,* and the *Westminster Review*.[26] Of these various offerings to the critical journals of Britain the most interesting is a series of articles on American writers which appeared in *Blackwood's* and which constitutes one of the earliest lengthy discussions of the literature of the United States to appear in Europe.[27] Another similar series of essays may be mentioned here, that which Timothy Flint contributed to the *Athenæum* for 1835.[28] Flint, it should be added, was not resident in England at the time.

Another American who contributed widely to the English magazines was N. P. Willis, whose sketches and poems were published during the 1830s by such journals as the *Court Magazine* and *Colburn's New Monthly,* for which he continued to write after his return

[25] Stanley T. Williams, *The Life of Washington Irving,* New York, 1935, I, 175–176; S. T. Williams and Mary A. Edge, *A Bibliography of the Writings of Washington Irving,* New York, 1936, p. 169.

[26] Irving T. Richards, "The Life and Works of John Neal," MS, Harvard University Dissertation, 1932, Vol. IV, Appendix F. For Neal in England see *ibid.,* Vol. I, chap. vii.

[27] For a reprint see *American Writers: a Series of Papers Contributed to Blackwood's Magazine (1824–1825),* by John Neal, ed. Fred Lewis Pattee, Durham, N.C., 1937.

[28] Nos. 401, 402, 405, 407, 409, 411, 412, 416–419 (July 4 to November 7, 1835). See also the preliminary series in *ibid.,* Nos. 375, 377, 380, and 382 (January 3 to February 21, 1835). These latter were written by N. P. Willis under pressure when Flint's manuscript was delayed (Henry A. Beers, *op. cit.,* p. 216). For later articles on American literature written by Americans but published in British journals see the Appendix of the present volume.

to New York.[29] Of course, almost any visitor from the United States who was handy with the pen was likely to contribute a few articles to a British journal, but Willis was for a while one of the luminaries on the horizon of London journalism, a close friend of Lady Blessington and her group, and a kind of Byronic hero to many a British admirer.[30] His success abroad led to his becoming probably the best-known prose writer in the America of the forties, and articles from his New York *Mirror* were very frequently reprinted in English newspapers and popular magazines. Even before the height of his fame in London he had been offered a salary to write for the *Morning Herald,* and in 1839, after a return to Europe, he estimated his receipts from British publishers for one year as amounting to $7,500.[31]

Proprietors of British magazines of the more entertaining sort, like *Bentley's Miscellany,* occasionally secured permission to publish Long-fellow, Charles Fenno Hoffman, and others, but often they merely pirated; and periodicals of a still less intellectual nature were delighted to pay for the sentimental drivel turned out by Mrs. E.D.E.N. South-worth.[32] But the practice of piracy was much more common on the part of the very cheapest of British magazines.

At the time of the outbreak of the Civil War a group of abolitionists in Boston sent as an agent to London a unique gentleman from Virginia, Moncure Conway, who hated the Trinity and slavery with an almost equal passion. He soon became prominent in England not only as the preacher of South Place Chapel but also as a well-known liberal who wrote for the reviews. During the several decades of his residence abroad he was from time to time a member of the staff of the *Daily News* and a prolific writer for *Fraser's,* the *Fortnightly,* the *Pall Mall Gazette,* the *Morning Star,* the *Academy,* and other magazines and newspapers. His articles for *Fraser's* alone run to about

[29] Beers, *op. cit.,* pp. 154–155.

[30] See Beers, *op. cit.,* and Irving T. Richards, "Longfellow in England," *PMLA,* LI (December, 1936), 1123–1140.

[31] Beers, *op. cit.,* pp. 129, 249. Part of this sum came from the royalties from several books published first in England.

[32] See the file of *Bentley's,* especially Vols. I to X. There are a few tales by Poe in *Bentley's.* Mrs. Southworth lived for several months in England during the middle of the century and wrote for various British journals. After her return to the United States, Robert Bonner, who published most of her products in his *Ledger,* regularly made arrangements for authorized reproduction in England (Southworth MSS in Duke University Library).

thirty in number.[33] One may recall also the early ventures in journalism of Henry Adams shortly after his return to the United States, and note how important to him—and to his American readers—were the articles on American politics and economics which he contributed to the *Westminster* and other British reviews.

After 1870, with the increasing number of American writers living abroad and with the development of the practice of "simultaning" (the simultaneous, or nearly simultaneous, publication of a book or article in both countries), the frequency with which one finds poems, stories, or essays by authors of the United States in the better English magazines increases. Thackeray at the outset of his career as editor of the *Cornhill* wrote to Longfellow, Halleck, Irving, and Motley for contributions, but the Civil War soon disrupted his plans.[34] During the period of Leslie Stephen's control of that journal a readiness was expressed to publish simultaneously work by Howells—and perhaps others of the contributors to the *Atlantic Monthly*.[35] The number of contributions by Americans to the *Cornhill,* however, is large enough to warrant its being mentioned as an illustration of the penetration of the transatlantic author into the highest class of British periodical literature. The *Contemporary Review* offers another good example of American contributors to the more intellectual British journals, for G. W. Cable, F. H. Underwood, Edward Bellamy, Albion Tourgée, and Gertrude Atherton were among the writers for that magazine during the late eighties and nineties.

Of course the inclusion of American authors among the contributors to the better journals necessitated a sympathetic attitude on the part of editors and publishers—and it may be said emphatically that few of the magazines of England were possessed of editors as friendly to America and Americans as Thackeray and Stephen. But toward the end of the century when the old-fashioned quarterly was driven to

[33] *Autobiography, Memories and Experiences of Moncure D. Conway,* Boston and New York, 1904, II, 149, 179, 200.

[34] J. G. Wilson, *Thackeray in the United States 1852-3–1855-6,* New York, 1904, II, 6–7. In 1861–1862 the *Cornhill* and the *Atlantic* "simultaned" Mrs. Stowe's novel *Agnes of Sorrento.*

[35] *Life in Letters of William Dean Howells,* ed. Mildred Howells, I, 277. The international interests of James T. Fields were a potent force. (*Macmillan's* was another British magazine interested in "simultaning.")

cover by the increasing popularity of the monthly magazine, the inclusion of American works, especially short stories, was considered good business practice to stimulate circulation; and the development of syndicates furthered the practice of "simultaning." But by the end of the century the practice declined. As Howells described the situation in 1902:

Formerly something could be got for the author by the simultaneous appearance of his work in an English magazine; but now the great American magazines, which pay far higher prices than any others in the world, have a circulation in England so much exceeding that of any English periodical that the simultaneous publication can no longer be arranged for from this side, though I believe it is still done here from the other side.[36]

The most widely discussed article dealing with a man of letters to appear in nineteenth-century England was one that was "simultaned" in the *Atlantic Monthly* and in *Macmillan's Magazine* for September, 1869—Mrs. Stowe's notorious attack on Lord Byron.

After 1870 there was an increase in the number of American contributions, induced by two factors: first, the rise in the number of English periodicals which, in imitating the methods of *Scribner's, Harper's,* and the *Century,* prized a short-story writer or essayist from across the sea; and, more important perhaps, the increase in the supply of American authors who resided for long or short periods in Europe. Of the writers of fiction, Francis Marion Crawford, Julian Hawthorne, Bret Harte, and Henry James appeared most frequently in the British periodicals, and in the largest number of them. Without aiming at completeness at all, one may note that Harte contributed to the *Cornhill, Macmillan's, Longman's, Temple Bar, Belgravia,* the *English Illustrated,* the *New Review,* the *Pall Mall Gazette,* the *Illustrated London News,* and many others. The range in the quality of the journals is amazing, as it is in the case of Henry James, whose stories or essays appeared not only in the *Yellow Book* and *Cosmopolis,* the latter perhaps the most ambitious magazine of the century, but also in *Black and White* and the *Illustrated London News.* After the extraordinary success of *The Red Badge of Courage* and its author's

[36] *Literature and Life,* New York and London, 1902, p. 12.

removal to England, the British editors hastened to secure stories by Stephen Crane. His work may be found in the *Cornhill,* the *Illustrated London News,* the *Pall Mall Magazine,* and a number of others. Frank Stockton, Sarah Orne Jewett, Mary Wilkins Freeman, Joel Chandler Harris, Constance Fenimore Woolson, and other story writers enjoyed a fair vogue in the English magazines. Mark Twain is represented in this type of publication by "The Tramp Abroad Again," which was serialized in the *Illustrated London News,* beginning in November, 1891, "Some Random Notes of an Idle Excursion" and a few other sketches which ran in *Belgravia* in 1877 and 1878, and "The American Claimant," which appeared in the *Idler* for 1892 and 1893.

Louise Chandler Moulton, who conducted a literary salon in London as well as in Boston, was a prolific contributor of inferior verse and of literary gossip to a variety of journals; and Brander Matthews was, likewise, fairly popular. Joaquin Miller, of course, was in great demand in the early seventies when he stunned the journalistic circles of London by combining the qualities of an Indian fighter and Lord Byron. Even the sophisticated *Dark Blue* published some of his poems—for example, "Kit Carson's Ride"—and followed up with an essay on the Oregon poet which begins with the words "a true singer from the New World," and ends with a eulogy of his verses, "imperishable as the peaks of the mountains or the melodies of the sea." The *Gentleman's Magazine,* however, seems to have led in the race for Miller's poetry.[37]

Compared with the bulk of British material the American contributions, of course, do not loom large, but they constitute a far from inconsequential element in such English periodicals as aimed at the same market which *Harper's* and the *Century* had won. *Longman's Magazine,* which began publication in November, 1882, offers an illustration better than the average. Its very first number contained a descriptive essay by Howells, whose work, however, was in general to be found only in American periodicals. John Burroughs, Bret Harte, Charles G. Leland, and Henry James were all among the early

[37] *Dark Blue,* II (September, 1871), 120–128. See, for example, *Gentleman's,* Vols. VII and VIII (1871 and 1872). In all cases merely samples are given, and no effort has been made to list all the contributions by any writer.

contributors, likewise Margaret Deland, whose novel, *John Ward, Preacher,* was widely sold in England and had made her name of value to the trade.[38] More material by James and a long serial by F. M. Crawford followed, but in the early nineties the American contributions disappeared. On the other hand, the *English Illustrated Magazine,* which issued its first number in 1884, shows an increase in its American element after 1891. During the eighties, James, Harte, and Crawford—the "big three" of American producers of fiction for British periodicals—are represented. From 1893 through 1895 Henry Harland, Robert Barr, Julian Hawthorne, and Mary Wilkins are among the contributors; and in 1896 one notes, with an unsatisfied curiosity, not only four contributions by Stephen Crane, but material by Julian Hawthorne, Longfellow, Harold Frederic, Joel Chandler Harris, Mary Wilkins, John B. Tabb, Frank Stockton, Brander Matthews, George Parsons Lathrop, Louise Moulton, and Louise I. Guiney. Such a concentration, however, is extremely rare. The American contributors usually appear rather sporadically; but the first volume or two of the magazines publishing fiction which were started after 1880 are likely to have something by Bret Harte or Henry James, if by no other American authors; and apparently there were no limits to the variety of authors from abroad, for even Ella Wheeler Wilcox is represented by poems in the *Pall Mall Magazine* for 1899.[39]

Closely allied to the history of the American contributors to the British magazines, and in part a factor in the increase in the number of such contributors after 1870, are the various attempts on the part of English publishers to establish international journals with an appeal to the entire English-speaking world. Efforts of the sort were made long before the Civil War. One of the earlier plans for an Anglo-American journal of a literary sort came as the result of the interest exhibited by British radicals in the transcendental *Dial,* which was edited by Margaret Fuller and Emerson during the years 1840 to

[38] Longmans had issued an authorized edition, but six pirates soon competed, one of whom sent the author a check for a thousand dollars (Margaret Deland, *Golden Yesterdays,* New York and London [1941], pp. 224–225).

[39] Her verses on "The Queen's Last Ride" were widely read in England at the time of Victoria's death (Jenny Ballou, *Period Piece: Ella Wheeler Wilcox and Her Times,* Boston, 1940, pp. 177 ff.). Professor Walter Graham has mentioned a number of American contributors to the Victorian journals in his *English Literary Periodicals,* New York, 1930.

1844.[40] This celebrated Boston quarterly, although possessed of only a few hundred subscribers at home, nevertheless always announced a foreign agent who took care of the British circulation—at first Wiley and Putnam, then John Green, and, for the last number in 1844, John Chapman, already mentioned as active in the importation and publication of American books. According to a letter written by Theodore Parker to Emerson on August 12, 1844, Chapman was eager to start "a *new* Dial" in London, for which Emerson, Carlyle, Tennyson, and others were to write; but nothing seems to have come of the project.[41] In December, 1846, Emerson reported that he had received three formal invitations to join in "an English-and-American Journal," the third of which had been extended by John A. Heraud, in those days associated with the *Athenæum*.[42] The year 1848 found Chapman still eager to publish a review "common to Old & New England," and Froude, Clough, and other Oxonians under the spell of Emerson were willing to "conspire"; but again this effort to renew the life of the *Dial* by making it international failed. Chapman, instead, took over the publication of the *Westminster Review*.[43]

Another attempt at an Anglo-American journal of English origin was made soon after the Civil War by one of the chief publishers of American books, the firm of George Routledge; and it may be used here as another illustration. This periodical actually came into being as a monthly entitled the *Broadway,* with offices both in New York and London. At the time of its first appearance, in September, 1867, the plan was to combine British and American contributors and by so

[40] Mudie's Library was begun with a collection of American transcendental works. A glance through the file of the *Westminster* will illustrate British awareness of the activities of the Boston group of liberals. See also the *Reasoner: a Weekly Journal, Utilitarian, Republican, & Communist,* edited by G. J. Holyoake. Vol. VI (1849), for example, contains material from the *Dial* (pp. 2–5), on Brownson (pp. 83 ff.), on and by Parker (pp. 146–149, 292–294), from Emerson (p. 270). Emerson's first little book *Nature* (1836) was at the outset more widely circulated in the United Kingdom than in the United States since much of it was reprinted in a Swedenborgian magazine (see the present writer's essay, "Some Remarks on Emerson's *Divinity School Address,*" *American Literature,* I, March, 1929, 27 n.).

[41] *The Letters of Ralph Waldo Emerson,* ed. Ralph L. Rusk, New York, 1939, III, 287.

[42] *Ibid.,* III, 363. In 1847 after the withdrawal of William Howitt from the editorship of the *People's Journal,* W. J. Linton asked Emerson to secure Bryant, Longfellow, Whittier, and others as paid contributors to that journal (*ibid.,* III, 378 n.).

[43] *Ibid.,* IV, 56 and 305.

doing appeal to the trade of both countries; political discussion naturally was to be eschewed.[44] But from the outset it was merely a London journal which devoted more than the average amount of space
to American topics and which included a few contributions by such
authors as the Cary sisters, Evert Duyckinck, and R. H. Stoddard.[45]
After a year's trial an announcement was made, in the number for
August, 1868:

"The Broadway" will cease to be specially an "Anglo-American" or an
"Americo-Anglican" magazine. We are convinced that there is a still
Broader way in Literature and Art than that which spreads itself under
the shadow of St. Paul's in London, or stretches from the Battery to
Harlem Bridge in New York.

The title was soon changed to fit the shift in policy—the *Broadway:
a London Magazine*. Routledge's New York office continued to han-
dle its sale in the United States, where, however, it seems to have had
little vogue. But contributions by Americans did not cease; as examples may be mentioned Whitman's "Whispers of Heavenly
Death," Mark Twain's "Cannibalism in the Cars," and Moncure
Conway's "Three American Poets" (one of them Howells).[46]

There are, of course, other examples of British attempts to produce
periodicals with a special American interest in the early seventies, a
period when "English-speaking Unions" and the like were being considered by advanced radicals, but we may pass these by in favor of a
few illustrations from the end of the century, when appeals to the
Anglo-American world were more insistent [47]—and probably more

[44] A prospectus appeared in the *Saturday Review* for June 29, 1867 (XXIII, 837).

[45] The first number contained an article on "William Cullen Bryant and American
Poetry," by W. Clark Russell, which begins: "The Americans have as yet, properly
speaking, no literature of their own." In the issue for November, 1867, Robert Buchanan wrote on Whitman, and in the number for the following month Russell
provided an essay on Longfellow.

[46] In the September, October, and November numbers for 1868. The numbering
of the volumes is very erratic.

[47] An *Anglo-American Times,* a weekly published in London 1865–1896, appears
to have been chiefly a sheet of financial and other news of interest to Americans abroad.
In 1872 a quarterly was begun in London as a guide to emigrants under the title
American Settler. In 1874 an *American Traveller* was started as a weekly intended to
give news to tourists and to list travelling Americans. Such numbers of these journals
as I have seen are without literary interest. For a list of these periodicals see Richard
H. Heindel, "Some Predecessors of 'Anglo-American News,'" *Anglo-American News,*
IV (December, 1937), 481, 513. In the January, 1887, issue of the *Westminster Re-*

cordial. The *Cosmopolis* advertised itself as "an International Review" when it began publication, as a monthly, in January, 1896, with T. Fisher Unwin as publisher; but despite the fact that it had a New York agent (the International News Company), it was primarily British and Continental. Henry James was represented in the first numbers with "The Figure in the Carpet," and there were a few more of his stories in later issues; but, except for him, Joseph and Elizabeth Pennell seem to have been the only other Americans who wrote for it.

Another example, *Literature,* is of slightly greater interest to the student of Anglo-American publishing. It began as a weekly under the editorship of H. D. Traill in October, 1897, with the subtitle "An International Gazette of Criticism." Published in England by the *Times* office and in the United States by Harpers, its purpose was really to take over the literary departments of the *Academy* as that excellent periodical had existed until the time of its revamping in 1896. The New York and London editions for 1897 and 1898 are identical except for the covers; but in 1899 the American edition, under the editorship of John Kendrick Bangs, went its own way—to an early death in November of the same year. The British edition lasted a little longer, and finally was merged again with the *Academy* in 1902. One must look twice to find anything especially indicative of an interest in America in the earliest issues of *Literature,* but with the number for March 26, 1898, Henry James started a series of articles on contemporary American books, a kind of gossip column with brief critiques. The first installment of this is extremely interesting to the student of James as a critic, for it demonstrates his appreciation of the possibility of viewing the literary output of the day as social history; [48] but subsequent installments indicate that, confronted with a variety of new—and often very inconsequential—books, James retreated to his nebulous irony and doubtless repented his rash agreement to supply a regular column. In the number for May 14, 1898, Howells supplied the "American Letter" instead of James, and for a time they seem to have alternated; but, as one might expect, the latter soon abandoned the task to his friend in New York—and he in turn

---

view an announcement states that with the April number the quarterly would become a monthly with a greatly increased claim on the American and Colonial public. A number of "Transoceanic" writers were to contribute (CXXVII, 3).

[48] II (March 26, 1898), 356–358.

passed the burden on to J. D. Barry. Previous to the new series which the American edition inaugurated on January 10, 1899, the "American Letter" by James or Howells and a few portraits of writers like Stockton, Crane, Hay, and Frederic were about all of the really American features of the magazine, although from the outset American books were reviewed. With the first number of the new series the New York edition became merely another American journal—and soon lapsed. Howells, however, remained one of its mainstays to the end.

Probably the best-known of the Anglo-American journals originating in England in the last years of the nineteenth century was the *Review of Reviews,* which was started as a monthly in January, 1890, by W. T. Stead, a disciple of James Russell Lowell and a friend of America. At the outset its function was to review the British and American periodicals, excerpting copiously, and to condense one novel each month. Among the journals of the United States covered during the first six months of its existence were the *Andover Review,* the *Arena,* the *Atlantic,* the *Century,* the *Chautauquan,* the *Cosmopolitan,* the *Forum, Harper's, Lippincott's,* the *New England Magazine,* the *North American Review,* and *Scribner's.* The novel condensed for the February number was Mark Twain's *A Connecticut Yankee,* a bold choice in view of the general charges of vulgar irreverence which early reviewers had made. Miscellaneous material from Holmes, Emerson, and other Americans also appeared. But the passage of the American Copyright Act of 1891 forced a readjustment in the contents of the *Review,* for the wholesale scooping of transatlantic offerings was no longer possible. An American edition was started with the issue for April, 1891—"republished, reëdited, and recast" by the Critic Company of New York under the editorship of Albert Shaw. After the separate publication in New York the American edition included more American materials and the English edition in turn became more thoroughly English; but transatlantic authors and magazines still continued to be levied upon. Nevertheless, the *Review of Reviews,* though it doubtless furthered the cause so dear to Stead, namely, the development of friendship with "English-speaking lands beyond the seas," never really became an Anglo-American entity.

Of very minor consequence compared with Stead's financially successful enterprise is the *Anti-Philistine,* a "little magazine" published in London from June to September, 1897. Its subtitle was "A Monthly Magazine & Review of Belles-Lettres. Also a Periodical of Protest," and it boasted the motto *castigare ridendo.* John and Horace Cowley were the publishers, with the former probably acting as editor. Of course the title was in part a slap at Elbert Hubbard's *Philistine: a Periodical of Protest,* but it seems to have owed a heavy debt to the Chicago *Chap-Book,* from which it occasionally borrowed material. Its verse, short stories, essays, and reviews for the most part have a sophisticated snap befitting the cosmopolitanism of the nineties, and a breezy air which no doubt was calculated to suit its interest in California and the authors of the Golden West. The first number contains some "Fables" by Ambrose Bierce, poems by Eugene Field, James Whitcomb Riley, and Joaquin Miller, an essay by Edgar Saltus, a critical article on Miller, a story by Opie Read, and a contribution by Francis Saltus. Later issues published work by Stanley Waterloo, Percival Pollard, Gertrude Atherton, and others; but Bierce, the two Saltuses, and a scattering of other Americans filled most of the pages. One portrait appeared in the *Anti-Philistine,* that of Bret Harte, along with an excellent biographical article which throws a ray of light on his early days in the West.[49] Viewed as a whole, the journal may be considered a kind of *Yellow Book* with a California slant, a bouquet of golden poppies and green carnations.

But so far as circulation is concerned the last decades of the nineteenth century were marked by the triumph of the American magazine in Great Britain, not that of the Anglo-American attempts initiated in London. Accordingly, we may now turn to a brief sketch of the magazine of American origin in the British trade. From the beginning of the nineteenth century, and before, copies of various journals from the United States were put on sale in England especially by such dealers as specialized in American books—Rich, Wiley and Putnam, Chapman, Trübner, Sampson Low, and others. One of the reasons for the interest on the part of these firms was that American magazines served to acquaint British publishers with books that might prove of a likely sort to reprint; and of course editors of the cheaper magazines were constantly on the alert for material to borrow. For

[49] I (August 15, 1897), 180–202.

example, an advertisement of the *American Monthly Review* appearing in a London booktrade journal in 1833 significantly stated: "This work is devoted entirely to criticisms of books printed in the United States"—and announced that copies could be obtained in the capital from Obadiah Rich or from Simpkin and Marshall; in Edinburgh from the firm of A. and C. Black.[50] Of the more weighty American organs a variety of religious journals and the *North American Review* were well known in England before 1840, and, judging from advertisements, could be found on the counters of a number of British bookstores.[51] In the forties Wiley and Putnam regularly advertised an array of American periodicals for sale in London, such as the *American Biblical Repository,* the *Democratic Review,* the *American Eclectic,* the *Christian World,* and the *National Preacher.*[52] And when Trübner and Sampson Low, later, became the chief specialists in the American import trade both announced a variety of transatlantic magazines, for some of which they were the official British agents. In his *American and Oriental Record* for 1868, as an illustration, Trübner synopsized the contents of the *Atlantic, Lippincott's,* the *North American, De Bow's, Putnam's,* and *Our Young Folks,* among others, and from the beginning of its existence—and for some years thereafter—announced copies of the *Overland Monthly* for sale. Bret Harte's reputation started from scratch in England; and it may well have been copies of the *Overland* received through Trübner that Dickens showed to his biographer with excited admiration for his California disciple. "I have rarely known him more honestly moved," wrote Forster.[53]

After 1870, and especially in the last two decades of the century, the chief American journals were regularly advertised, and practically all of the British magazines which contained "Notes on the Periodicals" or similar departments listed their contents with a fair degree of regularity—from *Punch* and the *Illustrated London News* to the *Academy.*[54] Such publications as had London agents or London edi-

---

[50] *Bent's Monthly Literary Advertiser* for June 10, 1833.

[51] See W. B. Cairns, *op. cit.,* chap. x.

[52] See, for example, the *Publishers' Circular* for August 1, 1842.

[53] *The Life of Charles Dickens,* ed. J. W. T. Ley, London [1928], p. 153.

[54] A sample from *Fun* for July 30, 1870, "Chats on the Mags": "*The Overland Monthly*—our favourite magazine—just to hand, shall stand first for notice this week,

tions were, naturally, the most favored. The history of the agencies has a place in the general picture of the American periodical invasion, and a few illustrations may be adduced. Thus, the *North American Review* in the middle of the century had Trübner as British agent until shortly after Appleton became the publisher, in 1878, when Sampson Low took over. With the number for June, 1882, the American Exchange in London became the London headquarters, and six years later G. E. Stechert succeeded. Brentano's English branch followed, to be replaced in 1893 by William Heinemann. The *Century,* which emerged from *Scribner's Monthly* in November, 1881, announced Frederick Warne as British publisher, but five years later T. Fisher Unwin succeeded, and in 1895 the London office of Macmillan's followed. *Harper's* during its earlier days as a pirating magazine could not be circulated in England, but when it shed its swaddling clothes and developed into one of the most powerful of the illustrated monthlies its sale in England grew by leaps and bounds. Sampson Low was its London agent. An English edition was started in 1880 with John Lillie as editor, and he in turn was succeeded by Andrew Lang in 1884. By April, 1882, *Harper's* had a British circulation of twenty-four thousand copies, and apparently gathered momentum throughout the decade.[55]

With the increasing coöperation between British and American publishing houses after 1870 the number of American periodicals with English agencies increased. *May's London Press Dictionary and Advertiser's Handbook* for 1871 lists four transatlantic journals, all handled by Trübner: the *Atlantic, Our Young Folks,* the *Overland Monthly,* and the *North American Review. May's Press Guide* for 1888 lists the following, with their London agents: *Atlantic* (Ward & Lock), *Century* (Unwin), *Harper's* (Low), *Harper's Young People* (Low), *Outing* (Carr), *St. Nicholas* (Unwin), *Scribner's* (Warne). By 1898 *Lippincott's* was added to the list; but there is no reason to believe that *May's Guide* mentioned all of the American in-

---

for it contains (from the pen of Mr. F. Bret Harte, we conjecture) a poem entitled 'Dickens in Camp,' which is one of the most graceful tributes yet paid to the memory of the great writer" (New Ser., XII, 34).

[55] J. Henry Harper, *The House of Harper,* p. 475; *Publishers' Circular* for April 1, 1882. Low was eventually succeeded by Osgood and McIlvaine, and then by the London branch of Harpers.

vaders, for early in 1890 *Lippincott's,* "like other American month-lies," had made a "strong bid for support" in England by booking more British novelists and by establishing a London editorial depart-ment under the direction of G. T. Bettany, with Ward & Lock as Lon-don publisher.[56]

To summarize from a quantitative point of view. From early in the century all varieties of American periodicals were imported into the United Kingdom in small quantities. Particularly popular before the Civil War were *Peter Parley's Magazine,* the *North American Review,* and several religious journals like *Brownson's Quarterly Re-view* and the *Bibliotheca Sacra,* several of which were reprinted or brought out in English editions.[57] With the rapid increase in the num-ber of magazines started in the United States in the fifties and sixties there does not seem to have been any comparable increase in British consumption.[58] Up to 1870 we were probably debtors to the English, from the quantitative as well as the qualitative angle; but for the rest of the century the situation is reversed. The editorial policies of the *Atlantic, Scribner's,* the *Century, St. Nicholas,* and *Harper's*—and the superiority of American methods of illustration [59]—won a larger transatlantic circulation than that acquired by any British rivals. It was the magazine of American origin which came nearest to solving the problem of an organ for the English-speaking world. Unfortun-ately, the figures on the number of copies sold cannot be obtained. It has been stated, however, that an English edition of *Scribner's* was begun in November, 1873, with twenty thousand copies, and that this

---

[56] *Athenæum* for November 30, 1889, p. 745.

[57] F. L. Mott, *op. cit.,* II, 130; I, 688; A. M. Schlesinger, Jr., *Orestes A. Brownson: a Pilgrim's Progress,* Boston, 1939, p. 198. For early indications of the small vogue of American journals see "The Periodical Literature of America," *Blackwood's,* LXIII (January, 1848), 106–112; and "American Periodical Literature," *Eclectic Review,* New Ser., V (February, 1839), 215–235.

[58] One of the estimates of the number of American periodicals follows: 1840 (830); 1850 (2,526); 1860 (4,051); 1870 (5,871); 1880 (11,314). From *Le droit d'auteur,* I (October 15, 1888), 103.

[59] For American contributions to the art of printing see Marjorie Plant, *The Eng-lish Book Trade,* London [1939], pp. 280, 285, 289, 294, 320; Henry R. Plomer, *A Short History of English Printing 1746–1900,* London, 1915, pp. 239, 240, 241, 267; and Henry Blackburn, "The Illustration of Books and Newspapers," *Nineteenth Century,* XXVII (February, 1890), 213–224. A writer for the *Academy* in noticing Lanier's *The Boy's Froissart,* issued in London by Sampson Low, observed that the work must be of American origin because of the excellent woodcuts (XVII, March 13, 1880, 194).

was "successful until *Harper's* entered the field in December, 1880"; but in 1898 it was asserted that the new *Scribner's* suffered no falling off in England because of the advent of the cheap monthly.[60] In 1892 the *Cosmopolitan* seems to have planned to send fifty thousand copies of its May issue abroad; and there is no reason to doubt the statement of Howells that at the beginning of the present century several American periodicals had circulations in England larger than any similar British journals.[61] Probably *Harper's* and the *Century* were the ones which he had in mind. The giants of the American periodical trade offered not only a canny combination of popularity and excellence, and often superior illustrations, but also the work of a large number of the ablest British writers.[62] One had to read them to keep up with *English* literature! Mudie's Select Library in the nineties circulated the current numbers of the *Century, Harper's,* and the *North American,* and offered to its customers bound volumes of the *Atlantic* and *Scribner's* as well.[63]

In 1875, in commenting on "Some Magazines for June," *Fun* observed:

The *Atlantic Monthly* contains, as usual, a list of contributors such as is not understood in this country, where one moderately good writer is supposed to compensate in magazine literature for the presence of a dozen duffers. . . . It is generally admitted that magazines are dying out here, and that the tremendous spurt made on the institution of the *Cornhill* was delusive. The reason is apparent. Here the really good writers— unless they be celebrated novelists, who can command their own price— never think of contributing to magazines, for reasons which must be obvious to the merest tyro. The *Cornhill,* which was started on a novel principle—that of paying fancy prices to fancy men, and general rates which could not possibly have been kept up for any length of time—was regarded as one of the wonders of the world when its first list of con-

---

[60] F. L. Mott, *op. cit.,* III, 467; *Illustrated London News,* CXIII (October 15, 1898), 562.

[61] *Life in Letters of William Dean Howells,* II, 22. See p. 57 of the present chapter.

[62] Prices paid had much to do with this fact. For example, George Eliot received $1,500—or about $4 per line—for her poem "Agatha," paid by the *Atlantic* in 1869 (Blanche C. Williams, *George Eliot: a Biography,* New York, 1936, p. 243).

[63] Catalogue for 1896. Many of the provincial public libraries circulated American magazines during the last quarter of the century. For example, the catalogue of the Nottingham Free Public Library for 1883 lists the *Atlantic, Century, Harper's, North American Review,* and *Harper's Weekly.*

tributors and their amounts was published. Yet in the *Atlantic Monthly* we see a miscellany, which every month is equal to our visionary ideal, going its way peacefully and quietly, and never evoking a word of wonder.[64]

Two years earlier John C. Dent in discussing the *Atlantic*, found it "quite up to the mark of any magazine of its class in the world," and repeated a well-worn critical judgment that the *North American Review* compared favorably with the best of the English quarterlies. *Appleton's, Scribner's, Putnam's, Harper's*, the *Galaxy*, and the *Overland* he described as "all ably-conducted"—and "all more or less known here."[65] *Blackwood's*, commenting on the invasion of the American journals, in 1883 decided that the *Century* was the best of the several "which England had accepted with cordiality." The illustrations were considered to be "excellent" and the literary matter, while "not of the highest," was yet possessed of novelty and freshness. A few years later the *Gentleman's Magazine* spoke of an article by Henry James in the *Century* as one of the most pleasant bits of reading to appear in a long time.[66]

St. Nicholas and several other of the American magazines for children were readily acknowledged superior to their native counterparts, which they frequently influenced.[67] Leslie Stephen in 1876 longed for a paper in England like the New York *Nation*, which he as an old contributor read "with great regularity"; and the London *Bookman* in 1893 casually referred to that weekly as maintaining "its undisputed supremacy among the literary journals of the world."[68] Walter Besant felt that the New York *Critic* might well serve as a model for British literary journals, but Frederic Harrison expressed a preference

[64] *Fun*, New Ser., XXI (June 19, 1875), 251. The policy of the *Cornhill* had been possibly modelled on that of the *Atlantic*.

[65] *Temple Bar*, XXXVII (February, 1873), 404–405. The *North American Review* had been praised in England from the early 1820s and during the editorial regime of Lowell and Norton seems to have been read by many of the British intellectuals.

[66] *Blackwood's*, CXXXIII (January, 1883), 136 f.; *Gentleman's*, CCLXVI (January, 1889), 104.

[67] *Athenæum* for December 20, 1884, p. 804; *Academy*, XV (January 18, 1879), 53, for example.

[68] F. W. Maitland, *The Life and Letters of Leslie Stephen*, New York and London, 1906, p. 295; *Bookman*, III (February, 1893), 143. (The motto of the *Bookman* came from Lowell.) Max Müller considered the *Nation* to be the most influential of the better journals of America (*Life and Letters*, ed. his wife, London, 1902, II, 231).

for the *Atlantic*.[69] When Mark Twain contributed to *Harper's,* gentlemen in the London clubs foregathered to hear the article read aloud and the *Evening Globe* might reprint the whole in order to spread the chuckles further—also to add several thousand extra copies to the afternoon sales.[70] Earlier in the century John Stuart Mill had been a subscriber to the *North American Review;* and one of Darwin's first efforts to create a vogue for the ideas in *The Origin of Species* was to circulate in England reprints of articles from the *Atlantic Monthly.*[71]

One effect of the invasion of the American periodical, its critical acceptance as well as its quantitative impact, was that authors from the United States were brought more and more to the attention of English readers.[72] Moreover, the indifference or condescension with which many of the leading reviews had traditionally viewed transatlantic literary products was undermined. A journal like the *Academy* tended to lean heavily on judgments of American authors passed by the *Critic*. Then, too, the obvious imitations of the *Century* or *Harper's* [73] which sprang up in London prove very well that of the English-speaking nations the one which specialized in journalism could very well show a few tricks to the one which consistently led in the number of new books. But the greatest effect, no doubt, was that of merely offering to hundreds of thousands of foreigners what was sufficient unto the day. America still does it through its movies and detective yarns—but it has a long tradition in this respect which seems to have been forgotten.

[69] *Autobiography of Sir Walter Besant,* with prefatory note by S. Squire Sprigge, New York, 1902, p. 195; Harrison to Morley, December 6, 1872 (*Early Life & Letters of John Morley,* ed. F. W. Hirst, London, 1927, I, 226).

[70] J. Henry Harper, *The House of Harper,* p. 567. The reprinting of material from American magazines by British newspapers was a common practice. Even the *Times* had been one of the organs to reprint Poe's "The Facts of M. Valdemar's Case," in 1846.

[71] *The Letters of John Stuart Mill,* ed. Hugh S. R. Elliot, London, 1910, II, 36; *The Life and Letters of Charles Darwin,* ed. Francis Darwin, New York, 1896, II, 147.

[72] In 1900 Richard Le Gallienne said that while an edition of Lanier's poems had been published in England seven years earlier he had come to know the poet through an article in an American magazine (*Academy,* LVIII, February 17, 1900, 147).

[73] See, for example, *Longman's,* the *Strand,* the *Pall Mall Magazine,* and the *English Illustrated Magazine.*

III. HUMOR

"The Americans are of our own stock, yet in their treatment of the ludicrous how unlike us they are!"—ANDREW LANG.

WHILE the sentimental school of authors like Mrs. Stowe, Susan Warner, E. P. Roe, Elizabeth Stuart Phelps, and Louisa Alcott probably accounted for more books sold in nineteenth-century England than any other group of American writers, the humorists also were not without their devotees among the British.

No one as yet has succeeded in isolating the first book of American humor. But the first group of American writers who have a connection, even though it now seems lukewarm, with the history of humor were the so-called Hartford or Connecticut Wits, and they may serve as pioneers in the present discussion. Of these by far the most widely known in England was Joel Barlow, who spent much time in London and Paris, abandoned the conservative attitudes fostered by Yale College, and made himself a political writer sufficiently popular to be proscribed by the Pitt ministry. But except for his political and economic pamphlets nothing by Barlow seems to have attracted wide attention in England, although his attempts in the field of verse were not unknown. *The Vision of Columbus* was brought out in a London edition in 1787, and when expanded into *The Columbiad* was likewise reprinted, in 1809. A friend even contributed some adulatory "Lines Written on Reading Mr. Barlow's Columbiad" to the *Monthly Magazine*.[1] But his best humorous production, "The Hasty Pudding," attracted little contemporary interest.

Timothy Dwight, another Connecticut Wit, was fairly well known in Scotland and England, but primarily as a theologian, although his *Travels* were read; and there were those who scanned the western skies for a poet and thought that Dwight might be the first American

[1] XXVIII (September, 1809), 191. Barlow had consulted with Richard Price about a London edition of *The Vision of Columbus* (Theodore A. Zunder, *The Early Days of Joel Barlow*, New Haven, 1934, pp. 228–229). At least five of the contemporary British magazines reviewed *The Columbiad*.

intruder on Parnassus. As Scott and Campbell levied upon the verse of Philip Freneau, so Erasmus Darwin borrowed a line from Dwight for *The Botanic Garden* and in a note referred to his *Conquest of Canaan* as a poem "which contains much fine versification." [2] David Humphreys was also known to a slight extent, but none of his works reprinted in England [3] created such a stir as John Trumbull's *M'Fingal,* the best product of the humorous and satiric propensities of the entire group. The first part of this spirited satire on the Tories was reprinted in London for J. Almon in 1776, and a so-called fifth edition of the completed work, with notes by Barlow, was brought out by J. S. Jordan in 1792, to be followed the next year by a "sixth edition" sponsored by Chapman & Company. To the credit of the Connecticut Wits as humorists it can be said that this jolliest of their satires surpassed all their other productions in the frequency with which it was reproduced in England during the early days of their vogue.

But the interest demonstrated by John Bull in the works of these men from Yale was trivial compared with the enthusiasm with which Irving's *Sketch Book* was greeted in 1819 and 1820. Of course the sentimental qualities of that work accounted for a great part of the popular acclaim, and such essays as "The Broken Heart" doubtless had the most telling effect, but the humor of its author was early appreciated. *Knickerbocker's History* was belatedly reprinted, and soon Master Simon and the Stout Gentlemen arose from Irving's pages to assure the British readers that the first American author to attract sensational interest in Europe was possessed of a characteristic which later in the century they considered to be the chief original element in the literature of the United States. There were those, too, in England who soon recognized in the earliest work of Charles Dickens the influence of the humor of Washington Irving, an influence which the creator of Pickwick himself apparently recognized, if one may judge by the tone of such letters as he addressed to his

---

[2] Canto IV of "Economy of Vegetation," l. 376. The panegyric on Franklin in this poem should not be forgotten.

[3] For the European editions see Frank L. Humphreys, *Life and Times of David Humphreys,* New York and London, 1917, Vol. II, Appendix. Godwin told Cooper that he had seen something of the work of Dwight, Humphreys, and Barlow (James Fenimore Cooper, *Gleanings in Europe, Volume Two: England,* ed. Robert E. Spiller, New York, 1930, p. 27).

eminent predecessor in the art of humorous caricature. A writer for the *Westminster Review* may be used to illustrate:

Our readers will, perhaps, be somewhat surprised when we mention Washington Irving as the writer, to the character of whose mind we find the greatest resemblance in "Boz." It is true, that they differ very greatly as to the subjects which they delight to treat. Washington Irving does not confine himself to depicting one particular class; and though, undoubtedly, his richest vein is in comic description, he exhibits an excellence in other styles, in which "Boz" has either made no efforts, or has attained only an inferior success. . . . But the two resemble each other in the most distinctive peculiarities of their minds. Both are endowed with the same remarkable susceptibility to impressions of what is passing around them; both seem to have the same power of detecting the ludicrous; and both have the same power of minute, accurate, and, at the same time, comic description. The field of "Boz" is the most limited; he is the Washington Irving of English low life. . . . In the writings of "Boz" there are fifty scenes in the style of the "Stout Gentleman," and exhibiting most of the excellencies of that most admirable comic sketch; but there is not one which we can procure quite equal to it.[4]

If one wishes a humbler proof of British recognition of Irving's humorous gifts it may be found in such collections as *Fun for the Million, or, The Laughing Philosopher,* a "new edition" of which was brought out in London in 1835; in its pages a selection from *The Sketch Book,* as well as a collection of supposedly ludicrous Indian names from Lewis and Clark, finds a place beside bits from Swift, Butler, and other older masters of the arts of satire and humor.

But astonishing as the reception of Irving was in the early twenties, a still more spectacular medium of transatlantic humor was the "entertainment" entitled *Trip to America* which the comedian Charles Mathews produced in London in March, 1824, after a visit to the United States. In his program he combined three of the outstanding personages identified with American humor—the Negro, the Irishman, and above all, the Yankee. There was also a Kentucky Colonel, although he is a far cry from the type as represented in Bret Harte's Colonel Starbottle, for he is depicted as a shoemaker—a connection as bizarre as the characterization of the "real Yankee," Jonathan W. Doubikins, as a slaveowner. The stage Yankee, one may be sure, was a pretty well-defined stock character already by 1824, and

---

[4] "The Works of Dickens," XXVII (July, 1837), 197.

the American-Irishman was merely an extension of the bogtrotter
who evolved from the Teague of the Restoration drama, and even the
Negro was by no means a novel comic figure. But Mathews succeeded
in creating such a hearty appreciation for the "coon song" and for
the shrewd Jonathan-type of yokel that he may well be considered as
deserving an important place in any sketch of British interest in
American humor. The number of London issues of the various booklets describing his *Trip to America* bears witness to the fact, and
the appearance of an edition in Baltimore in 1824 and two others by
different publishers in Philadelphia during the same year [5] indicates
full well that America itself was interested in its own humor as
adapted by a popular English actor. Indeed, the Jonathan of Yankee-
dom may well have been ultimately of English origin, borrowed by
the Colonials and later the Americans, finally to be converted into
the figure of Uncle Sam, the cartoonists' personification of our country.

However this may be, it is certain that the depiction of the Yankee
by the Charlie Chaplin of the London of the twenties created at home
and abroad a furore of interest. "We 'guess,' " observed a contemporary
press-notice, "that we may 'calculate' on a 'pretty considerable' inter-
mingling in our conversations of the American *colloquialisms* and
idioms." Such was the demand for the portrayal of Jonathan that
Mathews was forced to produce another, and this he did by adapting
a comedy by David Humphreys, *The Yankey in England,* in which,
according to tradition, a shrewd bumpkin from back-country New
England sings a variety of stanzas of "Yankee Doodle" and provides
the chief humorous element.[6] For years American jokes were referred
to in London as "Jonathans."

[5] Harvard has a splendid collection. One London publisher ran up to a "thirtieth
edition" in a short time. The one which I have examined most closely is *The London Mathews; Containing an Account of This Celebrated Comedian's Trip to America . . . ,* London, n.d. [1824?]. *Memoirs of Charles Mathews, Comedian,* by Mrs.
Mathews, London, 1839, contains a program of the *Trip to America* and other pertinent material, III, 442 ff.

[6] For Mathews's own acknowledgment of his source see Mrs. Mathews, *op. cit.,* III,
539. Frank Landon Humphreys gives Boston, 1815, for the publication of Humphreys's
play (*op. cit.,* II, 467–468). The Harvard copy is defective, but was apparently published in Connecticut. I have found no English edition. Professor Walter Blair has
kindly informed me that *The Yankey in England* was seen by Dunlap in 1805 and
reviewed by William Gifford in 1807. For other sources of Mathews's humor see H. E.
Dickson, "A Note on Charles Mathews's Use of American Humor," *American Literature,* XII (March, 1940), 78–83.

Early and late in the nineteenth century the British stage was constantly in debt to the United States for plays and for actors, on a scale only less extensive than the obligation of the American stage to London playwrights and performers. Assuredly, also, the history of American humor in England is intimately bound up with the history of the theatre, but for present purposes a mere mention of the fact will have to suffice.[7] Another aspect of the subject, Negro humor, will also have to be dealt with in the most slighting fashion.

When Mathews appeared in his *Trip to America* under the guise of a Negro reciting Shakespeare in a humorously garbled version anticipatory of Mark Twain's character in *Huckleberry Finn,* he introduced a number of songs, especially "Possum up a Gum-tree," which had an effect only less consequential than his portrayal of Jonathan W. Doubikins. He seems to have been one of the chief causes of the early—and long-enduring—vogue in England of the "coon song." The next period of this type of sensation was ushered into London when Rice and his fellow minstrels were in their fullest bloom. A student of "Musical Epidemics in London" in commenting on the craze describes a veritable orgy of such melodies from about 1836 to 1841, later revived from time to time. "Old Dan Tucker" and "Buffalo Gals" were succeeded by "Old Dog Tray" in the fifties, and not long afterward the "nigger melodies broke out again with redoubled fury." [8] It is well to remember that the popularity of *Uncle Tom's Cabin* was in part due to the widespread interest in the Negro as a humorous character, an interest which by the 1850s was almost an English tradition. *Punch* in 1865 could perpetrate the following "Americanism for Italy": "Situation of the Pope—*Non Possum-us* up a gum-tree"; and without doubt the attempt at humor was understood. After the Civil War—as well as before—one could find a variety of booklets for sale like this one: *Brudder Bones's Laughing Gas: a*

[7] For the enthusiasm over another Yankee on the stage see the notice of Moncrieff's *Tarnation Strange* in the *Monthly Magazine* for September, 1838 (New Ser., XXVI, 335–336); but this is only one in a legion. For an example of British deference to American comic actors later in the century see *Gentleman's Magazine* for October, 1884 (CCLVII, 415 f.).

[8] Charles Mackay, *Through the Long Day,* London, 1887, chap. vi. See also certain numbers in *The Book of American Songs,* ed. Howard Paul, London, 1857; and Harry Reynolds, *Minstrel Memories; the Story of Burnt Cork Minstrelsy in Great Britain from 1836 to 1927,* London [1928].

Reservoir of Nigger Wit and Humour, "comprising Darkey conversations, laughable jokes, comic anecdotes, and droll conundrums, as
given by Brudder Bones, in his celebrated Ethiopian entertainments,"
published in Glasgow and London by Cameron & Ferguson, n.d.
The same publishers offered seven other such compilations at threepence each, as well as a *Complete Nigger Entertainment* for a shilling. There was a long foreground to the interest that came later in
the century when some of the local-colorists gave new life to the
Negro dialect. *Punch* remarked in its number for July 16, 1881:
"Better than any one of 'em, or any Twain of 'em just now, is Mr.
Chandler Harris in his *Uncle Remus.* Difficult reading at first, on
account of the nigger spelling, but well worth mastering." Ten years
later *Punch* had mastered the spelling sufficiently well to attempt its
own story of "The Hibernian Brer Fox; or Uncle Remus in Ireland." [9]
To British and Americans alike the Negro was a humorous creature,
and the jokes and songs and stories attributed to him were a part of
our offerings to the comic muse.

But to return to the chronological outline. After the flood of interest
in American humor developed by Irving and by Mathews the next
wave of excitement fostered by books—not songs or plays—was due
to a Canadian, Thomas Chandler Haliburton, who, following the
tradition of the shrewd Yankee, produced in his Sam Slick of Connecticut a humorous character who did more than Davy Crockett,
Jack Downing, and all his other rivals to bring to British readers a
type of comedy that was generally accepted as non-European. Of
course the rivals of Sam Slick in this type of humor were also known
abroad. Murray, for example, in 1835 hired someone to write an
article on "Major Downing's Letters" for the *Quarterly Review,* and
the selections from the Davis epistles therein contained were calculated to arouse interest in an edition which the publisher brought out
the same year.[10] Obadiah Rich in 1834 sponsored a London edition of

[9] LXXXI, 21; and XCIX (December 20, 1890), 297. In connection with the study
of Negro humor in England see Helen de R. Troesch, "The Negro in English Dramatic Literature and on the Stage and a Bibliography of Plays with Negro Characters,"
MS, Western Reserve University Dissertation, 1940.

[10] In the late sixties and seventies there were a number of editions of the pseudo-
Downing material as well as of the "genuine" produced by Davis or Smith, e.g.,

Sketches and Eccentricities of Col. David Crockett, of West Tennessee, and three years later R. Kennett reprinted *Col. Crockett's Exploits and Adventures in Texas.*[11] Of course there were importations also, a fact which is apparent to one who looks at the earlier articles on American humor in the British quarterlies. An essay in the *Westminster* for December, 1838, by "H. W." may illustrate. Heading the discussion, in the usual manner, is the following list of books:

1. *American Broad Grins.* Second Edition. London: Tyas. 1839.[12]
2. *Yankee Notions.* By Timo Titterwell, Esq. Second Edition. Boston, 1838.
3. *The Clockmaker; or, the Sayings and Doings of Samuel Slick, of Slickville.* London, 1837; Second Series, 1838.
4. *Sketches and Eccentricities of Colonel David Crockett, of West Tennessee.* London, 1834.
5. *A Narrative of the Life of David Crockett, of the State of Tennessee.* Philadelphia, 1834.
6. *Colonel Crockett's Exploits and Adventures in Texas.* London, 1837.
7. *The Life and Writings of Major Jack Downing, of Downingville.* Boston, 1834.

Observing that "these books show that American literature has ceased to be exclusively imitative," the critic announces that "Democracy and the 'far-west' made Colonel Crockett: he is a product of forests, freedom, universal suffrage, and bear-hunts." As for Sam Slick, "H. W." continues, he is the result of "the Puritans and the American Revolution, joined to the influence of the soil and the social manners of the time." "The extensive circulation and notice which American humor has of late obtained in England," one may safely say, was due largely to Sam Slick, whose popularity during the late thirties and

Major Jack Downing, of the Downingville Militia, London: Warne, 1865; *Major Jack Downing to Lincoln,* London: Warne, 1865 [?]; and *Major Jack Downing of Downingville,* with an introduction by G. A. Sala, London: Routledge, n.d. J. C. Hotten also published Downing material separately and in the first series of *Yankee Drolleries.*

[11] The Beadle dime novels issued by Routledge in the middle of the century contained Crockett material, and in the sixties and seventies more of it was reprinted. In 1879 Frank Mayo took the play *Davy Crockett,* by Frank Murdoch, to England (*Davy Crockett & Other Plays,* ed. Isaac Goldberg and Hubert Heffner, Princeton, 1940, p. xix).

[12] The first edition of this work (1838) was described as "a volume of the most racy 'Jonathans,' carefully collected from the various newspapers" (*Monthly Magazine,* New Ser., XXVI, September, 1838, 331).

the following years may well have surpassed that of his cockney counterpart, Sam Weller.[13]

The enthusiasm for American humor in England was incited, encouraged, and spread widely during the forties and fifties chiefly by the popularity of Sam Slick, and throughout the latter half of the century cheap reprints of his works were readily available. Haliburton is important also as the editor of two anthologies—one consisting of authentic specimens of newspaper humor from the United States and the other of local indigenous yarns which occasionally border upon comedy. They were, respectively, *Traits of American Humour, by Native Authors,* first published in London by Colburn in three volumes dated 1852, and *The Americans at Home; or Byeways, Backwoods, and Prairies,* likewise first brought out in London as a three-decker, by Hurst and Blackett in 1854. Both were reprinted from time to time, especially the former, which seems to have commanded a steady sale throughout the rest of the century. These two anthologies are composed chiefly of material taken from the *Spirit of the Times,* a New York journal which specialized in news of the theatre and the turf and in tall tales gathered up from the newspapers, especially such as dealt with hunting. One could find in them such homespun classics as "Tom Wade and the Grizzly Bear" and "Colonel Crockett's Ride on the Back of a Buffalo." [14] But the novelty of these collections of backwoods yarns, sometimes spoken of as "frontier" or "native" humor, was not so great as one might imagine, for the English magazines and newspapers had already raided the American press for tall tales and glimpses of life in the border settlements. Moreover, in 1830 and 1832 Miss Mitford had edited two anthologies of native American stories containing, in part, material by Timothy Flint and others sometimes identified with the frontier, albeit her purpose was not to provide humorous reading. But in her search for the autochthonous element in American fiction, as she herself put it, she

---

[13] "H. W.'s" article appears in the *Westminster,* XXXII, 136–145. See Vernon L. O. Chittick, *Thomas Chandler Haliburton,* New York, 1924, especially pp. 326, 351–352, and the array of British editions in the bibliography, pp. 655 ff. For a contemporary estimate see "Notions of Sam Slick," *Bentley's Miscellany,* XIV (1843), 81–94.

[14] For the sources see the prefaces of the two anthologies, and V. L. O. Chittick, *op. cit.,* pp. 536 ff. For all aspects of American humor see the excellent bibliography and survey by Walter Blair in *Native American Humor,* New York [1937].

had grasped "at the broadest caricature" and the "wildest sketch." [15]
And during the fifties anthologists other than Haliburton were also
active in the field. Of these one of the more important ones was William Jordan, who edited *Yankee Humour, and Uncle Sam's Fun,*
published by Ingram, Cooke & Co. in 1853. The introduction to this
volume is very interesting in that it anticipates much that has more
recently been said about the frontier as a peculiar shaping force in
the history of the comic spirit in America, including the dubious
theory that the tall tale is the essential element.

Another English collection of the early fifties, but one not especially
confined to the "frontier" variety of American humor, was entitled
Dashes of American Humour, gathered, apparently, by the actor
Henry Howard Paul, with a preface by J. B. Buckstone, illustrated
by John Leech, and published in 1852 by Piper Brothers. Material
from Major Jones, Simon Suggs, and others is included; the featured
type is that of the Yankee, whom Paul depicted from time to time
on the stage at Egyptian Hall and elsewhere. Not all of the collection
is humorous, for it contains also a brief essay, "Who Reads an American Book?" in which the tremendous quantities of American writing
reprinted in London during the early fifties is the subject of comment.[16]

These compilations, which appear fairly frequently in the early
fifties, are evidence not only of the widespread interest in American
literary products induced by the success of *Uncle Tom's Cabin, The
Scarlet Letter,* and other transatlantic novels but of the broadly dif-
fused curiosity which Europeans always had felt in regard to life in
the Western democracy. The hunting story, the scalping yarn, and
all the paraphernalia of the frontier were always dear to British hearts;
and if they were merged into the ludicrous the attraction was doubled.
And though the number of anthologies is significant, and though before the Civil War many a volume of American humor was imported

[15] Preface to *Stories of American Life by American Writers,* 3 vols., Colburn and
Bentley, 1830, p. vi. The same publishers brought out her other collection, *Lights
and Shadows of American Life,* 3 vols., 1832.

[16] Pp. 237–240. Like most of these British anthologies, it was reprinted in the
United States, in 1853. Howard Paul produced another collection, published by Son-
nenschein in 1885: *Not Too Funny: Just Funny Enough.* Peck's Bad Boy, Brigham
Young, and Artemus Ward are involved in some of the anecdotes contained. Paul
also edited *The Book of American Songs,* London, 1857.

or reprinted, it may well be that the British newspapers and magazines supplied the British reader with an even larger quantity of comic tales and anecdotes from America. Reviewers of the anthologies edited by Haliburton sometimes objected on the ground that they were already familiar with his material, and one of them very properly observed that "a few specimens" had appeared in the journal for which he was writing.[17] The *Illustrated London News* not only reprinted passages from *High Life in New York*, by Jonathan (an imitator of Sam) Slick, but in its review of *Yankee Humour, and Uncle Sam's Fun* told its one hundred and twenty thousand subscribers:

We have no hesitation in acknowledging our keen relish for it [American humor]; we think it among the most racy and thoroughly diverting and exhilarating sorts of humour that ever obtained vogue, or prevailed among men. It is common to denounce it as extravagant. We praise it, and like it as extravagant.[18]

The *Westminster Review* in a "Retrospective Survey of American Literature," published in 1852, recognized the importance of the tradition of American comic writers and briefly surveyed the field as follows:

The writings of Franklin, "Modern Chivalry," written half a century ago by Judge Breckenridge [*sic*], Trumbull's "M'Fingal," and a dozen other works of the last age, abound with original and for the most part national comedy; and Irving may certainly be ranked with the first humourists who have written in the English language; while Paulding, Judge Longstreet, the late Robert C. Sands, Helleck [*sic*], Hawthorne (in the "Twice-Told Tales"), Mr. Davis and Seba Smith, (in the "Jack Downing Letters"), John P. Kennedy (in "Swallow Barn"), Willis Gaylord Clark (in "Ollapodiana"), John Sanderson, Charles F. Briggs, and Mrs. Kirkland (in a "New Home"), may well be said to have given American literature a fair infusion of this quality. But a school of comic writers in the southern and western states, amply represented in a series of volumes published in Philadelphia under the direction of William T. Porter, editor of the chief sporting journal in the Union, would quite redeem the

[17] V. L. O. Chittick, *op. cit.*, pp. 542–543; *Bentley's Miscellany*, XXXI (1852), 349. A writer for the *British Quarterly Review* for January, 1855, may also be cited (XXI, 60–78), especially since he was a competent folklorist who recognized the English element in the backgrounds of the sketches. He also suggested that English students should go to the United States to discover "precious fragments of old ballads."

[18] V (September 28, 1844), 202; and XXIII (September 3, 1853), 187.

fame of the Americans in this respect, though all the rest of their books were grim and stern as the most fanatical preacher in their pulpits.[19]

All of the authors mentioned had been reprinted in England, in excerpts in the cheap press if not in books. Even before the fifties, however, the books containing transatlantic mirth were plentiful in England. When Charles Dickens, as editor, and his friends arranged to supply copy for *The Pic-Nic Papers* in 1841 and Colburn, the publisher, needed more material, what was more simple than to make one of the three volumes a reprint of some humorous stuff from Philadelphia? [20]

By the middle of the century the critical conclusion was pretty generally fixed that the essence of American humor was exaggeration. We may use as an example a selection which, fittingly enough, comes from an article on P. T. Barnum, published in *Tait's Edinburgh Magazine:*

Their newspapers are "the largest newspapers in all creation"—their steam-boats are measured, not by the foot rule, but by the land-surveyor's chain, stretching so many fractions of a mile—their hotels are a conglomerate of desirable residences of which a traveller needs a map in order to find his way home after he has got within doors—their works of art for public view are panoramas stretching "a Sabbath-day's journey" or more. . . . Where the same tendency to monstrosity is not demonstrable by sheer bigness, the modest Yankee intensifies exaggeration in some analogous way: —when he takes it into his head to travel he "concludes to locomote" at the rate of greased lightning: —when he trots his prairie steed he passes the milestones so rapidly that to the astonished stranger from the old country, who sits by his side, they appear close together like the gravestones in a churchyard: —when he does battle he licks his adversary "slick," and "chaws him up" territory and all.[21]

John Bull wasn't always sure about American geography, but he felt pretty confident about the essence of the humor from abroad. Hear another critic, this one a little later:

---

[19] New Ser., I (January, 1852), 302. Note the influence of Rufus Griswold on this survey.

[20] Joseph C. Neal's *Charcoal Sketches* was the work pirated. See *The Letters of Charles Dickens,* ed. his sister-in-law and his eldest daughter, London, 1893, p. 479.

[21] XXII (January, 1855), 73. P. T. Barnum, like Theodore Roosevelt and Buffalo Bill, contributed to *Murray's Magazine.* See VII (January, 1890), 101–116.

The most obvious characteristic of American humour is its power of "pitching it strong," and drawing the long bow. It is the humour of exaggeration. . . . That place in the geography of United States called "Down East" has been most prolific in the monstrosities of mirth. Only there would a tree'd coon have cried to the marksman with his gun pointed, "Don't fire, Colonel, I'll come down." Only in that region do they travel at such speed that the iron rails get hot enough to serve the carriages with heat instead of hot-water bottles, and sometimes so hot, that on looking back you see the irons writhing about like live snakes, trying to wriggle off to the water to cool themselves.[22]

Late in the fifties, British interest in transatlantic humor received a new impulse in the discovery of two writers who could make even the Oxford dons chuckle—Holmes and Lowell. While volumes of verse by the latter had been brought out by Routledge, by John Chapman, and by Charles Mudie, all three in the year 1844, and subsequently more of his books, in both prose and verse, appeared in English editions, Mrs. Stowe on her visit to Europe in 1856 found him "less known" than she thought he deserved to be.[23] But in that very year, apparently, a new London publisher, John Camden Hotten, made arrangements with Lowell's friend Sydney H. Gay to prepare an edition of *The Biglow Papers* with notes to explain such terms as *White House* and *Bay State,* and a glossary with definitions of words like *consarn, tater patch,* and *skunk.* In 1859 the first issue of this piracy came from the press with the following on the title page.

The Choicest Humorous Poetry of the Age

THE

BIGLOW PAPERS

BY JAMES RUSSELL LOWELL

Alluded to by John Bright in the House of Commons
with
Additional Notes, an Enlarged Glossary
and
An Illustration by George Cruikshank

---

[22] *North British Review,* XXXIII (November, 1860), 465–466. *Fisher's River Scenes and Characters* had "the old family features" although the critic was not sure whether North Carolina was "Down East." (Sampson Low had issued Taliaferro's book in 1859, but it had been printed in the United States.)

[23] Annie Fields, *Life and Letters of Harriet Beecher Stowe,* Boston and New York [1897], p. 226.

In the autumn of the same year Thomas Hughes addressed an enthusiastic note to Lowell, asking for information to use in a preface
for another edition of *The Biglow Papers* which Trübner soon published.[24] From the outset these editions were successful, and issue
after issue was eventually run off. The second series of the *Papers*
was rushed into print as soon as it appeared in the United States, and
was likewise widely read, but in general was regarded as less striking
than the first. Parson Wilbur and Birdofredum Sawin began to be
talked of far and wide—as well they might be, for Hotten alone up
to his death in 1873 is said to have sold fifty thousand copies.[25] The
honorary degrees bestowed on Lowell by Oxford and Cambridge in
1873 and 1874 were primarily the result of his reputation as a humorist,
and even after he had forsaken satire and dialect and as Minister to
the Court of St. James's was recognized as perhaps the most popular
speaker on literary topics in London, it was still *The Biglow Papers*
that accounted for most of his fame. When the students at St. Andrews in 1883 nominated him for the position of Lord Rector of their
University, and objection was made on the grounds of his being an
alien, *Punch* entered into the controversy with some verses:

> An alien? Go to! If fresh genial wit
> In good sound Saxon speech be not genuine grit,
> If the wisdom and mirth he has put into verse for us
> Don't make him a "native," why so much the worse for us.[26]

Already in 1860 he was sometimes regarded as the "greatest of all
American humourists," and *The Biglow Papers* were asserted to be
independent of all European influence.[27] During the nineties there
were at least eight different editions of his humorous masterpiece in
England.

Holmes's reputation as a writer of light verse came before Lowell's.

[24] *Letters of James Russell Lowell,* ed. Charles E. Norton, New York, 1893, I,
275 and 295–297.

[25] Allibone, *A Critical Dictionary of English Literature,* Philadelphia, 1874. The
Athenæum published two reviews of the second series of *The Biglow Papers* (February 22 and April 19, 1862).

[26] LXXXV (December 1, 1883), 255.

[27] *North British Review,* XXXIII (November, 1860), 479. Cf. also, for example, the
Athenæum for February 22, 1862, pp. 251–253; the *Quarterly Review,* CXXII (January,
1867), 227–229, 231; G. Barnett Smith, "James Russell Lowell," *Nineteenth Century,*
XVII (June, 1885), 1003; John A. Steuart, *Letters to Living Authors,* London, 1892,
p. 58 *et passim.*

Miss Mitford in her *Recollections of a Literary Life,* largely a volume
of poetical selections with commentary, gave him space, and, while
she featured Longfellow among her Americans, it is obvious that her
personal preference was for the "healthy and cheerful masculine verse
of Dr. Holmes," whom she thought she was introducing to the English public.[28] But already in 1846 the firm of Obadiah Rich had issued
a volume of his poems, and Routledge six years later put his verse in
all the railway libraries in a cheap edition. After 1852 some of his
efforts, like the lines "On Lending a Punch-Bowl," seem to have been
well known abroad.[29] Hotten and others issued special collections of
his poetical "Wit and Humour" in the sixties and afterwards, but
it was the Breakfast-Table series, and particularly *The Autocrat,*
which led all his volumes in popularity. Sampson Low issued it in
1858 at three and six and soon followed with a cheaper edition. Strahan
brought out a rival edition in Edinburgh in 1859, and in the next two
decades a half dozen different publishers found profit in printing
and reprinting the work. Between 1890 and 1895 at least four different British firms reprinted *The Autocrat,* and in the eighties his
readers were judged to be in the hundreds of thousands.[30] The incomplete record of *The English Catalogue* reveals a decided preference
for Holmes's prose; his novels, especially *Elsie Venner,* were frequently reprinted, but the Breakfast-Table essays dominate. By the
end of the century there were at least twenty-five editions of *The
Autocrat,* fifteen of *The Poet,* and about the same number of *The
Professor.*

Even while *The Autocrat* was running as a serial in the first numbers of the *Atlantic Monthly* Thackeray was praising it at dinner
parties, maintaining that no Englishman alive could equal it; and

[28] *Recollections of a Literary Life,* New York, 1852, Preface; *The Friendships of
Mary Russell Mitford,* ed. A. G. L'Estrange, New York, 1882, p. 386; *Mary Russell
Mitford: Correspondence with Charles Boner & John Ruskin,* ed. Elizabeth Lee, Chi-
cago [1915], pp. 169 and 182. Cf. also Margaret Foster, *Hand-Book of American
Literature,* London, 1854, pp. 82–84.

[29] *The Correspondence of John Lothrop Motley,* ed. G. W. Curtis, New York,
1889, I, 205; *North British Review,* XXXIII (November, 1860), 476.

[30] George W. Smalley, *Studies of Men,* New York, 1895, p. 318; *Saturday Review,*
LVII (May 17, 1884), 651. Austin Dobson and Matthew Arnold joined a variety of
American authors in writing letters for the celebration of Holmes's seventy-fifth
birthday (*Critic,* New Ser., II, August 30, 1884, 97, 100).

Dickens boasted that he had read it twice.[31] Such critics as, later, found Artemus Ward or Orpheus C. Kerr rather vulgar, and Lowell occasionally profane, often put Holmes at the head of the troupe of jesters from across the sea, and many a penetrating reader claimed that his prose was thoroughly American.[32] His light verse, while admitted to be less distinctively national, was also very widely read late in the century, and was frequently judged to be of a very high order. In the sixties, Locker spoke of him as "perhaps the best living writer" of such verse; and in 1880 Edmund Gosse repeated the phrase, but without a "perhaps." [33]

Upon his trip to England in 1886 the enthusiasm ran high, and *Punch* welcomed him with some lines,

> Bigelow [*sic*] is here, to help us shout "Hooray!"
> For him who sang "The Wonderful One-Hoss Shay."

Men in the colleges stole fire from his torch to give him a poetical greeting; Parliament admitted him to the section reserved for ambassadors and foreign ministers; and when he attended the Derby he went out from London on the special train which carried the Prince of Wales.[34]

But although Lowell and Holmes were forming a reputation as humorists in England before the Civil War—a reputation which became indeed vast in the last two decades of the nineteenth century —they were swept along on a veritable avalanche of enthusiasm for fun from the West which developed rapidly in the late sixties and the years immediately following. A number of drolls and zanies of a less intellectual order suddenly achieved an amazing prominence. Of these by all odds the foremost was Artemus Ward. Correspondents

[31] *The Correspondence of John Lothrop Motley*, I, 226 and 369.

[32] For example, *North British Review*, XXXIII (November, 1860), 476; *Cornhill*, XIII (January, 1866), 42. The recent efforts to consider Holmes as not conforming to the tradition of American humor appear to need revision in the light of the British reaction to his works.

[33] *Lyra Elegantiarum*, London, 1867, p. xix; *Academy*, XVIII (November 6, 1880), 322–323.

[34] *Punch*, XC (May 15, 1886), 230; *Academy*, XXX (July 3, 1886), 9; *Our Hundred Days in Europe*, Boston [1892], pp. 34 and 63. The poems in *Punch* on the deaths of Lowell and Holmes may be noted (CI, August 22, 1891, 93; and CVII, October 20, 1894, 191).

like George A. Sala had occasionally quoted his remarks in dispatches to the London newspapers, but the first real excitement over the Genial Showman struck England in 1865, largely because of the cheap reprints issued by John Camden Hotten, whose profits from publishing humorous works by Americans, especially *The Biglow Papers,* led him in that year to bring out several editions of *Artemus Ward: His Book.* Within a few months rival publishers were in the field with competing collections of Ward's effusions, and the race was on.[35] On September 8, 1865, Hotten was eagerly writing to a friend who had sent him material, asking: "Have you any other scraps by 'A. Ward'? If not, do you know of the titles of any? I am anxious to secure all I can from his pen." [36]

In less than a year apparently everything that was known to have been written by the humorist had been reprinted in England—and was thereafter to be reprinted time and again. Even before he came to lecture in Egyptian Hall, and to contribute to *Punch,* he was a celebrated character in London; and his early death in that city was induced by an attempt to meet the demands of a popularity which had probably been without parallel in the United States. Within a few years Hotten alone had sold no less than 250,000 copies of one book by Artemus Ward.[37]

On the strength of the sales of Lowell and Ward, Hotten now became a focal point for the distribution of American humor in England, pirating whenever he could but sometimes issuing editions which were authorized. By 1869, one may discover from advertisements, he was printing also Hans Breitmann, Orpheus C. Kerr, Josh Billings, and Oliver Wendell Holmes and had gathered up some of these booklets into a larger volume called *Yankee Drolleries,* with a preface by G. A. Sala, containing *The Biglow Papers,* and material by Ward, Kerr, Jack Downing, and Petroleum V. Nasby. Shortly afterwards two more such anthologies appeared under his imprint:

[35] See the bibliography appended to Don C. Seitz, *Artemus Ward: a Biography and Bibliography,* New York and London [1919]. The *D.N.B.* contains about all the information on Hotten now available. It should be noted, however, that he had resided for a time in the United States.

[36] To T. Lace Caley, MS in Harvard College Library.

[37] George H. Putnam, *A Memoir of George Palmer Putnam,* New York and London, 1903, II, 236.

More Yankee Drolleries, with selections from Ward, Breitmann, and Josh Billings as well as *The Professor at the Breakfast Table* and the second series of *The Biglow Papers;* and *A Third Supply of Yankee Drolleries,* embracing *The Autocrat of the Breakfast Table* and material by Mark Twain and Bret Harte, together with more of Artemus Ward. Various portions of these compilations, it is to be remembered, were also published separately; and the three series of *Yankee Drolleries* were sometimes bound up together and sold as one book.

In rapid succession Hans Breitmann followed Artemus Ward into extraordinary popularity, with Mark Twain and Bret Harte hard at his heels. Of the three, Breitmann may be used for more extended illustration. As a specialist in the importation and publishing of American books, Nicholas Trübner arranged for an authorized edition of the Breitmann poems of Charles Godfrey Leland shortly after their first appearance in book form in Philadelphia; but, as had been the case with his 1859 issue of *The Biglow Papers,* he was soon in competition with Hotten, who had decided upon an annotated volume of the Germanic nonsense verses as a third sure-fire seller to follow Lowell's Down-East satires and Artemus Ward's effusions. Beginning in 1868, Trübner issued *Hans Breitmann's Party* and the other volumes which celebrated the beer-drinking hero, and after a "fifth edition" Hotten attempted to arrange with Leland, then in Philadelphia, for the sanction of rival editions; but, failing in his negotiations, he simply pirated whatever had first been published in the United States and brought out one volume after the other. A little later, when Leland had come to Europe and supplied new material which Trübner could copyright, Hotten nevertheless advertised his collection as "complete." Authorized publisher and author both protested in print, and the pirate merely pointed out that what he had published was by law free for the use of any British firm.[38] Nothing could be done but announce the fact that Trübner's editions were authorized and Hotten's were often incomplete, even ridiculous so far as the notes were concerned, but the sale of the piracies went merrily on. Mark Twain shortly afterwards went through precisely the same experience with Hotten, when Routledge discovered that

[38] *Athenæum* for April 3, April 24, May 1, and May 8, 1869.

the market for his authorized volumes suffered tremendous inroads from piracies.[39]

Leland's personal appearance in England was a real triumph, for he was all the rage in 1869 and for some years to come.[40] Personally he was affable, and, like Motley, so cultivated that his social success was assured. He stayed for ten years and after a sojourn in America returned, to become the first president of the Gypsy-Lore Society and to discover the British tinker's dialect known as Shelta. The controversy with Hotten, the Franco-Prussian War, and the infectious mirth of the verses all contrived to make Hans Breitmann a popular comic figure. Hans was introduced into three different London plays, all acting at the same time; imitations of the ballads appeared; a Liverpool tobacconist named a brand of cigars after him; and in 1871 Leland was forced to deny in a public letter that he had anything to do with a comic weekly entitled *Hans Breitmann*.[41] The editor of Tinsley's journal called *Mirth* considered himself lucky to get a contribution from Leland and proudly wrote to Tinsley: "His name is *very good.*"[42] During the latter part of the century Leland was a prolific contributor to a wide assortment of British periodicals, but wrote chiefly on serious subjects. At the height of the craze there were of course critics who were special partisans of his Germanic dialect and pronounced him to be the chief American humorist,[43] although there were others, impressed no doubt by the chronology of Hotten's imprints, who declared him to be an imitator of Lowell. After the death of Hotten in 1873 there were other firms ready to pirate such of the Breitmann verses as Trübner could not protect by copyright. In the eighties and nineties Leland and his publisher attempted to revive interest in the German droll, but the reaction was

[39] See communications in the *Spectator*, June 1, 1872, p. 698; June 8, 1872, p. 722; September 21, 1872, pp. 1201–1202; September 28, 1872, p. 1237. Mark Twain apparently departed from the whole truth in this affair with Hotten.

[40] Elizabeth R. Pennell, *Charles Godfrey Leland: a Biography*, Boston and New York, 1906, I, 358 ff.; II, *passim;* C. G. Leland, *Memoirs*, New York, 1893, chaps. vii-ix. Some selections from Leland's letters to G. H. Boker in which he comments on his popularity appear in Sculley Bradley, " 'Hans Breitmann' in England and America," *Colophon*, New Ser., II (Autumn, 1936), 65–81.

[41] *Athenæum*, September 16, 1871, p. 370.

[42] William Tinsley, *Random Recollections of an Old Publisher*, London and Paris, 1905, I, 222.

[43] *British Quarterly Review*, LII (October 1, 1870), 343–350.

fairly mild—as was the case with his creator's attempts at Pidgin English. That there was a steady sale for this humorous chinoiserie is indicated by the fact that *Pidgin English Sing-Song,* first published in 1876, reached a second edition ten years later, a fourth in 1897, and a seventh in 1904.⁴⁴ It should be remembered, however, that even though Hans Breitmann made the walls of London houses shake with laughter, especially during the late sixties and seventies, and "Leetle Yawcob Strauss" followed suit, the dominant type of humor enjoyed in England immediately after the Civil War was that which developed from the newspapers and was often identified with the West. Leland was sometimes confused with Bret Harte, and he himself soon after his arrival in Europe began writing letters with pseudo-phonetic spellings and locutions far removed from the dialect forms on which his fame is based.⁴⁵

If anyone doubted the popularity of American humor in England after the cordial reception of *The Biglow Papers, The Autocrat,* and Artemus Ward and Charles Godfrey Leland, the advent of Bret Harte and Mark Twain must soon have dispelled all doubts, for their welcome was perhaps even more spectacular. But it is sufficiently well known to require little illustration. Merle Johnson has already described the chief English imprints of Clemens's works,⁴⁶ but the reissues are in themselves more revelatory; and, accordingly, a list is here presented, for two years only, 1871 and 1872. Routledge had already issued *The Jumping Frog* volume in 1867, and Hotten had brought out in 1870 *The Innocents Abroad* in two parts, one bearing the title of the whole work and the other called *The New Pilgrim's Progress.* Here is the record of Mark Twain volumes issued in London for two years:

Mark Twain's Burlesque Autobiography	Routledge, 1871.
Eye Openers	Hotten, 1871.
Screamers	Hotten, 1871.
A Curious Dream	Routledge, 1872.

⁴⁴ Andrew Lang, like many another, found the work to be very clever and diverting (*Academy,* X, July 29, 1876, 104–105).

⁴⁵ Note his reference to the West in his letter published in the *Athenæum* for April 24, 1869.

⁴⁶ *A Bibliography of the Work of Mark Twain,* New York and London, 1910; revised and enlarged, 1935. The 1910 edition contains more extensive descriptions of the British imprints.

The Innocents Abroad	Routledge, 1872.
The Innocents at Home [really *Abroad*]	Hotten, 1872.
Roughing It	Routledge, 1872.
The Innocents at Home	Routledge, 1872.
The New Pilgrim's Progress	Routledge, 1872.
Practical Jokes with Artemus Ward	Hotten, 1872.
Screamers	Hotten, 1872.
Mark Twain's Sketches	Routledge, 1872.

These twelve issues or editions in two years could be increased if one were to add such volumes as represented combinations of two of the individual titles—but the popularity of Clemens is perhaps sufficiently demonstrated.

Of course many another American humorist was published in London during the avalanche of the sixties and seventies. The variety offered in the three series of *Yankee Drolleries* has already been mentioned. Routledge, whose dominance in the American booktrade at the railway stations was threatened by Hotten's cheap yellowbacks, advertised an entire series of American humorous works, although it was really only a portion of his enormous "American Library," but in the seventies his library of humor included not only Holmes, Lowell, Clemens, and Harte, but Edward Eggleston, Artemus Ward, Max Adeler, T. B. Aldrich, J. M. Bailey, Josh Billings, John Habberton, Will Carleton, and others. Before long the whole corpus of contemporary American humor was available in cheap editions in England—Routledge, Warne, Ward and Lock, Hotten, until his death in 1873, and then Chatto and Windus accounting for most of the publishing. One of the trade journals, the *Bookseller,* soon established a separate section in its list of new books, labelled "Facetiae," and the student who wishes to see the relative importance of the American production in this field may follow its monthly announcements.[47]

So impressive is the avidity with which the English consumed the

---

[47] A few samples: June 3, 1872, lists four items, two American; May 2, 1872, seven items, two American reprints and one an importation; March 2, 1872, three items, two American reprints and the third an importation. Later the American element runs to a much smaller proportion. In the late seventies there was a remarkable enthusiasm for John Habberton, the author of *Helen's Babies.* "The last passion here in American literature is *Helen's Babies* which sells by the 10,000 & is chiefly bought by the *haute noblesse*" (Henry James to T. S. Perry, London, April 18, 1877, MS).

products of transatlantic wits and drolls during the period immediately following the Civil War that the historian who attempts even such a superficial survey as the present one may well be asked to assign causes for the phenomenon. Of course no explanations of quirks in public taste are really adequate. The crocuslike flowering of British enthusiasm for Artemus Ward, Mark Twain, and other American humorists of the sixties and seventies is essentially similar to the recent vogue for cross-word puzzles or for plebeian wit attributed to Confucius—something for the social-psychologists, or even the sociologists, to generalize about. The student who ponders the problem of why many men have laughed soon finds himself confronted with that unresolvable question, "Why do I laugh?" Voltaire indicated the power of his intelligence as well as his skepticism when he opined that he who probes behind laughter for its reasons soon proves himself a fool. But whether folly or not, a few reasons, all perhaps of equal weight, may be advanced.

In the first place, a number of American humorists of undeniable abilities in drollery and satire confronted the British reader within a very short period. Ward, Leland, Clemens, and Harte struck the London bookmarts in quick succession after Lowell and Holmes. Moreover, the widespread interest in the Civil War led to a perusal of and reprinting from the newspapers of the United States on a scale much greater than ever before—and the newspapers provided the peculiar shaping force as well as the chief medium through which native American humor developed, the oral yarns of the frontier notwithstanding. Reports of Lincoln's enjoyment of the "funny fellows" were circulated in England, and some of his own pronouncements were esteemed to be of the order of the tall tale, such as his statement that the Mississippi gunboats were of such light draught that they could float wherever the ground was a little damp.[48] The British themselves recognized the influence from abroad. Consider, for example, the following statement from *Blackwood's* for October, 1867:

Of late years, partly in consequence of the great interest excited by the Civil War, and the more than usually copious extracts made by the English newspapers from those of America, and partly in consequence of

[48] See, for example, the *Saturday Review*, XIX (February 11, 1865), 164. In 1865 the firm of Frederick Farrah issued in London a collection of spurious anecdotes under the title *A Legacy of Fun by Abraham Lincoln with a Short Sketch of His Life.*

the popularity achieved by many American books—such as 'Sam Slick,' 'Uncle Tom's Cabin,' the 'Biglow Papers,' and the jests of Artemus Ward —a large number of American words and phrases, that ought not to be admitted into English literature, have been creeping into use amongst us, and exercising an influence upon the style of our popular journalists, our comic writers, and even of our ordinary conversation.[49]

Evidently the American cinema has had predecessors in its philological suggestiveness! Hear also the opinion of a writer for *All the Year Round,* delivered in 1878:

Everybody knows that the newspaper fun of the world is now mainly of transatlantic origin. The Americans regard drollery as an essential part of journalism—something absolutely indispensable, and to be indulged in at whatever cost; often at the sacrifice of good taste, not to mention graver considerations. . . . Over five thousand journals keep us pretty well supplied with mirth, even as the Gulfstream is said to warm our climate. They have, indeed, somewhat superseded, if not eclipsed, the native article. These facts are patent to everybody.[50]

The quotation serves also to illustrate another important factor in the heightened zest for comedy from the United States, the recognition of its superior quality. Of course not all the critics would admit any such thing as American superiority, even in popular humor, but many did. A writer for *Temple Bar,* surveying the literary products of the year 1871, noted: "As for funny books, humorous books, and comic books, we have had none this year at all of our own. But we have had certain American books of humour, and Leland, and Mark Twain, and Bret Harte have struck out new lines of humour which are sure to be immensely popular." [51] The *Spectator,* the following year, in a review of Mark Twain's *Screamers,* asserted that the "United States are taking a lead in the humorous literature of the day," and recognized the fact that Bret Harte, John Hay, and Artemus

[49] CII, 402; the article is entitled "Inroads upon English." In 1882 John Nichol charged that Mark Twain had "done perhaps more than any other living writer to lower the literary tone of English speaking people" (*American Literature: an Historical Sketch 1620–1880,* Edinburgh, 1882, p. 426). A reviewer for the *Spectator* was so struck by the humor of some of John Hay's verses that he copied them from the New York *Tribune* (July 29, 1871, p. 918). Cf. *Gentleman's Magazine* for June, 1883, for another recognition of American influence on the "style as well as the language" of British journalists (CCLIV, 592).

[50] New Ser., XXI (September 28, 1878), 298–299. The article is entitled "Caricature in America," and deals with the work of Thomas Nast and others.

[51] XXXIV (December, 1871), 110.

Ward came not as single spies. In 1873 the same journal, in a discussion of Josh Billings, reflected sadly: "the Americans are, in their way, more humorous than the English," but offered consolation in the thought that the Scotch could not enjoy Artemus Ward as keenly as their southern brethren.[52] Samuel Waddington, considering "American Vers de Société" in *Tinsley's* for June, 1876, remarked that transatlantic authors in the field surpassed their British fellows because of the possession of a "keener sense of humour" and a "witty quaintness which seems to be indigenous to the country." [53] Even after the peak of enthusiasm was passed one finds the *National Observer,* in 1891, gloomily wailing: "Fun we must have, of course. If we cannot import it, duty free and carriage paid, in bulk from America, it must be brought (O the pity of it!) from France." [54]

But another reason for the concentrated fervor of the sixties and seventies is the fact that a number of the humorists came to the British as men from the wilds of the Far West. The extraordinary interest in the border settlements which had existed in England since the day of the Noble Savage, and earlier, and which had been nourished by Fenimore Cooper and a variety of other writers, had received a remarkable stimulus during the period of the gold rush. After 1849 the Golden West was a veritable stamping ground for the European imagination. Anything on California in the way of a book was likely to have a sale; even the anthology of Western poets edited by Bret Harte was brought out in London, in 1866. The only subdivision of the United States which Mudie's Select Library recognized in its catalogues was California. Speakers in Parliament referred to its wealth in their debates, and, later, the Dean of Westminster described the redwoods in his sermons. On his deathbed Charles Kingsley, who abjured democracy and all its ways, babbled of the green fields near the Pacific. Even today the most intelligent type of Englishmen who visit our shores, the Commonwealth Fellows, regularly make their pilgrimage to the West Coast. In the sixties and seventies the first literary spokesmen of the region began to be heard in Europe. Artemus Ward lectured on the Mormons; Joaquin Miller sang of the landscape; Mark Twain spun yarns from Calaveras County and

---

[52] May 18, 1872, p. 633; June 27, 1873, p. 816.   [53] XVIII, 711.
[54] "The Decline of Humour," V (March 14, 1891), 425.

discoursed on Hawaii; Bret Harte immortalized the West-Coast Chinaman and revealed the tender hearts that beat beneath the red flannels of gamblers and miners. These authors from the West were expected to be in person exuberant and eccentric; and their subject matter as well as their method was received with acclaim. Charles Warren Stoddard and Ambrose Bierce soon followed Miller and Clemens from California, Bierce publishing his first three books in London, and becoming a staff writer for the rival of *Punch* called *Fun*.[55] Late in the century Gertrude Atherton was still able to profit from the traditional interest in Californians when she went to London to acquire a reputation, and Gelett Burgess likewise.[56] One can explain the extraordinary praise of Joaquin Miller's early verse in England only on the grounds of his subject matter; and it is reasonable to suppose that something of the fervor with which Ward, Harte, and Clemens were greeted was due to the belief that they were spokesmen of the romantic West.[57]

But another factor accounting for the craze for American humor during the period under discussion is the salesmanship of the publisher of the earliest books by Ambrose Bierce—again John Camden Hotten. His cheap editions of Lowell and Leland, of Clemens and Harte, and a dozen others, are as much responsible for the vogue of the "American Drolleries" as anything else. One might resist a book if it cost a good round sum, but all but the poorest could afford the sixpence or the shilling that bought from a railway stall an hilarious hour with Artemus Ward. Hotten is memorable to the student of American letters as the publisher of the first English edition of Walt Whitman, but he deserves to be remembered also as one of the chief agents responsible for the spread of British interest in one of our most distinctive intellectual products. It is an ironic fact that Mark Twain tried to satirize him out of business.[58]

[55] Vincent Starrett, *Ambrose Bierce; a Bibliography*, Philadelphia, 1929; Carey McWilliams, *Ambrose Bierce: a Biography*, New York, 1929, chap. vi.

[56] Gertrude Atherton, *Adventures of a Novelist*, New York [1932], pp. 227, 266 ff. English magazines rather than American ones accepted her stories (*ibid.*, p. 219). For an example of Burgess in English periodicals see the *Illustrated London News*, CXIII (September 17, 1898), 399, and the Christmas number of the same year.

[57] See, for example, an almost hysterical appreciation of Bret Harte in *Blackwood's*, CX (October, 1871), 422 ff.

[58] See Clemens's letter to the *Spectator*, September 21, 1872, pp. 1201–1202, reprinted in Merle Johnson, *op. cit.*, revised ed., pp. 160–162.

All through the seventies and eighties the interest in American humor continued, although there seem to have been no more sudden cataracts of enthusiasm comparable to the one which has just been described. The stream of transatlantic comic writing became broader with the development of the local-color story and the tremendous expansion of journalism which increased the supply of writers like Bill Nye or Frank Stockton.[59] Though the number of new books of humor from the United States declined later in the century and the Copyright Act of 1891 prevented the piracy of the latest offerings, the quantity of authorized editions is still very impressive. So far as books alone are concerned, very probably the early works of Artemus Ward, Mark Twain, and Bret Harte which had not been protected by copyright must have had the largest circulation, for they were constantly reprinted by several different firms. But Clemens and Harte soon acquired copyright by first publication in London, and it is doubtful whether many of their later productions had a wider sale than the books which first brought them an English reputation, in spite of the fact that the supply of readers increased by leaps and bounds throughout the eighties and nineties.

A number of the newer humorists who appeared after 1875 were protected by publisher's agreements or by prior publication in London, but many were not; and one may view an astonishing array in such a series as "Beeton's Humorous Books," issued by Ward, Lock and Company, one of the early competitors of Hotten. By 1885 this series had run to about eighty titles, three fourths of which were of American origin. The cheap libraries of Routledge, Warne, Ward and Lock, Chatto and Windus, and others offered a ready supply of transatlantic books of fun especially up to 1891; but the increasing production of anthologies of American humor in verse or prose is also deserving of mention. Compilations like Mark Twain's *Library of Humor* were of course issued also in London, and the British frequently made up their own.[60] It was the fashion also, as indeed it

---

[59] A British student of Americanisms declared in 1893 that 90 percent of the "purely comic" material printed in English periodicals came from the United States, an exaggeration which is nevertheless revelatory (T. Baron Russell, *Current Americanisms,* London [1893], pp. 5–6).

[60] A few examples: *American Humour: in Prose and Verse,* selected by John Hamer, London: Cassell, 1884; *Humorous Gems from American Literature,* ed. Edward T. Mason, London: Routledge, 1887; *American Jests and Anecdotes,* London: Paterson,

had been earlier, to combine both American and English authors in an anthology or "reciter." [61]

There were special lectures on American humor, too, such as those by Hugh R. Haweis, *mutatis mutandis,* a kind of Billy Sunday of London. In 1881 he delivered a series of discourses on transatlantic humorists for the Royal Institution, and repeated them the next year for the London Institution. They were soon gathered up into a book, published first in 1882 by Chatto and Windus under the title *American Humourists,* and reissued in the United States. Irving, Holmes, Lowell, Artemus Ward, Clemens, and Harte were the authors upon whom he lectured, a choice which the more intelligent of his audience must have approved. Speakers who discussed humor in general or British humor in particular sometimes indulged in an excursus on the American product, for example, William S. Lilly, who found place for a few remarks in his lecture on "The Theory of the Ludicrous" delivered at the Royal Institution in 1895. Like most critics after 1870, he found the transatlantic variety to be "distinctly a thing *sui generis*"—the "only intellectual province in which the people of the United States have achieved originality." Its distinctive charm, he supposed, lay in its "homely and fresh grotesqueness"; Lowell he considered to be "one of its chief masters." [62]

Late in the century the objections to the wholesale laudation of the more lowly types of American humor became more insistent and widespread. The freshness of the grotesquerie of the funny men seemed to be wearing out.[63] H. D. Traill in discussing "The Future of Humour" noted significantly: "The Dickensian humour, it would seem, is 'off': the American droll, after a vogue of a good many years, is apparently ceasing to amuse; the 'inverted aphorism' had but a short popularity . . . and nothing seems growing up to take

---

1887; *The Humour of America,* ed. James Barr, London: Scott, 1893; *American Humorous Verse,* London: Scott, 1891; *Humorous American Tales,* ed. Charles B. Neville, London: Simpkin, 1892; *American Humorists,* ed. Robert Ford, Paisley: Gardner, 1896. (The dates may not always represent the first issues.)

[61] E.g., *Poets at Play: a Handbook of Humorous Recitations,* ed. Frederick Langbridge, London: Eyre and Spottiswoode [1888?]; *Humorous Poems of the Century,* ed. Ralph H. Caine, London: Scott [1890?].

[62] William S. Lilly, *Studies in Religion and Literature,* London, 1904, p. 297. Cf. *Personal and Literary Letters of Robert First Earl of Lytton,* ed. Lady Betty Balfour, London, 1906, II, 374, for similar opinions.

[63] See, for example, the *Illustrated London News,* CX (January 2, 1897), 2.

its place." [64] Certainly *David Harum* and Mr. Dooley, though widely known, did not take England by storm,[65] but as the old century died Mark Twain was recognized as the outstanding humorist of the English-speaking world, and penetrating observers could still find evidences of American superiority, for instance, James F. Muirhead, who denied that *Life* was equal to *Punch* or that the average of British fun was below that of its American rival. But, he maintained:

When we reach the level of Artemus Ward, Ik Marvel, H. C. Bunner, Frank Stockton, and Mark Twain, we may find that we have no equally popular contemporary humourists of equal excellence; and these are emphatically humourists of a pure American type. If humour of a finer point be demanded it seems to me that there are few, if any, living English writers who can rival the delicate satiric powers of a Henry James or the subtle suggestiveness of Mr. W. D. Howells' farces, for an analogy to which we have to look to the best French work of the kind.[66]

Such an appreciation of the diffusion of the art of humor among American writers not especially professional mirth-makers was by 1890 almost a tradition. The sly touches of Hawthorne and the ethereal satire of such a work as "The Celestial Railroad" were early hailed as qualifying him; and Emerson had been found to be full of wit, capable of turning out humorous verses like those dealing with the mountain and the squirrel.[67] Henry S. Salt lashed fiercely at Lowell for insisting that Thoreau had no humor, and Longfellow was at times credited with the virtue of funmaking.[68] Even the stories of Poe were frequently published under the title, *Tales of Mystery, Imagination and Humour*. And when the swarm of local-colorists was unloosed, with the Stocktons, Bunners, and Aldriches besides, what could an Englishman say but that humor was almost all-pervasive in

---

[64] *The New Fiction and Other Essays on Literary Subjects*, London, 1897, p. 320.

[65] See, however, *Gentleman's Magazine*, CCLXXXII (December, 1900), 542–543. There were at least three piracies of *Mr. Dooley in Peace and War*. For the English reaction see Elmer Ellis, *Mr. Dooley's America: a Life of Finley Peter Dunne*, New York, 1941, pp. 121, 126, 134, 137.

[66] *The Land of Contrasts*, Boston, New York, and London, 1898, p. 142. Howells's plays were regularly printed in authorized editions by David Douglas in Edinburgh. For humor in his fiction see a very able article in the *Westminster Review* for October, 1884 (CXXII, 347–375).

[67] *North British Review*, XXXIII (November, 1860), 461–485.

[68] *Temple Bar*, LXXVIII (November, 1886), 375; *Fortnightly*, XXXIX (January 1, 1883), 103–104.

American literature—and, indeed, in American life? [69] Occasionally the utterances on this topic pass far beyond the bounds of belief. Grant Allen, for instance, declared that "embryo Mark Twains grow in Illinois on every bush" and that the "raw material of the *Innocents Abroad* resounds nightly, like the voice of the derringer, through every saloon in Iowa and Montana." [70] It was even asserted that English actors picked up a sharpened sense of comedy by a tour of the States, and book reviewers who wished to criticize an American novel without reading it felt pretty secure in animadverting on the general humorous tone of the work in question.[71] All this is, of course, as unconsciously humorous in its way as the account of Rhinthon of Syracuse viewed as the father of Greek burlesque tragedy which one reviewer used as a prelude to his appraisal of Orpheus C. Kerr.[72] But, stripped of all nonsense, the British argument that humor was more widespread in the United States was essentially sound. It is one conclusion which can be made from the "funny papers."

[69] Note the propriety of Bret Harte's contention that humor first diminished the power of English influence on American literature ("The Rise of the 'Short Story'," *Cornhill,* New Ser., VII, July, 1899, 3).

[70] *Fortnightly,* L (August 1, 1888), 249.

[71] See a splendid example in John Barrow Allen's discussion of *The Red Badge of Courage* in the *Academy,* XLIX (February 15, 1896), 135. The *Academy* retrieved itself in regard to Crane in a hurry; see LI (January 16, 1897), 76; LI (February 20, 1897), 231–232; and LI (May 22, 1897), 541.

[72] *Athenæum* for December 30, 1865, pp. 921–922.

IV. LONGFELLOW

"If there were only the name of Longfellow to plead against a war between his country and ours, we should abhor the man who would lift up his voice in its favour"—Introductory Notice in *The Song of Hiawatha,* published in London, 1855, by Knight and Son.

I F THE WALLS of the preceding chapters may be said to bulge and creak with the burden of their broad topics the same will prove to be true even of the present discussion, in which the field is narrowed to the reception in England of a single American author. Longfellow, the writer chosen for the purpose of illustration, attracted during his lifetime a number of readers throughout the world unequalled by any poet of his day, and the history of his popularity in the British Isles alone is a vast epic with a thousand and one episodes. When Franklin D. Roosevelt recently included a poetical quotation in a communication addressed to the Prime Minister of Great Britain he selected a passage from Longfellow's "The Building of the Ship," a poem which thousands of Britons have been familiar with from their youth and which they have heard sung in cantatas written by at least three Victorian composers. The President's choice was a good one, too, as coming from one naval enthusiast to another, for in 1869, twenty years after they were first published, the Chief Constructor of the British Navy declared the verses to be the "finest poem on shipbuilding that ever was, or probably ever will be, written." [1] Even today there must be in England ten thousand persons who can reel off from memory a dozen lines of Longfellow to every score who can name the title of one work by Arthur Clough, the poet whom Churchill quoted in reply to our President. [2]

The evidences of Longfellow's popularity in days gone by are not hard to find. His friends who visited England during the middle

---

[1] Samuel Longfellow, *Life of Henry Wadsworth Longfellow,* 3 vols., Boston and New York [1891], III, 135. (Hereinafter cited as *Life.*)

[2] Clough's *Bothie,* it may be of interest to note, was "directly prompted by a reading of Longfellow's *Evangeline*" (*The Letters of Matthew Arnold to Arthur Hugh Clough,* ed. Howard F. Lowry, London and New York, 1932, p. 91).

of the nineteenth century often mentioned it in their letters to the author, Hawthorne, for example, writing on May 11, 1855: "No other poet has anything like your vogue. Did you hear how the Harrow school-boys, a few months ago, decided by a formal vote (as I understood) that you are the first poet of the age?" [3] And a year later the novelist sent along a copy of the program of a Victorian night club which the proprietor had requested him to transmit, presumably because it included a number of Longfellow's poems used as songs. The owner of the "Supper Rooms" confessed that it had been the "dream and romance of his life" to see Emerson, Channing, and Longfellow seated with Hawthorne at one of his tables and listening to "the bacchanalian catches of his vocalists." [4]

So far as the poet's influence at Harrow is concerned, we have even more direct knowledge, for the father of Bertrand Russell, soberly reflecting at one of its desks in 1859, jotted down in his diary:

Oh! how can I waste one moment that the Almighty gives me? Well may Longfellow warn us to "trust no future," but to "act, act in the living Present"; well may he say,

> Let us then be up & doing,
> With a heart for any fate;
> Still achieving, still pursuing,
> Learn to labour & to wait.

The following year the young Russell took the same lines of "that beautiful & stirring stanza" as the motto for a Latin essay which won him a prize in the fifth form—the second prize, it may be added.[5] And lest one conclude that only the prep-school lads could really have been impressed, it may also be noted that in the late sixties both Oxford and Cambridge conferred honorary degrees on the author while the undergraduates shouted enthusiastically as they caught the titles of his chief works enumerated in the course of the Latin eulogies.

After Longfellow had ascended the British Parnassus there was no point in repeating Sydney Smith's notorious question. Even the London *Times,* in 1868, observed:

---

[3] *Life,* II, 287. [4] *Ibid.,* II, 308.
[5] *The Amberley Papers: the Letters and Diaries of Lord and Lady Amberley,* ed. Bertrand and Patricia Russell, London, 1937, I, 182, 196.

A guest is approaching our shores, or has already landed, whose name is a household word to the English people. No poet of our own or of any other land is so widely known and appreciated by strangely various classes of society. . . . He is not less the poet of the people than a chosen companion of the cultured and refined; and his words are in the mouths of thousands to whom our own Tennyson is only partially familiar, and to whom Browning is an unknown name.[6]

Ten years later William Michael Rossetti concluded that the American bard was still "by far" the most widely read poet of the English-speaking world, and shortly afterwards Samuel Waddington declared "A Psalm of Life" to be "the most popular composition in verse that has ever been written." [7] At the time of Longfellow's death, when men like Hall Caine, Austin Dobson, and others were writing verses in his honor, there were those who actually believed that the British pirates owed him more money than their American confrères owed any English author! [8] And at the end of the century the *Illustrated London News* reflected:

Perhaps the most entirely popular books in prose and poetry which have been read by the masses of the English people during the last fifty years have come to us from America—the poems of Longfellow and "Uncle Tom's Cabin," both largely tending to make our middle classes strongly sympathetic to the Stars and Stripes. Certain it is that Longfellow's sales in this country have far exceeded those of any one of our own poets.[9]

But the interest in his works was shared by all classes of English society. Dickens maintained that the workingmen were as widely acquainted with Longfellow's poems as the people above them, and the Queen herself declared that never had her servants and attendants exhibited such a peculiar interest in a distinguished visitor as they did

[6] June 10, 1868.

[7] *Lives of Famous Poets,* London, 1878, p. 387; *Chapters of My Life: an Autobiography,* London, 1909, p. 143.

[8] *Academy,* XXI (April 1, 1882), 232. Henry Bright and Dickens's friend Kent were others who wrote poems on Longfellow. A former M. P. for Chichester composed an *Elegy on the Death of Henry Wadsworth Longfellow* (by Humphry W. Freeland, printed for the author, Chichester, n.d.) which contains the following quatrain:

> "In Hiawatha's song the hopes and fears
> And legends wild of Indian life are seen,
> And many a heart hath sought relief in tears
> O'er the long sorrows of Evangeline."

[9] CVIII (January 18, 1896), 78.

on the morning in 1868 when the poet came to the Palace to gratify
her desire to see him.[10] A few years earlier George Gilfillan stopped
to visit an aged family servant and discovered that the old man was
ready to wax eloquent on the "lofty flichts" of Longfellow, whom he
was reading.[11]

The scholars, of course, were forced to discuss his translations or
his metrical experiments, and already in 1854 those who delighted in
Notes & Queries had started a prolonged discussion of the origin of
his name.[12] And as for the upper classes, Longfellow had to flee from
England in 1868 in order to avoid being fêted to death. Lord Houghton, friend of all American authors, took him to visit the House of
Lords, "where they treated him with great distinction, and gave him
a place under the throne"; and when his genial host proceeded to show
off his lion at a dinner at the Athenæum Club, the number of would-
be guests who had to be turned down caused extreme embarrass-
ment.[13]

The various and sundry British visitors to Cambridge, Massachusetts, who made their way out Brattle Street to pay their respects to
the poet in his own home included men like Sir Charles Fox, the
builder of the Crystal Palace, the Dean of Canterbury, the President
of the Royal Society, and Plumptre, the classical scholar. On October
9, 1879, Longfellow's diary records: "This forenoon fourteen callers;
thirteen of them English." [14] Lord Rosebery, with a Rothschild heiress

[10] Dickens to J. T. Fields, July 7, 1868, J. T. Fields, *Yesterdays with Authors,* Boston, 1893, p. 191; Amy Cruse, *The Victorians and Their Reading,* Boston and New
York, 1935, chap. xii, "Books from America," pp. 242–243.

[11] Robert A. Watson and Elizabeth S. Watson, *George Gilfillan: Letters and Journals, with Memoir,* London, 1892, p. 309. For Gilfillan's opinions of Longfellow see
his *Galleries of Literary Portraits,* Edinburgh and London, 1856, I, 217–223. (The
same work contains valuable critiques of Poe and Emerson also.)

[12] IX (February 25, 1854), 174. R. W. King states that other translators of Dante
have sometimes "closely" followed Longfellow (*The Translator of Dante: the Life,
Work and Friendships of Henry Francis Cary 1772–1844,* London, 1925, p. 326 n.).
Cf. also Paget Toynbee, "Chronological List of English Translations from Dante,"
Dante Studies, Oxford, 1921, pp. 156–280. The records of Routledge, the authorized
publisher of Longfellow's translation of *The Divine Comedy,* indicate a sale of over
seventy thousand copies of the whole or of the separate parts up to the year 1900.

[13] T. Wemyss Reid, *The Life, Letters, and Friendships of Richard Monckton Milnes,
First Lord Houghton,* London, 1890, II, 193–195.

[14] *Life,* III, 304. The first Englishman to call on Longfellow solely as a result of
reading his poems seems to have been a York Quaker, who visited him in 1845 (*ibid.,*
II, 27).

as a wife and three Derby winners in his stables, almost shocked Henry James out of his chair by announcing at the luncheon table that "his ideal of the happy life was that of Cambridge, Massachusetts, 'living like Longfellow.'" [15]

British musicians were, of course, interested in the American poet. *Hiawatha* and a few other of his longer efforts were made over into operas, a dozen more supplied the words for cantatas, for one of which Sir Arthur Sullivan wrote the music, but the most popular of all were the hosts of lyrics from his pen which tempted composers like Balfe and Hatton, in spite of Longfellow's own belief that his metres were not musical enough for the purpose. If an Englishman preferred the musical settings of foreigners, there were of course American versions to be had, as well as those by Brahms, Liszt, Gounod, and others on the Continent.[16] As the century ended, Coleridge-Taylor produced his choral-orchestral *Hiawatha's Wedding Feast* (1898), and followed this with *The Death of Minnehaha* (1899) and *Hiawatha's Departure* (1900). The painters, too, had their interest in this American, for practically every Victorian illustrator of consequence was called on to try his hand at a Longfellow subject, and Holman Hunt's "The Light of the World" is said to have been inspired by one of his translations.[17]

The vast number of parodies of his verses made by the English wits is of course another proof of popularity. They began to appear early —and still continue, their remarkable feature being the large number of different poems which have served as subjects. Shortly after the appearance of *Hiawatha* the chief British pirate of the poem in England brought out a small shilling-volume entitled *The Song of Drop o' Wather—a London Legend,* by Harry Wandsworth Shortfellow, to help add to his profits from the enormous success of the Red Indian saga. In 1879 the editor of the *World* offered two prizes for the best parodies of a selected portion of the poem, and among the

[15] *The Letters of Henry James,* ed. Percy Lubbock, New York, 1920, I, 77.

[16] Eric S. Robertson, *Life of Henry Wadsworth Longfellow,* London, 1887, Bibliography, pp. x–xi. Mr. H. W. L. Dana is preparing for publication a fuller list of the Longfellow music.

[17] Morley Stevenson, *The Spiritual Teaching of Longfellow,* London [1906], p. 14. "I knew Longfellow's volume fairly well, but I had no memory of having read the beautiful sonnet from Lopas [*sic*] de Vega" (William Holman Hunt, *Contemporary Review,* XLIX, June, 1886, 827).

one hundred and thirty-five contestants Lewis Carroll was judged to be third with his "Hiawatha's Photographing." Five years later a kind of parody journal was initiated with a definite plan calling for the treatment of one author after another, but the editor made the bad mistake of starting out with Tennyson and Longfellow, and so many of his readers began sending in new versions of these two authors that the original outline had to be held in abeyance. In his introductory sketch of Longfellow the editor also observed that the American poet had obtained in England "a popularity second to that of no English writer." [18]

While Longfellow's vogue developed rapidly in the forties and reached a startling height with the publication of *Hiawatha* in 1855, his popularity was sustained during the latter part of the century by the wide spread of reading among the lower classes and among children. The enormous expansion of the reading public in the British Isles during the last quarter of the century gave a renewed life to the old rank of popular writers that must be regarded as one of the chief general literary phenomena of the era. But Longfellow's reputation had roots that extended back even before the accession of Victoria. In 1831, for example, the *Athenæum* had reprinted his "Hymn of the Moravian Nuns," and after learning of his authorship of the poem referred to him as "an especial favourite of ours." [19] The newspapers and cheaper magazines soon began to share the opinion of the *Athenæum* and to follow its example; the chief favorites were the poems which were gathered together in *Voices of the Night* (1839) and *Ballads and Other Poems* (1841). Of the former volume "A

[18] *Parodies of the Works of English & American Authors,* collected and annotated by Walter Hamilton, 6 vols., London, 1884–1889, I, 62–63. Almost all the parodies of American authors in the earlier volumes are of British origin, except for selections from Bayard Taylor's *Diversions of the Echo Club.* Whitman, Harte, Poe, Whittier, Emerson, Holmes, Lowell, Hay, and others are represented. For Longfellow see especially I, 63–105; II, 6–24 and 246–255. Hamilton states that Lowell's *The Biglow Papers* were parodied chiefly by the Liberal newspapers (V, 248).

For examples of parodies of Longfellow published elsewhere see *Punch,* LII (February 23, 1867), 79 and LIII (October 12, 1867), 146; and *Our Miscellany,* ed. E. H. Yates and R. B. Brough, London, 1856, pp. 132–134. These are, of course, only a few of many. Probably the cleverest parody of Longfellow's hexameters was written by James Spedding (*Reviews and Discussions Literary, Political and Historical, Not Relating to Bacon,* London, 1879, p. 327).

[19] W. B. Cairns, *British Criticisms of American Writings 1815–1833,* Madison, Wis., 1922, p. 179.

Psalm of Life" was of course the best-beloved; and of the latter, "Excelsior." Their vogue was enhanced not only through reprintings but through constant quotation by clergymen and lecturers to mechanics' institutes and similar organizations. As a writer for the *National Review* later concluded: "He took the public ear at once and immediately; he required no introduction from critics and reviewers; he had not to convert or educate his audience, but found it ready and responsive from the first." [20] Bentley, with his usual capacity for selecting popular authors, ran a considerable number of his poems in the *Miscellany* for 1839 and the following years and paid their author for their use although he did not hesitate to alter titles when he saw fit.[21] Reviewers and other critics, of course, by wholesale quotation, spread the knowledge of Longfellow's lyrics. As early as 1850 periodicals like *Ainsworth's* did not hesitate to print verses avowedly based upon his.[22]

In book form his writings came to the British reader first in the shape of a prose miscellany modelled on Irving's *The Sketch Book* and entitled *Outre-Mer*. The first section of this work was issued in a London edition by Obadiah Rich, in 1833, and two years later Bentley brought out the whole in two volumes in an authorized edition consisting of the usual five hundred copies.[23] But the early reprintings of *Outre-Mer* did not bear its creator's name on the title page; and as a result certain of the reviewers inferred, not unnaturally, that Irving was the author.[24] Wiley and Putnam, and other importers, of course, disseminated copies of his works printed in America, but in the forties the deluge of British imprints began.

In 1843 Edward Moxon, the London specialist in the publication of

---

[20] VIII (January, 1859), 198.

[21] The rate of payment was £12. 12s. per sheet of sixteen pages. The number for January, 1853 (XXXIII, 101–102) also contains "The Warden of the Cinque Ports."

[22] XVIII (December, 1850), 550–551, "The Skeleton in Armour," by Caroline de Crespigny. No English poet of the order of Baudelaire seems to have been inspired by Longfellow (cf. his "Le guignon" and "Le calumet de paix"). The number of British poetasters who owed Longfellow a debt was legion.

[23] For all the material in this chapter dealing with authorized publications of Longfellow's works see "Longfellow and His Authorized British Publishers," by the present writer, *PMLA*, LV (December, 1940), 1165–1179.

[24] For samples of the early reviews see the *Athenæum*, No. 312 (October 19, 1833), p. 696; *Monthly Review*, IV (August, 1835), 544; *Gentleman's*, New Ser., IV (November, 1835), 529–530; and *Tait's*, New Ser., II (August, 1835), 553.

the newer poets, arranged for an edition of Longfellow's poems from sheets printed in Philadelphia, and in the same year H. G. Clarke began issuing numerous copies of his verse. Three years earlier Cunningham had already pirated the novel *Hyperion,* which three other publishers also reprinted before the decade was ended.[25] In the late forties the competition for his new productions became so keen, with publishers in London, Liverpool, and Edinburgh eager to follow the market, that certain tradesmen began to make payments to him for advance copy, proofs, or sheets; and in the vain effort to secure copyright most of his later volumes were brought out in Europe before appearing in the United States. John Walker of Liverpool, David Bogue, W. Kent, and finally Routledge became his authorized publishers.

The appearance of *Evangeline* in 1847 added materially to his popularity in England as well as in America, and of course stimulated the wholesale piracy of his works which, however, was already flourishing. During the early fifties Longfellow, along with Mrs. Stowe, Susan Warner, and Hawthorne, was an outstanding feature of the British booktrade; and the ground was prepared for the sensational recognition afforded *Hiawatha,* which Bogue, T. Nelson, Knight, and Routledge all issued in various editions in 1855 and 1856. But no sooner had a new Longfellow title appeared than it was incorporated in a "Poetical Works" or a "Complete Poems," and such collections provided the chief means whereby the authorized publisher or the pirate strove to meet an ever-increasing market. More than seventy different British publishers brought out one or more volumes by the poet in the years prior to 1901; the incomplete records of the house of Routledge plus the total of Warne & Co.—two of the chief firms which published Longfellow—added up to well over a million copies.[26] How many copies were sold by the seventy-odd other British publishers it is impossible to say.

The *Publishers' Circular* carried announcements of ninety-four

[25] For details of the publication of Longfellow's works in England see "A Check-List of Volumes by Longfellow Published in the British Isles during the Nineteenth Century," *Bulletin of Bibliography,* XVII (September, 1940–August, 1941), 46, 67–69, and 93–96. This list is based on copies now in the Bodleian, the British Museum, and several of the larger libraries of the United States.

[26] Gohdes, "Longfellow and His Authorized British Publishers," p. 1179.

editions or issues of Longfellow volumes during the fifties, forty-four during the sixties, fifty-two during the seventies, fifty-five in the eighties, and thirty-six in the nineties. The year 1878 marked the height of the publication in book form, and during its twelve months twenty-six items were announced. It is to be remembered, however, that these figures include reissues and some duplications. But disregarding these, the number of issues or editions appears staggering to those who know the history of the reception of Robert Frost, or even of Edgar Guest. Next to the general collections of his poems the individual work which attracted most reprinting was *Evangeline,* which was even brought out in a phonetic edition as an incitement to the study of Pitman's shorthand and in a French translation published on the island of Jersey. In the seventies, like various other works of the poet, it went into a variety of series issued for use in the new elementary schools. There were at least a dozen different editions of the novel *Hyperion,* and the other prose works of Longfellow were kept in print by a variety of publishers all through the century.

In prices the books indicate the wide range of the people who read them, for they ran from shilling or even sixpenny volumes to elaborately illustrated Christmas books costing a good round sum. One could purchase a copy of *Evangeline,* "decorated with leaves from the Acadian forests," or a sumptuous *Hyperion* with photographs of the Rhine and the Tyrol. The Leeds Antislavery Society issued some of the verses as propaganda, and the office of the *Review of Reviews* offered special reprints as prizes. In the eighties a collection of the poems was set up in "Dr. Moon's embossed type for the blind," and a volume of selections was also "printed and illuminated in gold." There were "recitation books," adaptations of the longer works for the use of amateur actors, "Gems," "Pearls," and even "Forget-me-nots" from Longfellow, to serve as birthday gifts. Notes were provided with various editions for the use not only of children but of serious students as well; and people like R. H. Shepherd, George Gilfillan, William Michael Rossetti, Henry Morley, as well as lesser fry, wrote introductions for one or more of his works. There was actually an abridged *Hiawatha* rendered into Latin by the radical brother of Cardinal Newman (1862).

There is no need for wonder that the *Annual Register* in its sur-

vey of British accomplishments for the year 1868 included Longfellow along with William Morris and Robert Browning in the section devoted to poetry, or that several different publishers announced
him in a series of "British" or "English" poets.[27] George McCrie in a
volume of essays on *The Religion of Our Literature,* published in
London in 1875, did not balk at Longfellow's nationality any more
than the *Annual Register,* and hailed the American as "the truest,
and in that sense, the greatest poet of our age." [28] Late in the century
an author of a standard textbook designed for the secondary schools
and for prospective teachers in the "training colleges" began his discussion of the recent English literature: "The six greatest poets of
the latter half of this century are Longfellow, a distinguished American poet, Tennyson, Mrs. Browning, Robert Browning, William
Morris, and Matthew Arnold," and added: "It may be said with truth
that Longfellow has taught more people to love poetry than any other
English writer, however great." [29] But this textbook man, after all,
was Professor of the Theory, History, and Practice of Education in
the University of St. Andrews. It was useless for William Rossetti
to cry out that "the real American poet" was Whitman, "a man
enormously greater than Longfellow," when people like Edwin Arnold and George Saintsbury were cogitating whether the author of
Hiawatha was the chief deputy of Apollo from the republic across
the sea.[30]

The reviewers began early to pronounce judgment on this poet who
impressed duchesses and mechanics alike, but the old quarterlies held
off from devoting a whole article to him until the 1850s. In 1844 Martin Tupper wrote a note suggesting that he be commissioned to prepare an essay on Longfellow for the *Quarterly Review,* and arguing

[27] For example, on February 3, 1869, William Rossetti called on J. B. Payne and
discussed the latter's plan for a series of English poets: "Longfellow would be the
first: followed by Scott, Byron, Shelley, Thomson, Keats, Selections, etc. etc." (*Rossetti Papers 1862 to 1870,* ed. W. M. Rossetti, London, 1903, p. 381).

[28] Page 181.

[29] J. M. D. Meiklejohn, *The English Language: Its Grammar, History and Literature,* 13th ed. enlarged, London, 1896, pp. 431–432, 433.

[30] Rossetti, in a sketch of Longfellow included in *Lives of Famous Poets,* London,
1878, p. 391. This work was designed as a companion volume to "Moxon's Popular
Poets," representing twenty-three writers, all English and all dead but Longfellow.
Arnold, *Seas and Lands,* New York, 1891, p. 95. Saintsbury in an obituary notice of
Emerson *Academy,* XXI (May 6, 1882), 320–321.

in favor of his proposal that the poet was the man of "chiefest mark" among American authors and that his verses had gone through "eight editions." But Lockhart, the editor, had made up his mind that the bard was "merely a cleverish imitator of the popular versification of the day," and later wrote: "I have always had a special contempt for Longfellow, and lately had a single combat with the fair Norton on that field"; but he weakened to the extent of adding, "If you have the fellow in one tome I will look him over again and try to make out what value is in him." [31] But when the Master of Trinity College and the Professor of Philosophy at Cambridge hailed *Evangeline* in *Fraser's Magazine* as "the first genuine Castalian fount which has burst from the soil of America" and described it as being "full of beauties of really indigenous" growth, the Lockharts were swept aside and all the bars were down.[32] When *Hiawatha* appeared seven years later Longfellow himself analyzed the reviews in his journal:

Six English papers I have already received on my side and as yet only one against me,—the Illustrated News. . . . More papers from England. Five of them in favor of Hiawatha; one, not very strong in opposition, but "disappointed." [33]

So far as one can judge from the little evidence available, the poet was of the opinion that British reviewers were more kindly disposed toward him than their American tribesmen.

But as time went on the average of enthusiasm in the reviews of his later books must have declined, for there were no more sensa-

[31] George Paston [E. M. Symonds], *At John Murray's: Records of a Literary Circle 1843–1892*, London [1932], pp. 44–45. Tupper visited Longfellow apparently in 1851 and again in 1877. His "admiration found its expression in his sending pips of an apple he ate at Longfellow's in America to England to be planted" (Ralf Buchmann, *Martin F. Tupper and the Victorian Middle Class Mind*, Bern, Switzerland, 1941, p. 29). Robert Bigsby falsely claimed the honor of first reviewing Longfellow (*Visions of the Times of Old; or, The Antiquarian Enthusiast*, London, 1848, I, 48 ff.).

[32] William Whewell, in a review published in the issue for March, 1848 (XXXVII, 295–298). He inquired of George Bancroft, then Minister to the Court of St. James's, as to the historical background of the poem and in 1856 sent Longfellow a volume of his own "privately printed" poems (*Life*, II, 108–109, 311).

[33] December 2 and 7, 1855 (*Life*, II, 296, 298). The *Illustrated London News* reviewed *Hiawatha* along with Tennyson's *Maud* and Bailey's *The Mystic, and Other Poems*, and while devoting the largest share of its attention to the American, announced a preference for his shorter pieces and attacked the metre of his new poem as a "marrowbones-and-cleaver measure, the song of the mill-clapper" (XXVII, November 10, 1855, 554–555).

tional works like *Evangeline* and *Hiawatha* in the offing. Even though *Miles Standish* did sell ten thousand copies on the first day of its appearance in London in 1858, by the time that *The Masque of Pandora* came along, in 1875, Routledge offered a contract which called for a relatively small sum plus a bonus "if the book proved acceptable." Of course the collections of his earlier works were still enjoying a very active sale, but reviewers in general were not inclined to deal with reprints. The tone of the reviews of the later books, however, is often more kindly than one would imagine; but the words "adds nothing to his reputation" appeared with ever-increasing frequency.

For a more detailed consideration of the opinions of the journalistic critics we may turn to the full-length articles on Longfellow which appeared in the British magazines, although many of them are nothing more than lengthy reviews and the variety of opinions expressed runs such a gamut that one is tempted to have done with them at once and say *quot homines tot sententiae*. But setting aside the chief factors biassing periodical criticism in the nineteenth century, namely, the religious, political, and business connections of the journals themselves, and disregarding the fact that an American could rarely receive justice at the hands of any but radical journalists in England until after the Civil War—and sometimes not even then—we may turn to the articles on Longfellow listed in the Appendix of the present volume and attempt a few generalizations along with more specific illustrations.

The largest group of these essays falls, of course, in the middle of the century, with a smaller number concentrated in the eighties after the poet had died and after both Poe and Whitman had waxed considerably in reputation among the critical classes of England. Perhaps the opinion most frequently found in the articles of both groups is that Longfellow's hexameters were not successful—an idea pretty firmly fixed in the minds of American critics, too. Nothing affords better proof that he never pandered to the taste of others than his return to the use of the hexameter after being told on all sides that his experiments with this metre were failures. Of his longer poems *Evangeline* was considered the masterpiece until after the appearance of

Hiawatha, which soon usurped its place; but early and late a large number of the essayists, like the lowlier folk, based his fame upon his shorter lyrics. Very few of the articles are completely laudatory or altogether condemnatory; their general pattern, established at the beginning and continued throughout the century, is a combination of pretty harsh detraction with praise for certain particulars, praise which today often appears extravagant if not ridiculous. Sometimes the magazines with a more popular appeal seem to have been less indulgent toward the poet than their more intellectual rivals.

For more specific illustration, one may begin with the *Eclectic Review* for 1849. The essayist writing in this journal praised the pictures of river and prairie scenery presented in *Evangeline* but urged its author to cultivate lyrical rather than narrative verse and expressed regrets at the "skeptical tone" of the subtitle of "A Psalm of Life." He chose "Nuremberg" as an example of the poet's best lyrical performance and contradicted a charge of imitativeness by counselling Longfellow to "keep as closely as possible to our fine old English models of style and versification." [34]

Ainsworth's, the next year, cavilled at an occasional word or metrical effect but drew attention particularly to the "healthful morality" and the "manly tone of faith" which characterized the bard. Everything in connection with *Evangeline* was praised except its hexameters—even the "life-like" characters. The *Dublin University Magazine,* also in 1850, reprinted "A Psalm of Life," and found a source in Richter for a number of ideas in the lyric, "every line of which" was proclaimed to be "full of touching beauty." The writer of the essay doubted whether Milton, Byron, Dryden, or Pope "could have produced lyrical effusions so simple and yet so full of sweet and touching beauty" as many of his poems, and quoted "Nuremberg" to prove the point. While lacking the higher imagination, except in "Excelsior," the American was full of fancy and possessed of a learning which made him inevitably an excellent translator. His novel *Hyperion,* so the critic stated, had enjoyed a popularity in England before it had been acclaimed in America, but was lacking in vigor.

[34] The volume and page numbers of the articles considered here may be found in the Appendix, under "Individual Authors: Longfellow."

The later novel, *Kavanagh,* however, was not unworthy of its author. Tennyson had more "quaintness and varied power" than Longfellow, but "The Footsteps of Angels" was an almost flawless lyric.[35]

Duffy's Fireside Magazine, in 1851, esteemed the author of *Evangeline* to be a very notable poet of nature; but his idyll lacked skill, although it was "self-reliantly sweet." *The Spanish Student* was believed to be a failure so far as characterization is concerned, but as for "Excelsior"—it was the critic's favorite: "simple, sublime, and beautiful." *Blackwood's,* during the following year, began its critique by affirming that Longfellow could be considered "an equal competitor for the palm with any one of the younger poets of Great Britain." Yes, there was "nearly as much fine poetry" in *The Golden Legend* "as in the celebrated drama of Goethe." But the man did not possess the art of "disguising stolen goods," and many of his original poems sounded like translations. In melody, feeling, pathos, and "exquisite simplicity of expression" he need not shun comparison with any living author, but his new poem on the Middle Ages wanted a life-like plot. (Here was at least one case where Longfellow had indeed disguised his source, for the plot of *The Golden Legend* was taken from *Der Arme Heinrich* by Hartmann von Aue.) But the charges of impiety which had been brought against the *Legend* could not be sustained, although the scene in which the monks were depicted as carousing did appear to be "coarse" and "vulgar."

Fraser's Magazine, in 1853, initiated its discussion of the poet with a charge that might be levelled at the metaphysical poets of the twentieth century, namely, a tendency toward the far-fetched and the extravagant. The very first extract chosen to exhibit the fine qualities of the author was one "in which that marvellous energy which characterizes young countries, and none more than America, receives from the poet a moral sanction that transforms it into something more than a 'go a-head' impulse, and modulates its march by the music of old and sacred experience"—"A Psalm of Life." The most important of Longfellow's minor poems, however, was "The Building of the Ship," and of all his works the outstanding one appeared to be *The Golden Legend.* The miracle play therein contained was not exactly

---

[35] Eric S. Robertson in 1887 spoke of "The Footsteps" as "probably the most successful domestic poem ever penned" (*op. cit.,* p. 81).

profane, but a few expressions were nevertheless "needlessly and pain-
fully coarse," and the orgy of the friars could be considered nothing
short of vulgar. The chief female characters created by the poet were
"nobly ideal creations," but psychology did not constitute one of his
strong points. The essay is pointed toward the opinion that the American was a good, though inconsistent, portrayer of medieval life; and
a comparison between *Faust* and *The Golden Legend* ensues, a comparison not especially to Longfellow's disadvantage.

The *New Monthly Magazine* for 1853 avowed a cordial admiration
for the "noble *Excelsior* strains" and *Voices of the Night,* "so sweetly
solemn, so tender and true," praised their author's figures of speech,
and hailed the characterization in *The Golden Legend* but regretted
the "flippant and irreverent" touches in it, meaning the miracle play
and the friars' scene, of course. *Evangeline* was considered to be so
excellent that its metre could be forgotten; and as for the novels,
Hyperion was too much like the *analecta* from a commonplace
book, but *Kavanagh* contained many good passages.

Skipping on to 1859, one finds a writer for the *National Review*
who is far more severe than any of his predecessors. The poems in
Voices of the Night, written from "every body's point of view,"
strike him as "commonplaces of intellectual character," and the longer
efforts appear to lack historical insight, *Hiawatha* alone demonstrat-
ing any creative or dramatic power. Longfellow's plays are bad and
his novels not very impressive. So far as his later lyrics are concerned, "The Two Angels" and "The Warden of the Cinque
Ports" stand out as the best. But, like all American poets, he is
"comparatively strong in depicting natural scenery" and he has the
merit of "genuine religious earnestness." Considered all in all, he is
a born poet, though not of the highest rank; and "his readers in-
sensibly acquire from his writings a very strong regard and affection for their author."

Of the batch of essays from the eighties we may choose one, that
by Henry Norman, in the *Fortnightly* for 1883, for they are all
alike in their essential nature. The convention was established for
handling Longfellow. One believed it to be a duty to undermine
the uncritical regard for the poet by analyzing his defects and then
to find merits which more plebeian taste had perhaps not discovered.

Cultured English opinion, Norman begins, has for a long while classed the man with the poets of mediocrity for at least three reasons. His patent didacticism is the first; and, secondly, he has been judged largely on the flimsy merits of his early poems, especially "Excelsior" and "A Psalm of Life." Finally, a number of his poems, essentially good lyrics, have been worn out by constant repetition. His prose is marked by clearness and originality of style, by erudition, humor, and "an unbounded fertility of imagination." But much of his verse, while unusually varied, has no permanent value. *Evangeline* indeed produces a refined and elevated impression, but *Hiawatha* has been vastly overpraised; its metre is wretched and its narrative uninteresting. Moreover, any poem containing such barbarous names as Mudjekeewis is bound to become even ludicrous. *"Paul Revere's Ride* suggests and can sustain comparison with Browning's *How They Brought the Good News from Ghent,"* and nothing in the English language has caught the Old Norse spirit better than "The Saga of King Olaf." Longfellow's sonnets in general have a good singing quality and are free from overadornment in imagery.

It is questionable whether the English language contains a series of six original sonnets equal in every point to those which are prefixed to Longfellow's translation of the *Divina Commedia.* They are perfect in form, splendid and yet moderate in language, and full of scholarly suggestion; they exhibit a distinct progression of thought, and, though they are of great virility, their singing quality never relaxes. The sonnets on *Giotto's Tower, Night, President Garfield, My Books, Possibilities,* the pathetic *Victor and Vanquished,* and several of his earlier ones, exhibit Longfellow's best work, and are surpassed by few modern sonnets, if by any.

Like almost every other critic of the period, Norman also praised Longfellow as a translator, and spoke of him as having "no living rival" in the field. But, unlike practically every other British intellectual who ever expressed a view on the subject, he described the translation of the *Divine Comedy* as "by far the best that we have, and probably the best that we shall have in English." The essay closes with the opinion that Longfellow was "entitled to a higher rank" than the one commonly assigned him.

Viewing the whole mass of Longfellow criticism, one may possibly conclude that the arbiters of the British Isles were more sympathetic and flattering to the poet than the American critics. Margaret Fuller and Poe had handled his wares pretty severely at the outset of his career and many another had followed suit. The more sophisticated American critic has for a long time—long before the era of "debunking"—dealt pretty harshly with his fellow countrymen, and Longfellow's muse has indeed erected a barn-door target.[36]

But what were the opinions of Longfellow held by the men of letters more distinguished—and perhaps more acute in their literary perceptions—than the mere journalists? Again the amount and variety of evidence is too great for more than partial illustration, for the literary men of England who failed to register an opinion of Longfellow were indeed few.

Unlike a number of other authors of the United States, Longfellow did not have an extensive personal acquaintance among British writers until after his reputation was firmly established, although through George Ticknor, Edward Everett, and Charles Sumner there was an opportunity of influencing the opinions of a relatively small circle of Englishmen with whom these friends of the poet were intimate. Most American authors who formed strong personal connections abroad did so as a result of their trips to Europe (Emerson's friendship with Carlyle is the outstanding example); but while Longfellow crossed the Atlantic in 1826, in 1835, in 1842, and again in 1868, his periods of sojourn upon British soil were fairly brief, for he preferred the Continent for purposes both of study and of recreation. Of course he met a very large group of the literary lights upon the occasion of his last visit, but for the most part his personal acquaintance among British men of letters was broad rather than deep.[37] In 1857 he asked Charles Sumner to remember

[36] For examples of the treatment of Longfellow by British critics in the present century see John C. Collins, *Studies in Poetry and Criticism*, London, 1905, pp. 53 ff.; George Saintsbury, *Selected Poems of Longfellow*, London, 1906, Introduction; John C. Francis, *Notes by the Way*, London and Leipsic, 1909, chap. xi; Oliphant Smeaton, *Longfellow & His Poetry*, London, 1913; Alfred Noyes, "The Undiscovered Longfellow," *Bookman* (London), LXXIII (October, 1927), 3–6.

[37] For his visits to England see Irving T. Richards, "Longfellow in England: Unpublished Extracts from His Journal," *PMLA*, LI (December, 1936), 1123–1140, and *Life, passim*. Professor Howard F. Lowry has kindly reminded me of Longfellow's friendship for Clough, but I do not consider the relationship as one which may be considered of real moment to either man.

him to only four men—Carlyle, Forster, Dickens, and Thackeray, the last two of whom he had first met during their visits to the United States. To Carlyle he had been introduced in 1835 through the instrumentality of Emerson, and Forster he had learned to know through Dickens. Up to 1868 Dickens was the only English author of considerable consequence with whom he may be said to have been on really intimate terms; and their friendship was in every way hearty and mutually enjoyed. Through letters, however, Longfellow broadened his connections with the English writers, for many sent copies of their works to him and he often reciprocated. Moreover, like the thorough gentleman that he was, the poet remembered any gesture of regard from abroad, and as a result the amount of his correspondence with European authors was rather large, the bulk of it of course following in the wake of his renown.[38] It was through letters that a friendly relationship developed with Tennyson, whom he did not see, however, until late in the sixties when he spent two pleasant days with the Laureate on the Isle of Wight. Accordingly, it may be posited that, with the possible exception of the Ticknor-Everett-Sumner connections and the Dickens circle,[39] English authors had no more to do with the spread of his reputation than the lesser lights among the journalists. Indeed, it seems to be the fact that the intrinsic qualities of his poetry, enhanced among the poorer classes by the cheap prices of numerous editions of his works, developed such a noisy acclaim that both the journalists and the better variety of authors were startled into attention by its echoes.

Dickens, like every Englishman who ever met Longfellow, was delighted with the poet's charming personality and wrote to Forster from New York early in 1842, saying that he had secured a volume of his verses to bring back as a present. "A frank accomplished man as

[38] In 1880 Palgrave, working on *The Visions of England,* remarked that a letter from Longfellow had given him "more encouragement than anything else" (G. F. Palgrave, *Francis Turner Palgrave: His Journals and Memories of His Life,* London, 1899, p. 164). Cf. also *ibid.,* pp. 143–160. The Dickens and Tennyson correspondence Mr. H. W. L. Dana is preparing to publish; and the Forster-Longfellow letters have been made ready for publication by Mr. J. Lee Harlan.

[39] Professor Emery Neff has reminded me of the tremendous influence of the Dickens circle, but I find no evidence of its "promoting" Longfellow especially. It is true, however, that Dickens and his friends undertook to "push" the anti-slavery verses of Longfellow.

well as a fine writer," was his initial reaction,[40] and remained his final verdict. No one rejoiced more heartily in the personal triumph of a friend than did Dickens in 1868, when the American was "everywhere received and courted." And the novelist himself varied the friendly gestures proffered by Gladstone, the Prince of Wales, the Archbishop of Canterbury, and others by dressing up a pair of postilions in the red jackets of the old royal Dover road for a ride after a jolly week-end at Gadshill. Eighteen years earlier, when Dickens was contemplating a title for his magazine which eventually became *Household Words,* he suggested "The Forge: A Weekly Journal," followed by four of the most didactic lines from "The Village Blacksmith," and the slight errors in his reproduction of them indicate that he was quoting from memory.[41]

Samuel Rogers was likewise an early admirer, for in 1842 he informed Sumner that he had read "again and again" the volumes of Longfellow. "Very few things, if any, have ever thrilled me so much," he gushed.[42] But the old gentleman was ever the "friend of American genius," as Washington Irving called him. Three years later George Darley encountered the bard's "ugly unpoetic name," but he was far from being, like Rogers, a lover of Americans. The transatlantic "metre-mongers," he wrote, "are mere apes of our poets, & of the worst among them, the modern, popular sort." And then he added a thought which today seems to have considerable novelty: "When they borrow our *mind,* I wish they would do as when they borrow our *money*—never give it us back again!" [43]

But the publication of *Evangeline* sent the estimate of Longfellow higher, for the Pre-Raphaelites, Hunt, Millais, and Dante Rossetti, in 1849 made a list of the names of people who seemed important to them—and they included the American. To Jesus Christ they awarded four stars, to Shakespeare and the author of *Job* three, to Raphael, Patmore, Elizabeth Browning, and Longfellow one each, while New-

[40] February 28, 1842, John Forster, *The Life of Charles Dickens,* ed. J. W. T. Ley, London [1928], p. 225.

[41] *The Letters of Charles Dickens,* edited by his sister-in-law and his eldest daughter, London, 1893, p. 214.

[42] *Life,* I, 439.

[43] To Laura Darley, February 8 [1845], Claud C. Abbott, *The Life and Letters of George Darley Poet and Critic,* London, 1928, p. 259.

ton, Bacon, and Phidias received none.[44] But Rossetti later changed his mind and, irritated by all the excitement over *Hiawatha,* wrote to Allingham:

How I loathe *Wishi-washi,*—of course without reading it. I have not been so happy in loathing anything for a long while—except, I think, *Leaves of Grass,* by that Orson of yours.[45]

But the Corn-Law rhymer, Ebenezer Elliott, was far from hostile. When Samuel Smiles visited the old radical in 1849 he expressed the desire to read the new poem that everybody was talking about, and accordingly Smiles sent along a shilling copy of *Evangeline.* The thank-you note indulged in a bit of criticism: "Longfellow is indeed a poet, and he has done what I deemed an impossibility; he has written English hexameters, giving our mighty lyre a new string! When Tennyson dies, he should read *Evangeline* to Homer." [46] The laureate ghost, however, would have demurred, for shortly after Longfellow's visit to Farringford Tennyson remarked of his guest: "I didn't compliment him—I told him I didn't like his hexameters: he rather defended them." [47] Hallam Tennyson has informed us that his father believed *Hiawatha* to be the most original of the American's poems and that he quoted a bit of one of his translations.[48] But the author of *Maud* was, apparently, chary of expressing his views. There were those who thought that he picked up an occasional idea from Longfellow, and it was very awkward when the *Times* circulated the false rumor that he had refused the Massachusetts bard permission to use

[44] William Holman Hunt, *Pre-Raphaelitism and the Pre-Raphaelite Brotherhood,* London and New York, 1905, I, 159. Emerson and Poe were mentioned but not starred.

[45] *Letters of D. G. Rossetti to William Allingham 1854–1870,* ed. G. B. Hill, London, 1897, p. 181. Longfellow later visited Rossetti, and "the good old bard," courteous "in the last degree," made the error of supposing that D. G. was only a painter while W. M. was the poet (Hall Caine, *My Story,* New York, 1909, pp. 177–178). Patmore, of *Hiawatha:* "Longwinded-fellow's last is, I think, his best." After pointing out certain choice lines, he added: "I don't understand how a man who can ever tumble on a good line can write such heaps of slush as he has done" (To Allingham, December 6, 1855, Basil Champneys, *Memoirs and Correspondence of Coventry Patmore,* London, 1900, II, 182).

[46] November 3, 1849, *The Autobiography of Samuel Smiles, LL.D.,* ed. Thomas Mackay, New York, 1905, p. 150.

[47] *William Allingham: a Diary,* ed. H. Allingham and D. Radford, London, 1907, pp. 182–183.

[48] *Alfred Lord Tennyson: a Memoir,* London, 1897, II, 55–56.

certain poems in an anthology, and there were apocryphal stories floating around, like the following one:

My father was dining one night at the Oxford and Cambridge Club with George Venables, Frank Lushington, Tennyson, and two or three others. After dinner the poet insisted on putting his feet on the table, tilting back his chair *more Americano*. There were strangers in the room, and he was expostulated with for his uncouthness, but in vain. *"Do* put down your feet!" pleaded his host. "Why should I?" retorted Tennyson. "I'm very comfortable as I am." "Everyone's staring at you," said another. "Let 'em stare," replied the poet placidly. "Alfred," said my father, "people will think you're Longfellow." Down went the feet.[49]

Browning, likewise, appears to have been reticent on the subject of Longfellow, but we know that in 1864 he inquired about him,[50] and later, when the two men met their relationship gave evidence of being very friendly. Browning was one of the few English authors of outstanding ability who was genuinely cordial to Americans; but he, too, was struck by their democratic manners, if one may judge by a story about Longfellow which he is alleged to have been fond of telling.[51]

The record of Wordsworth's reactions is equally slight, although there is no reason for supposing that his remarks concerning Longfellow were guarded—or needed to be. A correspondent of Longfellow's, in 1846, confided: "On a late visit to Ambleside Mr. Wordsworth inquired after you, & mentioned the pleasing interview he had with you at Rydal Mount, & passed a deserved eulogium upon your Poems." [52] But there is no evidence at all that Longfellow had visited the old poet, who may have confused him with another of the numerous visitors from America who came to the Lake District. The eulogium, on the other hand, can hardly be questioned since Emer-

[49] The *Illustrated London News,* for example, believed that Tennyson had "cited with approving assent" one of Longfellow's poems in *In Memoriam* (LV, July 17, 1869, 70). Tennyson promptly denied the *Times* report in a letter to the American (partially transcribed in *Life,* III, 265). The anecdote appears in Charles H. E. Brookfield, *Random Reminiscences,* London, 1902, p. 5.

[50] *Life,* III, 39.

[51] The two men were riding in a hansom cab when a heavy shower came up and the American poet pushed his umbrella through the trap in the roof so that the cabbie might protect himself from the weather. Browning thought the incident amusing (Marie Bancroft and Squire Bancroft, *The Bancrofts: Recollections of Sixty Years,* New York, 1909, pp. 394–395).

[52] Irving T. Richards, *op. cit.,* p. 1123.

son reported in 1848 that Wordsworth "spoke highly of Longfellow and regretted his name." [53] A fragmentary letter in which he commented on *Evangeline* reveals only his impression that the idyll was modelled "in metre and in manner and matter" on *Louise* by Voss.[54] It is ironic to contemplate the fact that in 1868, when it was thought for a time that copyright for Americans was more secure, Longfellow was paid by Routledge for one of his most inferior volumes a sum almost three times as large as Wordsworth's total income for the year 1844.[55]

The literary ladies of the mid-century who wrote fiction made their characters quote the poet upon occasion, and the greatest of them, George Eliot, ranked *Hiawatha* with *The Scarlet Letter* as "one of the two most indigenous and masterly productions in American literature." Informed by the learned men that the metre was Finnish, she spoke of it as "one of the greatest charms in the poem." [56] Mrs. Browning expressed her lack of interest in Miss Mitford's literary heroes, Irish and American, but hastily added: "Longfellow is a poet; I don't refer to *him.*" Apparently her early favorite among his poems was "The Arrow and the Song." [57]

Miss Mitford herself, as a special partisan of American authors,

[53] *Henry Crabb Robinson on Books and Their Writers,* ed. Edith J. Morley, London [1938], II, 678. Robinson himself found *Evangeline* to be modelled on Goethe but thought that Longfellow's lines ran "smooth" (p. 677).

[54] To John P. Nichol, August, 1848, *The Letters of William and Dorothy Wordsworth,* ed. Ernest de Selincourt, Oxford, 1939, III, 1317. Another version of the letter appears in *Some Letters of the Wordsworth Family,* ed. Leslie N. Broughton, Ithaca, N.Y., 1942, p. 90.

[55] Wordsworth informed Alexander Macmillan that his income was £350 per year (Charles L. Graves, *Life and Letters of Alexander Macmillan,* London, 1910, p. 319). Barry Cornwall was greatly surprised at the amount paid Longfellow when informed of it by Forster, who acted as agent in the transaction (R. W. Armour, *Barry Cornwall: a Biography of Bryan Waller Proctor,* Boston, 1935, p. 330). Proctor, who frequently corresponded with Longfellow, spoke of him as "a *very* agreeable man; and—within a certain limit—a pleasant writer." Several of the American's letters are to be found in *An Autobiographical Fragment and Biographical Notes,* ed. Coventry Patmore, London, 1877.

[56] For examples of the use of Longfellow by minor female writers see Amy Cruse, *op. cit.,* pp. 240–241. George Eliot in a review of a number of books for the *Westminster* (New Ser., IX, January, 1856, 297). She had the good sense to feature Browning rather than Longfellow in this review. For a discussion of the metre of *Hiawatha* see the *Athenæum* for 1855, pp. 1337, 1370, 1401, 1434, 1466–1467, and 1534.

[57] July 8, 1850, *The Letters of Elizabeth Barrett Browning,* ed. F. G. Kenyon, London, 1898, I, 454; Mary Russell Mitford, *Recollections of a Literary Life,* New York, 1852, pp. 69–70.

naturally had much to say about the poet. In her *Recollections of a Literary Life* she devoted an entire chapter to him, in the course of which she said that his "terseness of diction and force of thought delight the old; the grace and melody enchant the young; the unaffected and all-pervading piety satisfy the serious; and a certain slight touch of mysticism carries the imaginative reader fairly off his feet." She herself professed to like all these aspects of this man with such nearly universal appeal except the "mysticism." Since *Evangeline* at the time of her writing was still on trial she contented herself with commenting upon "its strange union of a semi-ideal passion with the most real and positive of all Dutch painting." The shorter poems, she believed, were enough to satisfy any one; and she forbore reprinting "Excelsior" and "A Psalm of Life" only because they had already found their way to so "many hearths and hearts." Instead, she chose "Nuremberg," "The Open Window," and a half dozen others.[58] But in her letters the old lady seems to have enjoyed a woman's privilege. Sometimes she expressed a preference for Holmes and Whittier over Longfellow, and while granting that some of his verses were as "fine as anything in Campbell or Coleridge or Tennyson or Hood," nevertheless objected to his "obscurity" and his "little dash of cant." His prose she dubbed "trash." [59] But when *The Golden Legend* came along in 1852, with the same emphasis with which Edward Fitzgerald exclaimed, "I may say I love" Longfellow, she declared, "I delight in Longfellow"— and babbled about the "rich, racy, graphic" qualities of the poem.[60] To Charles Boner she soon unburdened her enthusiasm in the following words:

I have just now a very fine racy poem by Longfellow, "The Golden Legend," breathing of Germany, and quaint old towers and grand cathedrals, and all the pageantry of the Middle Ages, full of local colour. I don't know that it will be popular, but in my mind it leaves all that he has done a million of miles behind. I know no living poet who could have written it.[61]

[58] *Ibid.*, chap. vi.

[59] James T. Fields, *Yesterdays with Authors*, Boston, 1893, p. 281; *The Friendships of Mary Russell Mitford*, ed. A. G. L'Estrange, New York, 1882, p. 386.

[60] To Mrs. Jennings, June 1, 1852, *The Life of Mary Russell Mitford*, ed. A. G. L'Estrange, London, 1870, III, 228; Fitzgerald to C. E. Norton, January 23, 1876, *Letters of Edward Fitzgerald*, London, 1907, II, 191.

[61] January 21, 1852, *Mary Russell Mitford: Correspondence with Charles Boner & John Ruskin*, ed. Elizabeth Lee, London [1915], p. 207.

Ruskin, who was in the habit of picking up suggestions from the good lady, also struck fire and in *Modern Painters* spoke of the "beautiful" use which Longfellow had made of the Dance of Death theme. Hailing Browning and Longfellow as the "truest" men, men who had actually recreated the Middle Ages, he went on in panegyric: "Thus Longfellow . . . has entered more closely into the temper of the Monk, for good and for evil, than ever yet theological writer or historian, though they may have given their life's labour to the analysis." [62] But Ruskin, too, had his reservations; his admiration for the poet was mixed—and rather utilitarian, as will be evident from one of his letters to Allingham, written in February, 1860:

I quite agree with you that neither Lowell nor Longfellow wrote finished—or even good poetry. Both of them are hard workers—to whom versemaking is a recreation—nevertheless I believe the "Psalm of Life" to have had more beneficial influence on this generation of English than any other modern composition whatever, except Hood's "Song of the Shirt."

I delight in "Hiawatha," and in bits of the "Golden Legend."

From Lowell I have myself received more help than from any other writer whatsoever. I have not learned so much—but I have got help and heart from single lines, at critical times.

For real utility, I think his shrewd sense and stern moral purpose worth all Keats and Shelley put together. I don't compare him with Keats, but I go to him for *other articles*—which I can't get from Keats—namely Conscience—Cheerfulness and Faith.

You might as well criticize one of Keats' idle rhymes in his letters as "Excelsior." [63]

As previously mentioned, Thackeray on taking over the editorship of the *Cornhill Magazine* asked a number of Americans to contribute, among them Longfellow; but if the memory of R. C. Jebb is correct, he believed that one of the translations in *Hyperion* was better than

[62] *The Works of John Ruskin,* ed. E. T. Cook and A. Wedderburn, London and New York, 1903–1912, VI, 394 and 446. In *Modern Painters* Ruskin makes two other references to *The Golden Legend (ibid.,* V, 229; VII, 179). Cf. also *Addresses on Decorative Colour* (1854), where Ruskin, still talking about monks, quotes a long passage from the same poem (*ibid.,* XII, 485–486).

[63] *Letters to William Allingham,* ed. H. Allingham and E. B. Williams, London, 1911, p. 261. Ruskin constantly praised Longfellow's "capacity of saying beautiful things at the level of the broad public" and in 1856 mentioned *The Biglow Papers* as one of his "favourite books" (*Letters of Charles Eliot Norton,* ed. Sara Norton and M. A. DeWolfe Howe, Boston and New York, 1913, I, 311, 146). It was not until 1869 that Ruskin and Longfellow met, in Verona.

any of the American's original productions.[64] The author of *Lucile,*
however, was not reluctant to discuss his views—and one needs no
memories, trustworthy or otherwise, to know that he disliked the
"display of moral purpose" in both Schiller and Longfellow. He
charged that any second-rate European poet could have written the
latter's verses; and as for "A Psalm of Life," it had a peculiar unsavori-
ness about it. Not only did the poem represent a "jumble" of imagery
but, worse still, it preached the "democratic fallacy" that all men can
make their lives like those of the great.[65]

But the novelist J. H. Shorthouse was a firm admirer. "Have you
ever tried how beautiful Longfellow's 'Seaweed' sounds when repeated to the music of the sea?" he asked a cousin in 1853; and thirty
years later he told Edmund Gosse that one of Gosse's poems reminded
him of Longfellow at his best. "You must not be angry at this comparison," he assured his correspondent, "because he has been, all our
lives (to both of us), very dear. In almost all of his poems I seem to
see something of that unique gift of *freshness,* both in thought and
expression, which I have always taken to constitute the *poet.*" [66]

Swinburne thought that Longfellow had a "pretty little pipe of
his own, but surely it is thin and reedy," and Frederic Harrison sniffed,
"lady's album"; but both men were impressed by the charm of Longfellow's personality, and the latter suggested that his features might
serve as the model for a Greek philosopher.[67]

As the century wore on, and the newer men strove mightily to scale
the heights achieved by the giants of the mid-century, the talk about
Longfellow in literary circles declined. He was committed to the
Philistines—or the school children. But unmitigated denunciations
of his artistry were still hard to find; for after all one could not turn

[64] Thackeray's letter inviting Hiawatha to shoot a "spare shaft" across the Atlantic
is published in *Life,* II, 394–395. Caroline Jebb, *Life and Letters of Sir Richard Claver-
house Jebb,* Cambridge, 1907, p. 162. Jebb states that an American professor of Greek
had described the translation as "borrowed" by Longfellow.

[65] *Personal & Literary Letters of Robert First Earl of Lytton,* ed. Lady Betty Balfour,
London, 1906, I, 213; II, 370–371.

[66] *Life and Letters of J. H. Shorthouse,* ed. his wife, London, 1905, pp. 37, 210.
Among many others, Henley was also impressed with Longfellow's poems about the
sea (W. E. Henley, *Views and Reviews,* New York, 1890, pp. 152–153).

[67] Swinburne to E. C. Stedman, February 20, 1875, *The Letters of Algernon Charles
Swinburne,* ed. E. Gosse and T. J. Wise, London, 1918, I, 201; Frederic Harrison,
Autobiographic Memories, London, 1911, II, 110. For Swinburne's reaction to Long-
fellow's personality see *Rossetti Papers,* p. 319.

against the friend of one's youth and say, "Go up, thou bald-head." It was too much like having the old family tutor put in jail for a misdemeanor.

Justin McCarthy recalled "how much I and many of my friends owed to him for the art with which he had brought us into sympathy and intellectual companionship with some of the minor German poets," and while acknowledging that it was "not the right sort of thing to say," honestly confessed, "I hold to it that Longfellow was, in his way and within his limits, a genuine poet." [68] To R. H. Hutton, and many another, his sonnets, at least were praiseworthy—and "a singularly classical" spirit seemed evident in his simplicity.[69] And Andrew Lang once affirmed that it was perhaps Longfellow who "first woke me to that later sense of what poetry means, which comes with early manhood," although at another time he made the American share the credit with Scott and Tennyson.[70]

Shortly after Longfellow's death in 1882 the men of letters were given an opportunity to pay their respects to his memory through a committee which arranged for the placing of a bust in Westminster Abbey. A few days after the newspapers had carried their obituary notices Canon Fleming remarked in a sermon preached in Westminster: "And in the death of Longfellow, just recorded across the Atlantic, we feel a touch of sorrow that bids us claim him, if not as one of our own to lie in our Abbey, yet as one of the men of this century who lived and talked and laboured and wrote for us all." [71] Before long the press began to discuss the desirability of a memorial of some sort, and many views of private individuals were expressed in letters to the editors of various newspapers. In conservative quarters a memorial to any foreigner in the British Valhalla was regarded as improper, even though ample precedent had long been established. There was already a slab in the floor of the Abbey honoring an American, the philanthropist George Peabody; but he had died in England,

[68] *Reminiscences,* New York and London, 1899, I, 202–203. For an amusing excoriation of "Excelsior" by James Thomson, B. V., see the pessimist's "Indolence: a Moral Essay," *Essays and Phantasies,* London, 1881, p. 163.

[69] *Criticisms on Contemporary Thought and Thinkers: Selected from the Spectator,* London, 1908, I, chap. ix.

[70] *Letters on Literature,* London and New York, 1893, p. 38; *Adventures among Books,* London, 1905, pp. 20–21.

[71] *Times* for March 27, 1882. Two days earlier the *Times* in an editorial had spoken of Longfellow as being "almost as much an English as an American poet," and had questioned whether he had been read more widely at home than in England.

and the case was different. But the proponents of the project, in spite of all objections, gathered increasing favor; for there was in progress an era of good feeling toward the United States and in vision the memorial was enlarged beyond the honoring of a mere man to a gesture of international comity.[72] As a consequence the opposition had to be extremely careful, for at the time British curses against democracy had to be confined to the drawing room.

Of course all enterprises of the sort rely upon the zealous activities of one man, and in the case of the Longfellow memorial the man was William Cox Bennett, a former watchmaker, possessed of literary aspirations, and with a trace of the cockney in his speech.[73] He became the secretary of a committee eventually formed, and was assisted chiefly by Francis Bennoch, who acted as treasurer. Both of these men, it may be added, had been very friendly to Hawthorne during his stay in England in the 1850s. When the committee was officially appointed on November 1, 1882, Lord Braye presided over a "large attendance," and Lord Granville made a speech in which he referred to Longfellow as one "whose works we prize as greatly as we do the works of Tennyson." [74]

Bennett hoped, not without reason, that the Queen herself would consent to act as honorary chairman, but because of the objections raised in certain quarters she refused. At her suggestion, however, the Prince of Wales was offered the position, and he agreed to accept it, provided no speechmaking would be required of him. A preliminary list of members was at once announced, with men like Tennyson, Arnold, Trollope, and Henry Irving heading it; and from time to time new recruits were added until eventually about five hundred names were obtained. A few of these people wrote in of their own volition, soliciting a place on the committee, but the vast majority were first sounded out by the industrious secretary. The final list included two dukes, two archbishops, ten earls, and lesser lights such as Alfred Austin, D'Oyly Carte, Wilkie Collins, Austin Dobson, Leslie Stephen, Froude, Hardy, Palgrave, and Jenny Lind. The Earl of Derby with

72 Goldwin Smith in November, 1882, pointed out to Sir Robert Collins that opposition to the memorial would be a stumbling block in the way of the "reconciliation of the English-speaking race" (*A Selection from Goldwin Smith's Correspondence,* ed. Arnold Haultain, London, n.d., p. 138; cf. also *ibid.,* p. 210).

73 *The English Notebooks by Nathaniel Hawthorne,* ed. Randall Stewart, New York and London, 1941, pp. 222-223.

74 *Times* for November 2, 1882.

the Baroness Burdett-Coutts and her husband, topping all the rest in their generosity, subscribed twenty pounds each.

The letters accepting a place on the committee written by scores of literary men are for the most part the merest of formalities; and there is little of interest to record in connection with them. Christina Rossetti, advised no doubt by her brother William, declined her nomination; and William himself in sending in his guinea felt that his position in the matter had to be made clear. After all, was he not one of the foremost champions of the claims of Whitman against Longfellow?

I regard Longfellow [he wrote] as a genuine poet & certainly one whose influence was constantly exercised for good, but still not a supereminently great poet: & it seems to me hardly reasonable that he shd. be recorded in Westminster Abbey while Shelley, Byron, & Keats are left without any such memorial. Still I like the project as a tribute to a distinguished & excellent man, & as an act of international courtesy.[75]

In February, 1884, a marble bust of the poet, sculptured by Thomas Brock, was exhibited, and early in the following month it was unveiled by the Sub-Dean, Canon Prothero, in the absence of the Dean. The Prince of Wales, Gladstone, and a number of others had to regret their absence from the ceremony, a fact which makes one a little suspicious; but the Earl of Granville was on hand with a few remarks. And Lowell, the favorite orator for literary occasions during his ministry in England, made a speech in which he repeated his happy idea that the British poet with whom his friend could best be compared was Thomas Gray. The humbler folk who flocked in later to stare at the bust of the author of "A Psalm of Life," placed beside the monuments of Chaucer and Dryden, must have approved heartily; for this American was the unofficial Laureate of Victorian England.[76]

[75] The various lists and the entire correspondence dealing with the memorial committee are now in the Craigie House, where I have been permitted to examine them through the courtesy of Mr. Henry W. L. Dana.

[76] *Times* for February 26, March 1, and March 3, 1884. Lowell's speech is reported in the last-mentioned issue. See also the account reprinted in *Life*, III, 346–351. For other monuments to Americans in England see J. F. Muirhead, *American Shrines on English Soil*, New York, 1925. Thackeray in 1860 had urged the case for an English memorial to Washington Irving ("Nil Nisi Bonum," *Cornhill Magazine*, I, February, 1860, 132).

V. OF CRITICS AND INFLUENCE

"There is the world of ideas and there is the world of practice"
—MATTHEW ARNOLD.

FOR SOME YEARS after the Revolutionary War the official opinion of literary production in the United States held by the British arbiters of taste was that there was no such article as American literature. The paucity of our authors was a factor in the formation of this opinion, but probably more important was the political animosity inspired by a democratic form of government. In much the same fashion as in our day the idea has been rife in the capitalist countries that Soviet Russia because of political and social viciousness could produce no army of consequence, so the monarchists argued that governmental and social conditions prevailing in the United States were likely to hamstring the development of learning and the arts. A leader in the *Athenæum* for 1829 on "America and American Writers" supplies a neat illustration in its concluding words: "We do not believe America has a literature. . . . We do not believe that it can have one till its institutions are fundamentally changed." [1] When Washington Irving, Fenimore Cooper, and William Ellery Channing attained a very considerable popularity in the twenties and thirties they could be disposed of by dubbing them mere imitators of English models; and, like the chief American painters of the entire century, they were quietly absorbed into the "British School." The critics in the United States themselves seemed to be proud of hailing their own writers as the "American Goldsmith," the "American Scott," and so on; and their docility may have served to reassure the European arbiters of the essential accuracy of their judgment.

Moreover, there was a pretty firmly fixed idea that the presses in the New World merely turned out pirated editions of the works of

---

[1] October 14, 1829, p. 639. Nevertheless, this journal became one of the chief organs for the reviewing of American books. This fact is partially recognized by Leslie A. Marchand, *The Athenæum: a Mirror of Victorian Culture,* Chapel Hill, N.C., 1941.

British authors; and this idea was not entirely shaken until long after the Civil War. But during the fifties the quantity of American books consumed in England became so large that only a minority of the British intelligentsia thereafter maintained the tradition of denying that the United States could produce its own supply of writers. Confronted by the vast popularity of Mrs. Stowe, Hawthorne, Longfellow, Emerson, and many another, and perhaps somewhat disturbed by the readjustments of a political sort which followed the reforms of 1832, the critics shifted their attack on the literature of America and rang the changes on the theme of imitation. Unmindful of the fact that the currents of the Romantic movement were as influential in New England as in Kent and that Shakespeare had only occasionally dealt with the English scene and Milton but rarely, John Bull pointed a finger and demanded a full-grown national literature. Of course, the renewed clamor for the autochthonous was motivated primarily by the desire to demonstrate the intellectual dependence of the United States. But there was also a curiosity about the New World which, it was thought, its authors might well gratify, travel books written by Englishmen being somewhat of a weak substitute. Later in the century the spread in England of the doctrines of Taine may also have served to bolster up the belief that the American bard should be a voicer of something *sui generis,* perhaps in a way self-taught, like the minstrel of Odysseus. Whitman was, of course, to many an Englishman of culture an interesting poet merely because he was thought to be the "answerer" to the clamor for an original Western genius.

But, when several American authors actually presented the American background in their works, only the middle class of readers—and few of the intellectuals indeed—seem really to have been impressed, once the immediate sensation of novelty subsided. Not many who represented the official voice of English criticism were ready to hail Fenimore Cooper or Bret Harte as important authors merely because they seemed to satisfy the demand for non-European materials. *The Marble Faun* to many a critic appeared to be the *chef-d'œuvre* of Hawthorne simply because its Italian setting was more familiar than the New England of the old Puritans depicted in *The Scarlet Letter*. A reviewer could heave a sigh of relief when he discovered that *Transatlantic Sketches,* by Henry James, dealt with Europe, not the United States;

and Matthew Arnold, upon reading the essays of John Burroughs condemned the "American disease of always bringing into comparison his country and its things." [2] In the last quarter of the century when the local-colorists from the United States were flourishing in England as well as at home, the critics often objected to the obscurity of their works, an obscurity due to their preoccupation with the language and manners of sections of America unfamiliar to the British. James Lane Allen's book, *A Kentucky Cardinal,* needed the explanation that no humor was intended.

While many an individual American work was considered "original" from the early decades of the century to its close, as a class, the humorists impressed the English arbiters as being the least imitative of American authors; but they were in general regarded as too vulgar, irreverent, and eccentric—in a word, too distinctively American, to be rated high in the literary scale. A man like Thomas Hardy could see that Mark Twain was more than the chief buffoon of the English-speaking world, and William Archer could assert that *Huckleberry Finn* was the long-awaited great American novel, but their opinions were exceptional. [3]

While the large number of minor poets produced by the new country attracted respectful attention from time to time, [4] the charges of imitation could be well sustained; and this fact, no doubt, had an important bearing upon the general assumption that all American literature was unoriginal, for the classical tradition of viewing a national literature solely in terms of its poetry was maintained in England long after the novel had become the distinctive literary genre of the age. Our novelists, in general, were better received than our poets, [5] and in the eighties there was in certain quarters a conscious recogni-

[2] H. G. Woods in *Academy,* VIII (October 16, 1875), 398; *Letters of Matthew Arnold 1848–1888,* ed. George W. E. Russell, London, 1895, II, 362.

[3] Hardy asked Howells in 1883: "Why don't people understand that Mark Twain is not merely a great humorist?" (*Life in Letters of William Dean Howells,* ed. Mildred Howells, Garden City, N.Y., 1928, I, 349). "If any work of incontestable genius, and plainly predestined to immortality, has been issued in the English language during the past quarter of a century, it is that brilliant romance of the Great Rivers" (William Archer, *America To-Day,* London, 1900, pp. 178–179).

[4] For a good early example see the *Times* for January 24, 1835, p. 5.

[5] The earliest British criticism of Cooper is discussed by Marcel Clavel, *Fenimore Cooper and His Critics,* Aix-en-Provence, 1938. For Hawthorne see Bertha Faust, *Hawthorne's Contemporaneous Reputation: a Study of Literary Opinion in America and England 1828–1864,* Philadelphia, 1939.

tion of a new American school, of which Howells and James were considered the leaders.[6] Its specialty was considered to be "analysis." But the wider acceptance of these realists was impeded even in more discerning circles by the absence of plot interest in their works, and when Howells calmly asserted the obvious truth that the art of Henry James was a finer art than that of Thackeray or Dickens the British critics unsheathed their swords for an onslaught against such heresy.[7] There was a hesitant sort of recognition in England that the Americans were ahead so far as realism is concerned, but realism was disliked.[8] The artistic qualities and the cleverness of the new school of fiction writers from the United States were, however, widely appreciated, and a few Englishmen recognized the fact that the outstanding novelists and short-story writers of America during the last quarter of the century had transferred their allegiance from the British tradition to that of the French. A number of these New World authors were, of course, identified with another modern trend disliked by the old guard, namely, the doctrine of art for art's sake. Henry James, it may be remembered, was not only a contributor to the *Yellow Book* but the only author who was made the subject of an article in it. But a review by James Ashcroft Noble of *The King of Folly Island* by Sarah Orne Jewett may illustrate more pointedly:

Miss Jewitt's [sic] volume is very able, and, to us, very irritating. It contains, in addition to *The King of Folly Island,* seven elaborate examples of the new American story, which is not a story at all, but rather an episode in a story of which the beginning, or the end, or both, remain untold. Our children may learn to delight in this kind of thing—and unless rumour errs we have among us living adults who, at any rate, pretend to delight in it—but there are those of us who are too old to learn new tricks

[6] "Recent Fiction in England and France," *Macmillan's Magazine,* L (August, 1884), 253.

[7] For example, *Academy,* XXIX (April 3, 1886), 233; *ibid.,* XXX (December 25, 1886), 423–424; *Macmillan's Magazine,* LV (March, 1887), 358; *National Review,* I (April, 1883), 257–268; *Quarterly Review,* CLV (January, 1883), 201–229; *Illustrated London News* for August 8, 1891, p. 175; John Nichol, *American Literature: an Historical Sketch 1620–1880,* Edinburgh, 1882, pp. 452–453.

[8] Hardy and Meredith, like George Eliot, were more cordially received in the United States than at home, Meredith being of the opinion that the run of his novels "started from American appreciation" (To Eugen Frey, February 19, 1909, *George Meredith: Letters,* ed. his son, New York, 1912, II, 633). Howells was probably the chief critical protagonist of realism in the English-speaking world (cf. *Life in Letters of W. D. Howells,* II, 161).

of appreciation, and to whom the game of pretension is not worth the candle. Some people object to the doctrine "Art for art's sake" because they consider it dangerous to morality; but we may fight shy of it on the ground that it is all but fatal to interest. The "finish" of these stories, for such in default of another name we must call them, is so delicate and perfect that connoisseurs of "craftsmanship" will probably be thrown into ecstasies of admiration; but one commonplace middle-aged critic feels inclined to ask the brutal question, "What is the use of finishing a thing which is really not begun?" [9]

As the Americans, especially in fiction, devoted themselves more and more to native materials the more astute British cannot be said to have valued their works accordingly. The vast body of readers and the lesser lights in the critical firmament alone appear to have taken the cry for the autochthonous seriously—and the subject matter and themes dealt with by the transatlantic authors had to be somewhat sensational really to please. For most of the century the scholars of England knew more about Babylon than Chicago, and while four American historians had been made Honorary Fellows of the Society of Antiquaries as early as 1850, they were esteemed almost in indirect ratio to their absorption in the history of their own country. Prescott was the most widely read during the century, but Motley was regarded as the most eminent, and Parkman received scant critical attention, although in the nineties he had a certain following among people who were preparing for a trip to the United States.

In the last decades of the century the charges of imitation subsided, though they never entirely disappeared, and it became the fashion to consider America as possessing a very large number of minor writers, many of them able and artistic but lacking perhaps what Quintilian called the *summa manus*. Its past was believed to be illumined by a half dozen authors of consequence, yet its promise for the future was considered excellent.

So much for the official view. Like all bodies of critical opinion it was contradictory and illogical—and, of course, subject to innumerable exceptions. Sydney Smith could decry the woeful state of American intelligence and still urge his daughter to read Benjamin Franklin or treat George Ticknor with the appreciative kindness which one bestows on an equal. Many a critic damned American literature as

[9] *Academy,* XXXIV (August 18, 1888), 100.

feeble stuff and promptly proceeded to hail *Uncle Tom's Cabin* as a great original work. A peculiar Tory like Ruskin would denounce the denizens of the New World as republican barbarians and then confess his indebtedness to James Russell Lowell or his affection for Charles Eliot Norton. Gladstone, returning from a dinner party at which the vulgarity of American society had been the conversational *corpus vile,* could write a letter to a publisher urging the acceptance of a book by an American or invite Joaquin Miller for a week-end visit. Early and late in the century there were some critics who dealt very fairly with the literature of the United States.

So far as any generalization can be made, it appears that the chief devotees of American literature among the critical classes of Great Britain were likely to be extreme liberals or radicals in politics or Scotchmen by birth, sometimes both. The susceptibility of the radicals requires no explanation, and the receptiveness of the Scotch may perhaps be accounted for on the grounds that they, too, felt the weight of English condescension, and their school system and religious establishment were more akin to the transatlantic counterparts. A third category of critics was also inclined to dissent from the official view, namely, the journalists who fingered the pulse of the great middle class of readers. But always, whether radicals, Scotchmen, or panderers to Demos, there was a tendency on the part of a writer, once established, to assume the long-nosed attitude toward all things American. Dickens is, of course, a notorious example; [10] and the Chartist Thomas Cooper another. The latter as a young man read Irving, and in 1842 taught essays by Channing to a Sunday School class but found himself, in regenerate days, disposed to recall that Emerson was the only American in whose company he had ever felt "real enjoyment." [11] But as the years went by and people in London and Manchester knew better what "shooting Niagara" meant, the supply of critics who dealt fairly sympathetically with the literature of the Western democracy

[10] Alfred Noyes has advanced the theory that Dickens's attitude toward America "is only to be accounted for on physical grounds" (*New Essays and American Impressions,* New York [1927], p. 216). It should be remembered that Dickens transported Martin Chuzzlewit to America merely to stimulate sales (Arthur Waugh, *A Hundred Years of Publishing,* London [1930], pp. 58–59).

[11] *The Life of Thomas Cooper,* by himself, London, 1882, pp. 65, 164, 311–312. Passages from Emerson appear in *Cooper's Journal,* I (March 2 and 9, 1850), 135 and 151.

increased. The Langs, the Sharps, the Saintsburys, and the Henleys were more respectful than their predecessors; and many of them had even crossed the Atlantic to see the Americans in their own home. Moreover, with the deluge of books from America in the eighties and nineties one could scarcely refrain from discussing the works which were so widely read, and political or religious bias was diluted by the currents of the new journalism, a journalism which made book reviewing, if not less ephemeral literary discussion, more and more an accessory of the publishing business. No one was surprised when various of the book-reviewing magazines devoted special departments to "American Novels," or included an "American Letter" as a regular feature, for no reviewer who seized his pen with any frequency could escape dealing with a book from the United States.

Many of the British men of letters, of course, counted an American author or two among their friends, and this aspect of the reception of American literature abroad must not be forgotten. It may seem odd to us today to realize that Mrs. Wordsworth asked George Ticknor to urge her husband to cease frittering his time away on "sonnets and other trifles" and to finish his *Recluse,* but the friendship of the poet with the American historian must have been close enough to warrant her doing so.[12] Carlyle never forgot the sympathetic assurances of the angelic Emerson delivered in the early days when his career was in doubt, and was consoled in his last years of solitude by the disciple-like affection of Charles Eliot Norton and Moncure Conway. George Eliot kept up a friendly correspondence with Mrs. Stowe, as did Fitzgerald with Lowell, William Sharp with Stedman, Tennyson with Whitman, to name only a few. But the English authors who most cordially extended their friendly offices to a large number of transatlantic authors were minor figures indeed, Samuel Rogers and Richard Monckton Milnes.[13] Likewise minor among the literary men of

---

[12] *Life, Letters, and Journals of George Ticknor,* Boston, 1877, II, 167.

[13] Certain details of Rogers's relations with American authors are to be found in Joseph J. Firebaugh, "Samuel Rogers and American Men of Letters," *American Literature,* XIII (January, 1942), 331–345. An English newspaper, commenting on Joaquin Miller's return to England, referred to Milnes as a man raised to the peerage "on the understanding that he would promote kindly feelings between the Great Republic and the 'Old Country' by giving breakfasts and dinners to celebrities in London hailing from the other side of the great ocean" (unidentified clipping, n.d., in collection of Lord Crewe).

the century was the most ardent advocate of an Anglo-American
Union, Thomas Hughes, the author of *Tom Brown's School Days.*[14]

Occasionally a British author turned out a preface or an introduction for an English reprint of an American work, or even edited a
volume from over the ocean. Emerson's name was thus associated with
that of Carlyle, Whitman's with that of William Rossetti, Willis's
with that of Barry Cornwall, Harte's with that of Tom Hood, Cable's
with that of Barrie, and so on. While the publishers frequently used
American introductions for their reprints of American books, the desire for a special feature sometimes led to the hiring of an Englishman
to add a prefatory essay or to supervise an edition. Such essays constitute a fairly large body of critical and biographical material, but for
the most part the British editors and introduction writers were people
of less renown, like Ernest Rhys, who prepared several volumes by
Americans for the "Camelot Series," published late in the century by
Walter Scott, or H. R. Haweis, who frequently acted as a hack for
Routledge. In the middle of the century the English introduction writers, like other critics abroad, derived much of their factual material
from the various anthologies compiled by Rufus Griswold, but later
on a few examples of critical writing of a high order appeared as front
matter in the reprints, for example, John Morley's essay prefixed to an
edition of Emerson's works published by Macmillan in 1883 and
1884.[15]

The number of complete books devoted to individual American
authors and written by Englishmen is small, and practically all of
them appeared late in the century. Of the several volumes on Whitman probably the most important was the study (1893) done by John
Addington Symonds, who confessed that *Leaves of Grass* had influenced him more than any book except the Bible. Emerson was also
the subject of several volumes, the most valuable being that by Richard

---

[14] Hughes was greatly interested in an English community established in Tennessee.
See his *Rugby Tennessee,* London, 1881, especially pp. 16–17, 23–24, 117–118, 108,
125. Note also his praise of Lowell in *Memoir of a Brother,* Boston, 1873, p. 119.

[15] Among the British editors or introduction writers for volumes by Emerson were
Percival Chubb, Ronald J. McNeill, H. R. Haweis, and Walter Lewin. The last-
mentioned was one of the ablest reviewers of American books in England. Andrew
Lang was one of the essayists on Holmes; Thomas Hughes and Richard Garnett
were among those who wrote on Lowell; W. H. Dirks and H. S. Salt on Thoreau;
James Hannay and H. Noell Williams on Poe; the Earl of Carlisle on Mrs. Stowe.
These are only a few examples chosen at random from several scores.

Garnett (1888); but another little work, by George Searle Phillips, should also be mentioned since it is the very first book on the Concord sage which appeared in print ("January Searle," *Emerson, His Life and Writings,* 1855). The earliest volume on Holmes was, likewise, of English origin: James Ball, *Dr. Oliver Wendell Holmes and His Works* (1878), and before the century was ended Walter Jerrold had produced another (1893). Two Englishmen also made Thoreau the súbject of books, A. H. Japp and Henry S. Salt; and there is a varied assortment of other studies of individual American authors, for example, Edward P. Hingston's *The Genial Showman,* on Artemus Ward, John H. Ingram's biography of Poe, and Eric S. Robertson's volume on Longfellow in the "Great Writers Series." The series included books on other Americans—Whittier (by W. J. Linton), Thoreau (by H. S. Salt), Emerson (by Richard Garnett), and Hawthorne (by Moncure Conway).

Of all these works none carries much authority today, and perhaps the most important for its period was the biography written by John H. Ingram—*Edgar Allan Poe: His Life, Letters, and Opinions,* published in two volumes in 1880. Although the literary activities of Henry S. Salt and of William Rossetti in connection with Thoreau and Whitman respectively have given them a high place among the English students of American authors, Ingram's work as a Poe enthusiast was probably more important. Not only was his biography for a period the most thoroughgoing study of the poet to be found on either side of the ocean, but his editorial activities in connection with various editions of Poe, his articles, letters, and reviews published in a variety of important journals were so numerous that many of his countrymen associated him with Poe in the same way that Lord Houghton was connected in their minds with Keats. For many years all writers on Poe, whether English or American, were so zealously —and jealously—criticized by Ingram that he may be said to have forced a modicum of accuracy into the legendary accounts which viewed the poet as a combination of moral leper and literary genius.[16]

---

[16] Most of the early British critiques of Poe had followed Rufus Griswold not only because his introduction was frequently reprinted but because he was regarded as a good authority on American literature. Professor Arthur H. Quinn has pointed out the effect of his lies on the English critics in *Edgar Allan Poe: a Critical Biography,* New York and London, 1941, pp. 678–686. After the book by Sarah H. Whitman,

While most of the anthologies of American literature circulating in the British Isles during the nineteenth century were reprints of collections originating in the United States, there was a fair sprinkling of such works compiled under British auspices. In the first half of the century one could find, for example, *Specimens of the American Poets,* London, 1822, edited by one of the sons of William Roscoe, with a prefatory essay which argued that the Republican form of government was very favorable to the development of a literature. "We ought," argued Roscoe, "to regard the advances of the Americans in all honourable pursuits as an eldest son would watch the fortunes of a younger brother." [17] There was, in 1834, a volume of *Selections from the American Poets* with a Dublin imprint, and the publishers in London and Edinburgh turned out sundry others. After the Civil War the supply became more bountiful, and there are occasional examples of very useful anthologies, such as *Poetry of America* (1878), edited by W. J. Linton [18] and published by George Bell as one of the volumes in "Bohn's Standard Library," or *American Sonnets* (1889), edited for Walter Scott by William Sharp, or *American Poems* (1872), edited for Moxon by W. M. Rossetti. But readers of anthologies may have found the American authors more frequently in collections including both European and American writers, for it was a common practice for an editor or publisher, confronted by the difficulties of copyright, to reach out freely and fill up space with selections from abroad. One should not be surprised, then, to find the literature of the United States represented in a collection devoted to *Poems of English*

Ingram's was the first volume to attack Griswold's contentions. In England at least two writers had questioned the reliability of Griswold's account before Ingram— Joseph Gostwick, *Hand-Book of American Literature,* London and Edinburgh [1856]; and W. Moy Thomas, "Edgar Allan Poe," *Train,* III (1857), 193–198. For Ingram's persistent activity see, for example, *Academy,* XXIV (October 13, 1883), 248–249; *Athenæum* for July 29, 1876, pp. 145–146, July 20, 1878, p. 80, August 17, 1878, p. 210, October 26, 1878, p. 531, May 15, 1880, p. 632, July 24, 1886, p. 115; and Appendix of the present volume under *Poe.* These are only a few examples.

[17] Page xxi. This introduction is as fair an estimate of the difficulties and possibilities of literature in the United States as its period produced.

[18] Linton was probably attracted to American writers by way of his political radicalism. In 1866 he removed to the United States but returned to England from time to time. One of the most charming stylists among the Victorians, Alexander Smith, supplied an introductory essay to one of the several British reprints of John W. S. Hows, *Golden Leaves from the American Poets* (London: Warne, 1866).

Heroism (1882).[19] And the practice, of course, affords another illustration of the readiness with which American literature was absorbed into the body of English writing.

Entire volumes devoted to the history and criticism of American literature were very rarely produced by British authors. But there are a few examples which are superior to the work of Philarète Chasles or Madame Blanc in France. A very able *Hand-Book of American Literature* was prepared by Joseph Gostwick and published by W. and R. Chambers in 1856, based largely on a series of sketches of American authors which the Scotch firm had included in a *History of English Literature*.[20] But without question the chief work on American literature produced in the British Isles during the century was a volume by John Nichol,[21] Professor of English Literature in the University of Glasgow, where he had been an undergraduate acquaintance of James Bryce. During the sixties and seventies Nichol had lectured on the subject and had acquired sufficient reputation as an expert to be asked to write the sketch on the literature of the United States which was included in the 1875 edition of the *Encyclo-*

[19] Following are a few examples of the practice of combining American with European authors:

The Casquet of Literary Gems, ed. Alex. Whitelaw, First Ser., Glasgow: Blackie and Son, 1839 (1st ed., 1828); 2d Ser., 1838 (1st ed., 1829).

The Casquet of American and European Gems, Glasgow: John Reid, 1835.

Poets of England and America, London: Whittaker, 1853.

Nightingale Valley, ed. "Giraldus," London: Bell & Daldy, 1860.

Lays and Lyrics of the Nineteenth Century, ed. John W. Gregg, Dublin, 1863.

A Household Book of English Verse, ed. Archbishop Trench, London: Macmillan, 1868.

A Thousand and One Gems of English Poetry, ed. Charles Mackay, London: Routledge [1867].

Songs of Society, ed. W. Davenport Adams, London: Pickering, 1880.

Poems of English Heroism, ed. Arthur C. Auchmutz, London: Kegan Paul, 1882.

The Children of the Poets, ed. Eric S. Robertson, London: Walter Scott, 1886.

The Blue Book of Poetry, ed. Andrew Lang, London: Longmans, 1891.

Lyra Heroica: a Book of Verse for Boys, ed. W. E. Henley, London: Nutt, 1892.

Pen and Pencil Pictures from the Poets, Edinburgh: Nimmo, n.d.

Beeton's Great Book of Poetry, London: Ward, Lock, n.d.

Only two of these examples contain selections from Whitman.

[20] Gostwick acknowledged his indebtedness to Griswold and to the critical opinions of the *North American Review.* Chambers' *Cyclopedia of English Literature* in the later revisions regularly included American authors.

[21] *American Literature: an Historical Sketch 1620-1880,* Edinburgh: Adam and Charles Black, 1882.

pædia Britannica. His interest in the New World had been encouraged not only by his youthful radicalism and a trip across the Atlantic in 1865 but by the ardor of his father, who during the fifties had made plans for a study such as Bryce eventually published in 1888.[22] At the time of his death, in 1894, his work was deemed inferior, especially since it had failed to win critical approval in America, and today its chief value lies in its reflection of academic opinions held in days gone by. Melville is barely mentioned in the book, and Whitman is viewed as a violent egotist whose "provoking rudeness" made him sadly inferior to Blake, but Poe and Hawthorne are accorded a high place. *The Scarlet Letter* Nichol considered to be "the most profound, the boldest, the most riveting analytical romance of our tongue, in our century."

So far as articles on American literature in the British journals are concerned, they may be said to have doubled in number during the fifties, the period when the consumption of American books in England became so great that critical attention was inevitable. The following decade, that of the Civil War, was marked by a slight dropping off in number, and thereafter there was a constant increase, so that the nineties produced the greatest amount of critical discussion. As one would expect, the liberal journals, like the *Westminster,* and certain of the Scotch magazines devoted a fair number of pages to the literature of the United States. Our historians, of course, fared best in the old quarterlies, their books being more weighty than those of poets and fiction writers. The authors who received the greatest amount of attention were those of the older school who came to be regarded both at home and abroad as the chief literary men of whom the new nation could boast. Channing, Irving, and Cooper were the first of our writers to arouse any considerable amount of critical discussion in the British magazines. N. P. Willis followed, and then came a larger number of authors who were made the subjects of special articles, Emerson leading them all in the frequency with which he was discussed, with Mrs. Stowe and Longfellow following him most closely. But Mrs. Stowe's record would not be so high if one were to eliminate the articles occasioned by her attack on Lord

---

[22] *Ibid.,* Preface. Nichol acknowledged his obligations to Griswold, to G. W. Curtis, to the Duyckincks, and to M. C. Tyler.

Byron. Hawthorne, Whitman, and Poe were dealt with less frequently than the authors of *Uncle Tom's Cabin* and *Hiawatha,* and Lowell and Holmes were written about only less than they. Whittier, Melville, Thoreau, and Bryant trailed, in that order. The newer writers of the century ran up a smaller number of articles especially devoted to them not only because the period of their fame was of shorter duration than that of authors like Irving or Emerson, but, presumably, also because the American magazines circulating in the British Isles in the last quarter of the century added a bountiful supply. Of the younger writers Mark Twain, Bret Harte, Joaquin Miller, William Dean Howells, and Henry James—in about that order—led all the others. Of the ladies, other than Mrs. Stowe, Margaret Fuller [23] and Louise Chandler Moulton were most frequently made the subjects of special articles. Emily Dickinson was almost unknown.[24]

Emerson was pretty generally regarded in the better critical circles as the outstanding writer of America, but Hawthorne was proclaimed the leading artist: as Sidney Colvin described him, "one of the masters who in his English, has seemed classical with the most ease." [25] After 1850 approval of Hawthorne was all but universal in British critical circles. The century ended somewhat in doubt as to whether Poe or Whitman should be called the chief poet of the United States, and, likewise, there was a question as to whether Howells or James

---

[23] Some of the earliest reviews of Margaret Fuller's works have been discussed by Frances M. Barbour in "Margaret Fuller and the British Reviewers," *New England Quarterly,* IX (December, 1936), 618–625. George Eliot wrote an interesting discussion of Margaret Fuller's *Woman in the Nineteenth Century* for the *Leader* (No. 290, October 13, 1855).

[24] My assumption in these estimates is that the list of articles included in the Appendix of the present volume is representative. One should note that I have not considered the ordinary book reviews or the discussions in the British newspapers.

[25] *Fortnightly Review,* XIX (February 1, 1873), 280. Jowett recommended *The Scarlet Letter* to the Amberleys; Fitzgerald regarded Hawthorne as the "most of a man of genius America has produced"—"a man of fifty times Gray's genius"—but never found him to his own taste; George Eliot called him a "grand favourite of mine," and Meredith admired his "deliberate analysis" and his "luscious, morbid tone." Already in 1860 the *Illustrated London News* could assert that he had "established so complete a reputation in this country as well as in his own that the only introduction a new tale from his pen needs is a congratulation" (XXXVI, March 24, 1860, 276); and in 1872 Keningale Cook began an article for *Belgravia* with these words: "Hawthorne ought to have been born in England" (XIX, 72). The casual references are also illuminating; for example, *Punch* in reviewing *Dorian Gray* remarked, "a finer art, say that of Nathaniel Hawthorne, would have made a striking and satisfying story of it" (XCIX, July 12, 1890, 25).

could be considered our greatest living novelist. Lowell was easily selected as the foremost critic of the older school, an honor which came naturally to the man whom certain Englishmen had been willing to nominate for the first professorship of the English language and literature established at Oxford.[26]

The tendency to include discussions of American writers along with their British fellows in volumes of criticism is, of course, another proof of the fact that transatlantic authors were progressively absorbed into the body of English literature. The collections of essays by George Gilfillan, R. H. Hutton, Andrew Lang, and Leslie Stephen are only a few examples of many.[27] Despite the official condescension, a number of American writers commanded such respect abroad that occasionally the British critics made a point of rebuking their brethren of the New World for failing to recognize the merits of their own countrymen. Thus, George Saintsbury, objecting to a few *obiter dicta* of Henry James on the author of "The Raven," stoutly defended Poe and animadverted on the "incomprehensible fancy of American critics for depreciating" him.[28] Whitman also was often thought to have been unjustly dealt with by his fellow countrymen, and claims were not infrequently made that Stephen Crane and several other of our authors were first really appreciated in England. But with the possible exception of Washington Irving it is doubtful whether any American author of great consequence developed a considerable reputation among critics abroad earlier than he did at home. With all the British interest in Whitman, it should be remembered that Moncure Conway really did as much for the poet in England as even William Rossetti, and assuredly Emerson and certain of his friends recognized the genius of the Good Gray Poet long before the enthusiasts in London

[26] H. E. Scudder, *James Russell Lowell: a Biography,* Boston and New York, 1901, II, 318. Lowell refused to be considered. During his ministry in England he had been the chief speaker at the dedication of memorials to Fielding, Coleridge, and Pepys, and had acted as President of the Wordsworth Society. A window and a bust in the Chapter House of Westminster Abbey stand as a memorial to him (dedicated November 28, 1893).

[27] The essays on Lowell, Holmes, Whittier, Howells, and Mark Twain in *Letters to Living Authors,* by John A. Steuart, new ed., London, 1892, ought to be better known.

[28] *Academy,* XIII (April 20, 1878), 337. The Virginian Moncure Conway was very unsympathetic with Ingram's attempt to "vindicate" Poe's life (*ibid.,* XVIII, July 24, 1880, 55–56).

turned to their inkwells. Early in their careers both Carlyle and Tennyson had a larger following in the United States than at home,[29] and the best counterpart that may be advanced is probably the case of Joaquin Miller, who during the early seventies was undoubtedly regarded more seriously by British intellectuals than by the critical class of America. But certainly the English were ahead of their trans-marine rivals in rating the peculiar virtues of American humor.

So far as the quantity of books sold is concerned, the readers of the United States were, for the century as a whole, more numerous than those of the British Isles, and it may be consequently assumed that they read more works by American authors than did the British; but for limited periods the consumption of certain American works in England must have surpassed that at home. For example, both *Uncle Tom's Cabin* and *Dred* had a larger sale in the British Isles within a year or two of first publication, as did *The Scarlet Letter* and *Hiawatha,* and, during the fifties, Emerson's essays. And there can be little doubt that Henry Adams's *Democracy* sold more copies in the cheap British reprints than in the original edition. Similarly, for limited periods the critical approval of certain American authors, while rarely prior to acclaim at home, waxed more enthusiastic abroad; Hawthorne, Cooper, Bret Harte, Mark Twain, and the humorists in general, are examples. Indeed, despite the official skepticism toward American intellectual pretensions, a number of authors of the United States from the time of Irving on would have received a good many votes for places in a British Academy, if there had been any such society. When, in 1897, one of the magazines actually proposed an Academy of Letters and presented forty names selected by its editorial staff the list included Henry James; and in the correspondence elicited by the proposal little objection was made on the grounds of his nationality;[30] and Bret Harte and Captain Mahan were added to the roster of nominees. In viewing the books of a quarter or of a year the British journals frequently mentioned works by Americans

[29] William Silas Vance, "Carlyle and the American Transcendentalists," MS Dissertation, University of Chicago, 1937; H. D. Widger, "Thomas Carlyle in America: His Reputation and Influence," MS Dissertation, University of Illinois, 1940; John O. Eidson, *Tennyson in America,* Athens, Ga., 1943.

[30] *Academy,* LII (November 6, 1897), 376, and the immediately subsequent numbers.

as being among the outstanding productions, and whenever it suited their purposes the critics treated the authors of the United States as if they were Englishmen.[31] Late in the century it was assumed, however, that the final word on the writers of the New World would have to be pronounced by the Americans themselves.

But the criticism of our authors offered by the British arbiters exerted a powerful force upon literary opinion in the United States, as did also the republication of books. Mark Twain and Lowell were, like many another, flattered by the earliest piracies of their works, and Poe merely reflected the attitude of his day when he exerted himself to spread the news that his stories had been reprinted and discussed in Europe.[32] Assuredly Emerson's reputation at home received a noticeable fillip after his successful debut in the literary coteries of Edinburgh and London, and Hawthorne's countrymen were much surer that he was a genius when they knew that the English also considered him to be such. Cooper himself recalled how a distinguished citizen of New York crossed the street to inquire after his health because of a puff in a British journal.[33] Until the time of the Civil War there was a strong tendency in the United States to accord its authors an importance only as the British critics and readers seemed to indicate. Later in the century, while still effective in promoting a literary reputation, the British accolade possessed less value.

In outlining the effect of a British reputation upon an American author it should also be observed that the results were by no means confined to criticism, for a number of our writers kept a weather eye on their European audience. Mark Twain is a good example; his transition from the humor of his earlier works may be considered a result not only of his graduation from the newspaper level to that of the illustrated magazines but also of his huge transatlantic market. Longfellow wrote poems on Florence Nightingale and on the Duke

[31] Occasionally a reviewer was unaware of the fact that the book he was considering had been written by an American, but more often the style betrayed the fact even after the spelling had been Anglicized. For an amusing confusion of a Unitarian from the United States with Samuel Johnson, the lexicographer, in the present century see Henry W. Foote, *Three Centuries of American Hymnody*, Cambridge, Mass., 1940, p. 241.

[32] See, for example, A. H. Quinn, *op. cit.*, pp. 513, 516.

[33] *Afloat and Ashore*, 1844, chap. xxvii. For the difficulties of maintaining an original opinion in the face of British critics see *Southern Literary Messenger*, I (October 15. 1834), 51–52.

of Wellington primarily for his British readers, and Bret Harte ground out yarns with a background in the Far West long after he had forgotten that California poppies were yellow simply because his agent must have told him that "Westerns" succeeded best in the English magazines. And Henry James and William Dean Howells may possibly have continued to exploit the American girl primarily because she was such a sensation abroad.[34]

But more pertinent to the subject of the present volume is the influence of American literature in the British Isles, and, as before, the general features of the topic may be outlined with a few illustrations. Since the literature of the United States is English literature "with a difference," as Lowell expressed it, one rightly expects the parent stock to have influenced the scion rather than the reverse. Of none of the major English poets or prose writers can be said what Valéry affirmed of Baudelaire when he named an American (Poe) as the "principal agent de la modification des idées et de l'art" of the author of *Les fleurs du mal*. Nevertheless, the extensive perusal of American writers even in the select circles of England could hardly fail to exhibit an occasional effect. The hostile Charles Kingsley had known Bryant's poetry from his youth, took pot shots at Maria Cummins and Susan Warner in the first edition of *Water-Babies*, was led to write *The Heroes* because of his dislike of Hawthorne's versions of the Greek myths, delighted in Longfellow, damned Whitman as being coarse and sensual, claimed Irving's prose to be as graceful as that of Lamb, thought *A Fable for Critics* worthy of Rabelais, and in three of his works devoted himself to counteracting the heresies of Emerson.[35] Even Matthew Arnold did not confine his New World authors to Emerson, for the casual references in his letters show that, like George Eliot, he was impressed by Margaret Fuller, invited Longfellow to visit him at Harrow, dipped into Prescott and Burroughs, and during the last year of his life read Cooper's *The Pioneers* aloud to his family.[36] Though in 1860 he was firm in the conviction that

[34] See George W. Smalley, "The American Girl in England," *London Letters and Some Others,* New York, 1891, II, 101–117.

[35] Margaret F. Thorp, *Charles Kingsley 1819–1875,* Princeton, N.J., 1937, pp. 185, 171, 170, 96; Ellis Yarnell, *Wordsworth and the Coleridges,* New York, 1899, pp. 192–193.

[36] *Letters of Matthew Arnold 1848–1888,* I, 31, 394, 49, 115; II, 360, 375.

"few stocks could be trusted to grow up properly without having a priesthood and an aristocracy to act as their schoolmasters," he was nonetheless flattered and delighted by the perspicacity of the judgments pronounced on his own works by certain of the American periodicals.

Poe, to think of his influence alone for a moment, suggested the motif of "The Blessed Damosel," as Rossetti himself pointed out; and traces of his effect may be seen in a variety of British works of fiction, ranging from Stevenson's *Treasure Island* and Conan Doyle's detective yarns to George Eliot's "The Lifted Veil." With the reinforcement of French approval, his critical theories became gospel to the new school of the nineties.

The influence of the ideas of Whitman upon men like Stevenson, Symonds, Edward Carpenter, and Havelock Ellis has often been noted,[37] but his free verse had little to offer to the English poets excepting perhaps by way of the French writers of *vers libre*. And that topic belongs chiefly to a study of the present century, as does also the perhaps more consequential one of the influence of Henry James, whose effect upon the most artistic novelists of both England and the United States has given him a position in fiction somewhat analogous to that formerly occupied by Edmund Spenser in the sphere of poetry. No fictionist who has ever used the English language can be said better to deserve the appellation "the novelists' novelist." But James's chief disciple was an Anglicized Pole, and he himself became a British subject before he died.

One may recall that Bret Harte was the chief model for the early work of Kipling in both prose and verse,[38] that Lowell was responsible for the literary career of Leslie Stephen, that Bartram gave suggestions to Wordsworth and Coleridge, that Irving influenced the youthful Dickens, that Mrs. Stowe supplied Kingsley and many another with ideas for propagandist fiction—and so on. There is probably an abundant store of such examples to be found if one stoops to

[37] See especially the excellent study by Harold Blodgett, *Walt Whitman in England,* Ithaca, N.Y., 1934.
[38] In his autobiography Kipling simply says: "Bret Harte, to whom I owed many things" (*Something of Myself,* Garden City, N.Y., 1937, p. 39). As a schoolboy he had read Emerson's poems with avidity and had written verses imitative of Longfellow and Joaquin Miller (*ibid.,* pp. 22, 37–38, 41).

a lower level, say, that of Robert Buchanan.[39] But the sum total of such illustrations can at best make only a minority report, hardly more impressive than the fact that Whistler introduced French impressionism into the salons of London or that the British socialists of the late century owed a far greater debt to Henry George and Edward Bellamy than to Karl Marx.[40]

The American author who probably exerted the greatest influence on the intellectuals of the British Isles was the same writer who numbered Whitman and Thoreau among his disciples—Emerson. In 1849 an organ of the High Church and Tory party began a discussion of "The Emerson Mania" with these words:

> The reputation enjoyed by that "transatlantic thinker" . . . suggests matter for grave reflection. When we find an essayist of this description, who seems to be "a setter forth of new gods," belauded alike by Tory and Radical organs, by the friends of order and disorder—when we find his words reproduced in every possible form, and at the most tempting prices, proving the wide circulation they must enjoy amongst the English public generally—we feel that we too should not leave them disregarded. . . . We are credibly informed that these essays find many readers and admirers amongst the youth of our universities.[41]

Emerson was right in believing that his audience would include young men in search of their way of life, and the young men of Oxford were no exceptions. When he visited his friend Clough at Oriel College, Froude was already an admirer and soon laid his religious problems before the visitor, who, somewhat embarrassed no doubt, recommended a reading of the *Vedas*. It was at one of Emerson's lectures that Froude first saw Carlyle, and he is alleged to have confessed later in his life that the Concord essayist had emancipated him from the confines of the Church of England: "He broke the fetters. I owe my freedom to him." [42]

John Morley, whose friends sometimes detected "something of Emersonian sententiousness" in his writings, recalled that at Oxford

---

[39] Longfellow and Bret Harte, among others, seem to have shaped some of the verse of the Scotchman (cf. *The Poetical Works of Robert Buchanan*, London, 1884, pp. 496–500, and 504–508).

[40] R. C. K. Ensor, *England 1870–1914*, Oxford, 1936, pp. 157, 334.

[41] *English Review*, XVIII (December, 1849), 546.

[42] Herbert Paul, *The Life of Froude*, New York, 1905, p. 41; George W. Smalley, *Studies of Men*, New York, 1895, p. 294.

the senior commoner, Cotter Morison, "pressed Emerson upon us"; and, viewing college life in retrospect, he commented on "the transcendentalists, of whom in every University you find a small set fervently attached to Emerson and to the less valuable parts of Carlyle's teaching." [43] A. C. Benson in his disguised autobiography describes his hero at Cambridge in the early seventies as possessed of a "unique devotion" to Shakespeare, Bunyan, and Emerson; and in 1874 the students of Glasgow invited the American to be a candidate for the office of Lord Rector of their University.[44]

The professors, too, were not without regard for the friend of Carlyle, for Tyndall began his daily tasks with a reading of Emerson's poems [45] and Max Müller dedicated a volume of *Lectures on the Science of Religion* (1873) to him "in memory of his visit to Oxford, and in acknowledgement of constant refreshment of head and heart derived from his writings during the last twenty-five years." Herbert Spencer was eager to have Emerson's favorable opinion as an aid in gaining acceptance in England for his projected work on synthetic philosophy, and Matthew Arnold expressed his devotion not only in an early sonnet but also in a letter in which he spoke of "the refreshing and quickening effect your writings had upon me at a critical time of my life." [46] When preparing for his lecture tour in the United States, Arnold reread the essays and his "strong sense" of the value of their author was "deepened," and he meant his remarks on Emerson to be as high praise of a transatlantic thinker as an Englishman of his class and background could bestow. It should be remembered, also, that some of the halfhearted limitations imposed by him on the friend of the spiritual-minded were as violently attacked in England as in the United States.[47]

Like William Ellery Channing and Theodore Parker, Emerson became one of the established saints for the most intelligent religious

[43] John, Viscount Morley, *Recollections,* New York, 1917, I, 11; F. W. Hirst, *Early Life & Letters of John Morley,* London, 1927, I, 31, 48.

[44] A. C. Benson, *Memoirs of Arthur Hamilton, B.A.,* New York, 1907, p. 14; *The Letters of Ralph Waldo Emerson,* ed. Ralph L. Rusk, New York, 1939, VI, 258, 259.

[45] *Letters of Charles Eliot Norton,* ed. Sara Norton and M. A. DeWolfe Howe, Boston and New York, 1913, I, 313.

[46] *The Letters of R. W. Emerson,* V, 219 and V, 361 (Arnold to Emerson, June 19, 1864).

[47] An example: C. A. Ward, "Emerson," *Temple Bar,* LXXII (October, 1884), 236–248.

radicals known to the English during the century, the Unitarians. Augustine Birrell, addressing the British and Foreign Unitarian Association, could say with truth that many of his audience knew Emerson's books better than their Bibles.[48] The circle of friends who helped to form the early intellectual milieu of George Eliot were nearly all Emersonians, and she herself spoke of him as the "first *man* I have ever seen." At times she picked up his works "for my spiritual good," as she phrased the idea; but he can hardly be said to have meant as much to her as he did to Tyndall, Arnold, Clough, or James Hutchinson Stirling.[49]

Sometimes the minor writers of the day acknowledged the stimulus received from a perusal of Emerson's works, and even a Lord Mayor of London professed to have owed his success in life to the preacher of self-reliance.[50] Late in the century, when John Lubbock selected his "one hundred best books" Emerson was included, and the critics spilled little gall.

But interesting as the reaction of the intellectual classes to American literature may be, its effect on the middle class of readers who consumed the shilling libraries may have been more considerable. With Emerson still in mind for another moment, one should recall that many of his hearers and readers in England, especially in the pro-

---

[48] *The Collected Essays & Addresses of the Rt. Hon. Augustine Birrell 1880–1920,* New York, 1923, II, 69. The same work contains another essay, dated 1887. Birrell concluded that Emerson "must be content with a small allotment" in England. James Martineau was little indebted to Emerson, but owed much to Channing (James Drummond and C. B. Upton, *The Life and Letters of James Martineau,* London, 1902, I, 204; II, 270, 314–315; and the section on his philosophy in Vol. II). For the early interest in Channing in England see, for example, *Correspondence of W. E. Channing, D.D., and Lucy Aikin, from 1826 to 1842,* ed. Anna L. LeBreton, Boston, 1874, p. 7; and *Life, Letters, and Journals of George Ticknor,* I, 479; II, 150. For the importance of Parker to his chief editor, see *Life of Frances Power Cobbe,* by herself, Boston and New York, 1895, I, 87–88, 92.

[49] For the interest of the Hennells in Emerson see Moncure D. Conway, *Autobiography, Memories and Experiences,* Boston and New York, 1904, II, 156–158. For her own statements on Emerson see *George Eliot's Life as Related in Her Journals and Letters,* ed. J. W. Cross, New York, n.d., I, 139, 360; II, 196. Her friend, and possibly lover, Dr. John Chapman, was one of the early publishers of Emerson's works. For the importance of Emerson to Clough, Allingham, John Sterling, *et al.,* see Townsend Scudder, III, *The Lonely Wayfaring Man,* London and New York, 1936, especially pp. 60 ff. and 209–211.

[50] For example, Vernon Lee, who volunteered: "I am aware of his exceptional influence in maturing my thought" (*Contemporary Review,* LXVII, March, 1895, 345); Moncure D. Conway, *op. cit.,* II, 282.

vincial centers, were the kind of people whom Carlyle despised as canaille.[51] It was a member of a class at the Working Men's College, and not an Oxfordian, who pointed out to Ruskin that many of his ideas were similar to those of Emerson's poems,[52] and the lads who attended the meetings of the Mechanics' Institutions could probably have bested the boys at Cambridge in an examination on Longfellow. For many years the middle class of the British citizenry must have acquired their knowledge of the New World almost entirely from the works of American authors, and the stories of Cooper and Bret Harte created a romantic illusion which even yet has not been dispelled.[53] When it is remembered that a powerful middle-class journal like the *Illustrated London News* gave the death of Channing more space than the demise of Southey or the appointment of Wordsworth as Poet Laureate, and that the most widely read poet and novelist of the fifties were both Americans, there is reason for speculation about the possible effect of such phenomena. If the widespread consumption of the literature of another country has value as propaganda it must be concluded that the British middle class was favorably disposed toward the United States not only because of the migration thither of friends and relatives but because of the romantic escape found in Cooper, the sympathy compelled by Mrs. Stowe, and the moral elevation preached by Longfellow. The force of American literature may well have been an important element in preventing the furthering of the designs of the British Government at the time of our Civil War.[54] And certainly it aided in the promulgation of liberal political views, for in the English sense of the word these popular American authors were all "radicals."

[51] Townsend Scudder, III, "A Chronological List of Emerson's Lectures on His British Lecture Tour of 1847–1848," *PMLA,* LI (March, 1936), 243–248: "Emerson's British Lecture Tour, 1847–1848," *American Literature,* VII (March, 1935), 15–36; VII (May, 1935), 166–180; "Emerson in London and the London Lectures," *ibid.,* VIII (March, 1936), 22–36.

[52] See "Plagiarism," *Modern Painters,* Part IV, Appendix III (*The Works of John Ruskin,* ed. E. T. Cook and A. Wedderburn, London, 1903–1912, IV, 427).

[53] Douglas Woodruff, "Expansion and Emigration," *Early Victorian England, 1830–1865,* ed. G. M. Young, London, 1934, II, 357, proves the case for Cooper's influence.

[54] Arnold was of the opinion that the feeling of sympathy toward Americans held by the middle class was "based very much on the ground of their common radicalness, dissentingness, and general mixture of self-assertion and narrowness" (To his mother, December 18, 1861, *Letters of Matthew Arnold 1848–1888,* I, 157).

Later in the century a critic occasionally stumbled upon the problem of the international effects of literature, for example, a writer for the *Quarterly Review,* who insisted that from the time of Irving and Cooper

to this day, the common influences of letters have been in action till the English railway-stalls contain more American than native productions— Bret Harte and Mark Twain shouldering Thackeray and Dickens, and Miss Wetherall [sic] and Miss Alcot [sic] making our different classes more intimate with American domestic life than they are with that of any class among their countrymen beyond their own.[55]

The political results of the consumption of American literature in England assuredly were not insignificant even though the bulk of readers came from the mute, inglorious elements of society which leave few records for the historian. Who knows but that the laughter induced by Artemus Ward and Mark Twain may not have facilitated the settlement of the Alabama Claims? Yet if one still doubts that the pen of an American author could affect the political life of the British Empire let him remember that a mild Hindu, editing and agitating in South Africa, discovered Henry Thoreau, and from him picked up a very workable idea known as "Civil Disobedience." [56]

In viewing the effect of American writing upon the mass of readers in the British Isles, one would infer that American experience was not without value to the journalists, since the levelling of the press of the United States in the direction of "average" taste was further advanced, say, in 1840, than it was abroad. As the English were confronted more and more by the awful apparition of the semiliterate reader it was natural that they should find a few ideas and methods already tested across the Atlantic. The British themselves before the century was ended spoke dolefully of the "Americanization" of their newspapers.[57] And there can be no doubt that the transition from the old quarterly to the more modern monthly was stimulated by the model of the illustrated magazine from the United States. Humorous

[55] "Social Relations of England and America," CXLII (July, 1876), 277.

[56] Gandhi has acknowledged his indebtedness. Cf., for example, "Gandhi and Thoreau," *Nation & Athenæum,* XLVI (March 1, 1930), 720. For the interest shown by the friends of Gandhi in Thoreau see their periodical *Young India.*

[57] Occasionally one of the dominant figures in the "new journalism" was vitally affected by an American author. Cf. W. T. Stead, *James Russell Lowell: His Message, and How It Helped Me,* London: John Haddon & Co. [1891].

journalism in England was also affected by the tactics of the "funny fellows" from the New World, as one may see if one takes the trouble to read George Eliot's essay with the revealing title "Debasing the Moral Currency." [58] A very considerable part of the influence of American literature upon the British during the nineteenth century may have been in the technique of appealing to the masses. And that, for better or for worse, is a democratic influence.

[58] In *Theophrastus Such*. Already in 1863 a critic had charged *Punch* with a new tendency toward "wild exaggeration, vulgar anti-climax, and outrageous punning" (*Temple Bar*, IX, November, 1863, 591).

APPENDIX

ᵗ

REPRESENTATIVE ARTICLES ON AMERICAN LITERATURE
APPEARING IN BRITISH PERIODICALS 1833 TO 1901

THE PRESENT LIST, compiled almost entirely from the holdings of the Library of Congress, is intended to illustrate the popularity of various American authors among the critics who wrote for the magazines published in the British Isles during the period indicated. Book reviews of the ordinary type, obituary notices, and discussions of international copyright are not included. Nor are the legions of "American Letters," "Notes from America," and so on unless such a department consists of an entire essay. For examples of British critical articles published prior to 1833 the reader is referred to the two studies made by the late William B. Cairns.

All articles dealing at some length with two or more authors and classified under the heading *General* are indexed also under the names of the individual authors except where their titles are sufficiently revelatory. For example, an article under *General* which is entitled "American Essayists" is not cross-indexed under *Irving,* but one entitled "Three Prominent American Authors" is referred to again under *Irving* if he happens to be one of the authors discussed at some length.

Under each heading the arrangement is chronological.

General

1835. N. P. Willis, "Literature of the Nineteenth Century in America," *Athenæum,* Nos. 375, 377, 380, 382 (Jan. 3–Feb. 21, 1835), pp. 9–13, 52–55, 105–107, 147–150.

Timothy Flint, "Sketches of the Literature of the United States," *Athenæum,* Nos. 401, 402, 405, 406, 409, 411, 412, 416, 417, 418, 419 (July 4–Nov. 7, 1835), pp. 511–512, 526–527, 584–586, 624–625, 666–668, 696–698, 714–716, 782–783, 802–803, 817–819, 831–832.

1838. "American Lions," *Bentley's Miscellany,* IV (1838), 405–412. [Irving, Cooper].

1847. "The American Library," *Blackwood's,* LXII (Nov., 1847), 574–592. [Hawthorne, Simms, Margaret Fuller, Poe.]

1848. R. L., "Literature of the United States," *Westminster Rev.,* XLIX (July, 1848), 333–348.

1852. "Retrospective Survey of American Literature," *Westminster Rev.,* New Ser., I (Jan., 1852), 288–305.

1852 (continued)

"Contemporary Literature of America," *Westminster Rev.*, New Ser., I (Jan. and April, 1852), 305–322, 663–677; II (July and Oct., 1852), 272–287, 583–598; III (Jan. and April, 1853), 287–302, 605–617; IV (July and Oct., 1853), 274–288, 593–609.

1853. "English and American Literature," *Illustrated London News*, XXII (Feb. 12, 1853), 121–122.

"American Literary Celebrities," *Bentley's Miscellany*, XXXIII (June, 1853), 633–642.

1854. "A New Phase in American Life," *Eclectic Rev.*, 5th Ser., VII (Feb., 1854), 171–192.

1857. "Prescott and Motley," *Edinburgh Rev.*, CV (Jan., 1857), 1–45.

"Literary Style," *Fraser's Mag.*, LV (April, 1857), 424–437. [Carlyle, Emerson, Whitman, Ruskin.]

1858. "Literary Celebrities of New York," *Illustrated London News*, XXXII (March 6, 1858), 245–246.

"Literary Celebrities of Boston," *Illustrated London News*, XXXII (March 20, 1858), 295–296.

1859. "New England Provincial Life and History," *North British Rev.*, XXXI (Aug., 1859), 175–196.

1862. "British and American Literature, with a View of Their Mutual Relations and Obligations," *Scottish Rev.: A Quart. Jour.*, Jan., 1862, pp. 120–134.

1863. "American Literature and the Civil War," *Fraser's Mag.*, LXVII (April, 1863), 517–527.

1864. "New Englanders and the Old Home," *Quart. Rev.*, CXV (Jan., 1864), 42–68. [Emerson, Hawthorne.]

"The Transcendentalists of Concord," *Fraser's Mag.*, LXX (Aug., 1864), 245–264.

1868. George M. Towle, "The American Literati at Home," *Broadway*, I (Aug., 1868), 869–886.

An American, "American Literature," *Cassell's Mag.*, IV (1868–1869), 93–95, 301–303, 382–384, 430–432, 685–687, 714–716. [Humourists and Satirists, Essayists, Poets, Historians and Biographers, Novelists, Female Writers.]

1870. "American Literature," *Westminster Rev.*, New Ser., XXXVIII (Oct., 1870), 263–294.

1871. "The Literature of the United States in 1870," *Athenæum*, No. 2254 (Jan. 7, 1871), pp. 13–15.

"American Books," *Blackwood's*, CX (Oct., 1871), 422–442. [Harte, Miller, Leland, Elizabeth S. Phelps, Louisa Alcott.]

"The Literature of the United States in 1871," *Athenæum*, No. 2306 (Jan. 6, 1872), pp. 14–16.

1873. John C. Dent, "America and Her Literature," *Temple Bar,* XXXVII (Feb., 1873), 396–406.

Lady Juliet Pollock, "The Imaginative Literature of America," *Contemporary Rev.,* XXII (Aug., 1873), 347–371.

1876. Richard M. Milnes, "Social Relations of England and America," *Quart. Rev.,* CXLII (July, 1876), 251–289.

1877. Henry Holbeach, "Transcendentalism in England, New England, and India," *Contemporary Rev.,* XXIX (Feb., 1877), 469–488.

1881. George E. Woodberry, "The Fortunes of Literature under the American Republic," *Fortnightly Rev.,* New Ser., XXIX (May 1, 1881), 606–617.

1882. Stuart J. Reid, "A Summer Day at Concord," *Manchester Quart.,* I (Jan., 1882), 1–13. [Alcott, Emerson.]

"Letters in America," *Scottish Rev.,* I (Nov., 1882), 30–51.

1883. "American Literature in England," *Blackwood's,* CXXXIII (Jan., 1883), 136–161. [Howells, C. D. Warner, James.]

1885. James Gooden, "Concord and Its Worthies," *Manchester Quart.,* IV (July, 1885), 300–335.

1887. Francis H. Underwood, "Recollections of American Authors," *Good Words,* XXVIII (1887), 29–34, 154–159, 289–304, 521–527, 664–671, 807–816. [Whittier, Longfellow, Holmes, Lowell, Hawthorne, Emerson.]

1888. Francis H. Underwood, "The Awakening of New England," *Contemporary Rev.,* LIV (Aug., 1888), 257–278.

1891. William Sharp, "American Literature," *National Rev.* [monthly], XVII (March, 1891), 56–71.

Theodore Watts, "The Future of American Literature," *Fortnightly Rev.,* New Ser., XLIX (June, 1891), 910–926.

George P. Lathrop, "Literature in the United States," *New Rev.,* V (Sept., 1891), 244–255.

1892. Douglas Sladen, "New York as a Literary Center," *English Illustrated Mag.,* X (Nov., 1892), 137–144.

1893. W. Morris Colles, "The Future of English Letters," *New Rev.,* VIII (May, 1893), 577–586.

1896. W. R. Nicoll, "The Present State of American Literature," *Bookman,* XI (Dec., 1896), 62–63.

1898. George W. Smalley, "Among My Books: Old Lamps for New," *Literature,* II (Feb. 19, 1898), 204–205.

"Literature in America," *Literature,* II (March 19, 1898), 303–304.

Henry James, "American Letter: the Question of the Opportunities," *Literature,* II (March 26, 1898), 356–358.

—— "American Letter," *Literature,* II (April 9, 1898), 422–423.

William D. Howells, "American Letter: American Literary Centres," *Literature,* II (June 4 and 18, 1898), 649–651, 704–706.

1898 (continued)

William D. Howells, "American Letter: the Southern States in Recent American Literature," *Literature,* III (Sept. 10, 17, and 24, 1898), 231–232, 257–268, 280–281.

—— "American Letter: the Nature of American Literary Criticism," *Literature,* III (Oct. 22 and Nov. 5, 1898), 378–379, 424–425. [Poe, Lowell, C. E. Norton, James, Harte, G. W. Curtis.]

1899. Frederick Rockell, "Three Anarchists of American Literature," *University Mag. and Free Rev.,* XI (April, 1899), 176–191. [Whitman, Emerson, Thoreau.]

1900. William Wallace, "The Coming War of American Dreams," *Scottish Rev.,* XXXVI (Oct., 1900), 270–292.

Poetry

1835. "American Poetry," *Dublin University Mag.,* V (Jan., 1835), 93–112.

"American Poets and Poetry," *Court Journal,* No. 297 (Jan. 3, 1835), pp. 1–2.

"American Poetry," *Edinburgh Rev.,* LXI (April, 1835), 21–40.

1843. "A Night at Peleg Longfellow's," *Fraser's Mag.,* XXVIII (Aug., 1843), 160–168.

1844. "American Poetry," *Foreign Quart. Rev.,* XXXII (Jan., 1844), 291–324.

1850. "American Poetry," *People's and Howitt's Jour.,* New Ser., III (1850), 101–104.

1852. "American Poetry," *North British Rev.,* XVII (Aug., 1852), 394–421. [Longfellow, T. B. Read, Poe, Byrant.]

1853. "The American Poets," *Eclectic Rev.,* 5th Ser., VI (Sept., 1853), 307–321. [Lowell, Poe, T. B. Read, Holmes.]

1854. "Recent Poets of America," *London Quart. Rev.,* II (June, 1854), 440–459. [Lowell, Longfellow, Poe.]

1855. "The Poets of America," *Irish Quart. Rev.,* V (June and Sept., 1855), 193–220, 561–590.

1857. "American Poets and Poetry," *Scottish Rev.: A Quart. Jour.,* Jan., 1857, pp. 1–19.

1861. "American Poets," *London Quart. Rev.,* XVII (Oct., 1861), 36–72.

1867. "Characteristics of American Literature—Poetry," *North British Rev.,* XLVI (June, 1867), 456–487.

"War Poetry of the South," *Dublin University Mag.,* LXX (Oct., 1867), 424–431.

"American Poets," *People's Mag.,* I (Nov. 2 and Dec. 7, 1867), 748–750, 777–779.

1868. "Some Recent Pieces of English and American Poetry," *Eclectic*

Rev., 8th Ser., XIV (March, 1868), 227-253. [Emerson, Mrs. Stowe.]

George Smith, "On Three Contemporary Poets," *Bentley's Miscellany,* LXIV (July, 1868), 61-69. [Longfellow, Bryant, Tennyson.]

M. D. Conway, "Three American Poets," *Broadway,* New Ser., I (Oct., 1868), 240-248. [J. A. Dorgan, Myron Benton, Howells.]

1874. "American Poets," *Dublin Rev.,* New Ser., XXII (April, 1874), 302-325; New Ser., XXIII (July, 1874), 65-86.

1876. S. Waddington, "American Vers de Société," *Tinsley's Mag.,* XVIII (June, 1876), 705-711. [Saxe, Holmes, Aldrich, Stedman.]

1877. "Critical History of the Sonnet," *Dublin Rev.,* New Ser., XXVIII (Jan., 1877), 141-180.

1884. Percy Greg, "American Poetry," *National Rev.* [monthly], III (April, 1884), 256-269.

1885. Percy Greg, "American Poets and Poetry," *British Quart. Rev.,* LXXXII (Oct., 1885), 302-324.

1886. "American Poets," *Quart. Rev.,* CLXIII (Oct., 1886), 363-394.

1889. William Sharp, "The Sonnet in America," *National Rev.* [monthly], XIII (April, 1889), 191-201.

1891. Andrew Lang, "Some American Poets," *Illustrated London News,* XCVIII (March 7, 1891), 307. [Emily Dickinson, Aldrich, Lanier, Field.]

1894. Thomas Bradfield, "Characteristics of America's Chief Poets," *Westminster Rev.,* CXLII (July, 1894), 48-57.

1895. "Transatlantic Bardlets," *Saturday Rev.,* LXXIX (March 30, 1895), 408-410.

1898. Archer, William, "Recent American Verse," *Pall Mall Mag.,* XV (Aug., 1898), 471-482.

Fiction

1843. "American Works of Fiction," *Foreign and Colonial Quart. Rev.,* II (Oct., 1843), 458-488.

1849. "Jonathan in Africa," *Blackwood's,* LXVI (Aug., 1849), 172-182. [Melville, W. S. Mayo.]

1853. "American Novels," *North British Rev.,* XX (Nov., 1853), 81-109. [Hawthorne, Mrs. Stowe, Susan Warner, Longfellow.]

1856. "A Trio of American Sailor-Authors," *Dublin University Mag.,* XLVII (Jan., 1856), 47-54. [Cooper, R. H. Dana, Melville.]

1867. "Fictions of Home Life—American and English," *Eclectic Rev.,* 8th Ser., XII (Feb., 1867), 107-123. [D. G. Mitchell, Bayard Taylor.]

"Two Novels of New England Life," *Eclectic Rev.,* 8th Ser., XIII (Dec., 1867), 445-467. [H. W. Beecher, Holmes.]

1875. Agnes Macdonell, "The American Heroine," *Macmillan's Mag.,* XXXII (Oct., 1875), 544–551. [Hawthorne, Louisa Alcott.]

1882. "American Society in American Fiction," *Edinburgh Rev.,* CLVI (July, 1882), 170–203.

1883. "American Novels," *Quart. Rev.,* CLV (Jan., 1883), 201–229.

Arthur Tilley, "The New School of Fiction," *National Rev.* [monthly], I (April, 1883), 257–268.

1884. Karl Hillebrand, "About Old and New Novels," *Contemporary Rev.,* XLV (March, 1884), 388–403.

"The New School of American Fiction," *Temple Bar,* LXX (March, 1884), 383–389. [James, Howells.]

W. Clark Russell, "Sea Stories," *Contemporary Rev.,* XLVI (Sept., 1884), 343–363. [Melville, Dana, Cooper.]

Lady F. P. Verney, "The Americans Painted by Themselves," *Contemporary Rev.,* XLVI (Oct., 1884), 543–556. [James, Howells.]

1887. Alice Meynell and William Coyne, "A Discussion on American Novels," *Irish Month.,* XV (Oct., 1887), 560–566.

1889. William Watson, "Fiction—Plethoric and Anaemic," *National Rev.* [monthly], XIV (Oct., 1889), 167–183.

1891. "American Fiction," *Edinburgh Rev.,* CLXXIII (Jan., 1891), 31–65.

1898. "Novels of American Life," *Edinburgh Rev.,* CLXXXVII (April, 1898), 386–414. [Mary Wilkins, Harold Frederic, Gertrude Atherton, H. B. Fuller, J. L. Allen, Stephen Crane.]

William D. Howells, "American Letter: Puritanism in Fiction," *Literature,* II (May 14, 1898), 563–564. [The Misses Wilkins, Jewett, Brown, Cooke.]

—— "American Letter: Chicago in Fiction," *Literature,* II (July 2, 1898), 758–759. [Herrick, H. B. Fuller, George Ade.]

—— "American Letter: the Politics of American Authors," *Literature,* III (July 16, 1898), 41–42. [Bellamy, Hale, T. W. Higginson, Cable, Garland.]

1899. H. H. Bowen, "Religion in Novels: the Existence of This Characteristic in Stories of New England Life," *Westminster Rev.,* CLI (May, 1899), 558–564.

Bret Harte, "The Rise of the 'Short Story,'" *Cornhill Mag.,* New Ser., VII (July, 1899), 1–8.

Humor

1838. H. W., "Yankeeana," *Westminster Rev.,* XXXII (Dec., 1838), 136–145.

1852. "American Humour," *Irish Quart. Rev.,* II (June, 1852), 171–196.

1854. "Yankee 'Screamers,'" *Eliza Cook's Jour.,* XI (June 10, 1854), 99–100.

1860. F. G. Stephens, "American Humorous Poetry," *Macmillan's Mag.,* I (Jan., 1860), 203–211. [Saxe, Lowell, Holmes.]

1865. "American Wit," *Saturday Rev.,* XIX (Feb. 11, 1865), 164–166.

"The Comic Periodical Literature of America," *Trübner's American and Oriental Literary Record,* I (Sept. 21, 1865), 118–119.

1866. Leslie Stephen, "American Humour," *Cornhill Mag.,* XIII (Jan., 1866), 28–43.

1867. "Yankee Humour," *Quart. Rev.,* CXXII (Jan., 1867), 212–237.

1870. "American Humour," *British Quart. Rev.,* LII (Oct., 1870), 324–351.

1871. "American Humour," *Graphic,* III (April 1, 1871), 295.

"The Political Influence of Humour in America," *Spectator,* XLIV (Dec. 16, 1871), 1522–1523.

1872. "Modern Poets," *Dublin University Mag.,* LXXIX (May, 1872), 573–580. [Lowell, Leland.]

1876. Matthew F. Turner, "Artemus Ward and the Humourists of America," *New Quart. Mag.,* VI (April, 1876), 198–220. [Ward, Twain, Harte.]

"Cope's Mixture," *Cope's Tobacco Plant,* I (Aug., 1876), 931–932. [Sam Slick, Ward, Lowell, Twain, Cooper, Emerson.]

"Cope's Mixture," *Cope's Tobacco Plant,* I (Oct., 1876), 954–955.

1899. R. M. Sillard, "Transatlantic Whimsicalities," *New Century Rev.,* VI (July and Aug., 1899), 62–68, 110–113.

Journalism

1839. "American Periodical Literature," *Eclectic Rev.,* 4th Ser., V (Jan., 1839), 215–235.

1842. "The Newspaper Literature of America," *Foreign Quart. Rev.,* XXX (Oct., 1842), 197–222.

1843. "The Answer of the American Press," *Foreign Quart. Rev.,* XXXI (April, 1843), 250–281.

1848. "The Periodical Literature of America," *Blackwood's,* LXIII (Jan., 1848), 106–112.

1855. C.A.B., "The Political Press of America," *Fraser's Mag.,* LII (Dec., 1855), 678–685.

1857. "The Press in America," *New Monthly Mag.,* CXI (Dec., 1857), 412–426.

1863. "The British Newspaper: the Penny Theory and Its Solution," *Dublin University Mag.,* LXI (March, 1863), 359–376.

"The Periodical Press of the United States of America," *Fraser's Mag.,* LXVIII (Sept., 1863), 325–334.

1864. "The American Newspaper Press," *Leisure Hour,* XIII (July 23 and 30, 1864), 477–480, 493–495.

1865. R.K., "The Newspaper Press of America," *Temple Bar,* VII (Jan., 1865), 190–201.

The Author of 'Dangerfield's Rest,' "The Transatlantic Press," *St. James's Mag.,* XII (Feb., 1865), 303–311.

1868. Robert Tomes, "The New York Press," *Broadway,* I (April, 1868), 582–590.

"The New York Associated Press," *Broadway,* I (May, 1868), 690–693.

1870. "Curiosities of American Newspaper Literature," *Tinsley's Mag.,* VI (June, 1870), 558–564.

"American Newspapers," *Chambers's Jour. of Popular Literature,* 4th Ser., VII (June 25, 1870), 406–409.

1871. "The American Press," *British Quart. Rev.,* LIII (Jan., 1871), 1–26.

"American Newspapers," *London Quart. Rev.,* XXXVI (July, 1871), 390–408.

1872. John C. Hutcheson, "The American Press," *Belgravia,* XVII (March, 1872), 101–112.

1873. "American Journalism," *Saturday Rev.,* XXXV (Jan. 18, 1873), 79–80.

Emily Faithful, "American Journalism," *Victoria Mag.,* XXI (Aug., 1873), 289–302.

1876. "Modern Newspaper Enterprise," *Fraser's Mag.,* New Ser., XIII (June, 1876), 701–714.

1885. Theodore Child, "The American Newspaper Press," *Fortnightly Rev.,* New Ser., XXXVIII (Dec. 1, 1885), 827–839.

1887. An American Journalist, "Journalism in the United States," *Time,* New Ser., V (Jan. and Feb., 1887), 22–28, 152–158.

Arnot Reid, "The English and the American Press," *Nineteenth Century,* XXII (Aug., 1887), 219–233.

Whitelaw Reid, "A Decade of American Journalism," *Westminster Rev.,* CXXVIII (Oct., 1887), 850–862.

1892. Edward Delille, "The American Newspaper Press," *Nineteenth Century,* XXXII (July, 1892), 13–28.

1898. Elizabeth L. Banks, "American 'Yellow Journalism,'" *Nineteenth Century,* XLIV (Aug., 1898), 328–340.

"English and American Journalism," *Literature,* III (Oct. 8, 1898), 313–314.

Individual Authors

Adams, Henry. Mrs. Humphrey Ward, "Democracy: an American Novel," *Fortnightly Rev.,* New Ser., XXXII (July 1, 1882), 78–93.

Aldrich, Thomas Bailey. "Arnisto," "A Famous American Poet and Humourist: Thomas Bailey Aldrich," *Scots Mag.*, New Ser., XXV (May, 1900), 447–453.

See also under *Poetry:* 1876, 1891.

Allen, James Lane. "James Lane Allen. An Inquiry," *Academy,* LIX (July 14, 1900), 35–36.

See also under *Fiction:* 1898.

Atherton, Gertrude. "Gertrude Atherton," *Academy,* LV (Dec. 10, 1898), 431–432.

See also under *Fiction:* 1898.

Audubon, John James. "Audubon," *Athenæum,* Nov. 30, 1833, pp. 817–818.

"Audubon, the Ornithologist," *Eliza Cook's Jour.,* V (May 24 and June 7, 1851), 53–56, 89–92.

"The Adventures of Audubon," *Edinburgh Rev.,* CXXXIII (July, 1870), 250–275.

"A Great Naturalist," *Blackwood's,* CLXIV (July, 1898), 58–69.

Bailey, James Montgomery. "The American View of England," *Macmillan's Mag.,* XXXIX (Feb., 1879), 299–303.

Bancroft, George. "Bancroft's History of America," *British and Foreign Rev.,* V (Oct., 1837), 321–366.

"Bancroft's *Memoirs of General Washington*," *Eclectic Rev.,* 4th Ser., IV (Nov., 1838), 489–518.

"Bancroft's History of the United States," *Foreign Quart. Rev.,* XXVII (July, 1841), 327–361.

"Bancroft's *History of the United States*," *Edinburgh Rev.,* LXXXV (Jan., 1847), 115–142.

Bellamy, Edward. "Looking Forward," *Rev. of Reviews,* I (March, 1890), 230–241.

H. S. Salt, "The Socialist Ideal: Literature," *New Rev.,* IV (Jan., 1891), 19–28.

See also under *Fiction:* 1898.

Brown, Charles Brockden. George B. Smith, "Brockden Brown," *Fortnightly Rev.,* New Ser., XXIV (Sept. 1, 1878), 399–421.

Bryant, William Cullen. Sir Nathaniel, "William Cullen Bryant," *New Monthly Mag.,* XCIX (Nov., 1853), 306–311.

W. Clark Russell, "William Cullen Bryant and American Poetry," *Broadway,* I (Sept., 1867), 40–45.

E. S. Nadal, "William Cullen Bryant," *Macmillan's Mag.,* XXXVIII (Sept., 1878), 369–375.

Thomas Bradfield, "William Cullen Bryant," *Westminster Rev.,* CXLIII (Jan., 1895), 84–91.

See also under *Poetry:* 1852, 1868.

Burnett, Frances Hodgson. Clementine Black, "The Novels of Frances Hodgson Burnett," *Time,* New Ser., I (Jan., 1885), 72–85.

Burnett, Frances Hodgson (continued)

Marie A. Belloc, "Mrs. Hodgson Burnett. A Famous Authoress at Home," *Idler,* IX (June, 1896), 644–648.

Burritt, Elihu. "Elihu Burritt, the Learned Blacksmith," *London Journal,* III (Aug. 8, 1846), 358.

"Elihu Burritt," *Hogg's Weekly Instructor,* V (May 1, 1847), 153–155.

"Elihu Burritt in 'Our Old Home,' " *Eclectic Rev.,* 8th Ser., VI (June, 1864), 694–702.

"Burritt's Walk from London to Land's End and Back," *Eclectic Rev.,* 8th Ser., X (Feb., 1866), 162–171.

Burroughs, John. H. S. Salt, "John Burroughs' Essays," *Gentleman's Mag.,* CCLXVI (April, 1889), 349–360.

Carleton, Will. "An American Crabbe," *Chambers's Jour. of Popular Literature,* 4th Ser., X (Sept. 6, 1873), 618–620.

Cable, George Washington. "Mr. G. W. Cable," *Academy,* LI (June 12, 1897), 15.

W. P. Ridge, "Mr. G. W. Cable and His Passon Jones [*sic*]. A Sketch," *Bookman,* XIV (June, 1898), 64–65.

See also under *Fiction:* 1898.

Channing, William Ellery. "Channing's Literary and Political Essays. Remarks on Milton," *Fraser's Mag.,* XVII (May, 1838), 627–635.

"Channing's Literary and Political Essays. Remarks on Napoleon Bonaparte," *Fraser's Mag.,* XVIII (Sept., 1838), 286–297.

"Pulpit Eloquence in America," *British and Foreign Rev.,* X (April, 1840), 608–644.

"Dr. Channing's Works," *British Critic and Quart. Theological Rev.,* XXIX (Jan., 1841), 201–239.

"Memoir of William Ellery Channing," *Tait's Edinburgh Mag.,* XV (July, 1848), 432–441.

"Memoir of Dr. Channing," *British Quart. Rev.,* VIII (Nov., 1848), 295–328.

"Memoir of Dr. Channing," *Eclectic Rev.,* 4th Ser., XXIV (Dec., 1848), 432–457.

"Life of Channing," *Westminster Rev.,* L (Jan., 1849), 317–348.

Charles Whitehead, "The Literary Career of William Ellery Channing," *Bentley's Miscellany,* XXV (1849), 88–90.

"Dr. Channing," *Eliza Cook's Jour.,* VI (Jan. 17, 1852), 187–190.

Thomas Hughes, "Dr. Channing, the Abolitionist," *Macmillan's Mag.,* XLII (May, 1880), 59–64.

Cooper, James Fenimore. "Cooper's England," *Quart. Rev.,* LIX (Oct., 1837), 327–361.

"Epaminondas Grubb, or Fenimore Cooper, versus the Memory of Sir Walter Scott," *Fraser's Mag.,* XIX (March, 1839), 371–377.

"Cooper's Novels," *Dublin Rev.,* VI (May, 1839), 490–529.

Leumas Derfla, "Cooper and Modern Romance," *Duffy's Fireside Mag.*, II (Dec., 1851), 43–50.

"The Works of Fenimore Cooper," *Eclectic Rev.*, 5th Ser., III (April, 1852), 410–422.

Keningale Cook, "James Fenimore Cooper," *Belgravia*, XVIII (Sept., 1872), 379–387.

George Saintsbury, "The Historical Novel," *Macmillan's Mag.*, LXX (Oct., 1894), 410–419.

T. E. Kebbel, "Leather-Stocking," *Macmillan's Mag.*, LXXIX (Jan., 1899), 191–201.

See also under *General:* 1838; *Fiction:* 1856, 1884; *Humor:* 1876.

Crane, Stephen. H. D. Traill, "The New Realism," *Fortnightly Rev.*, New Ser., LXII (Jan. 1, 1897), 63–73.

Edward Garnett, "Mr. Stephen Crane: an Appreciation," *Academy*, LV (Dec. 17, 1898), 483–484.

"Stephen Crane," *Academy*, LVIII (June 9, 1900), 491.

See also under *Fiction:* 1898.

Crawford, Francis Marion. "Mystic Novels," *Scottish Rev.*, IV (Oct., 1884), 302–323.

"Three Young Novelists," *Blackwood's*, CXXXVI (Sept., 1884), 296–316.

Edgar Attkins, "Marion Crawford's 'Doctor Claudius,'" *Manchester Quart.*, X (Oct., 1891), 303–323.

Janetta Newton Robinson, "A Study of Mr. F. Marion Crawford," *Westminster Rev.*, CXXXVII (April, 1892), 378–393.

"Marion Crawford: a Short Biography," *Bookman*, VIII (April, 1895), 11–13.

Ouida, "The Italian Novels of Marion Crawford," *Nineteenth Century*, XLII (Nov., 1897), 719–733.

Crockett, David. "Colonel Crockett," *Fraser's Mag.*, XVI (Nov., 1837), 610–627.

"Colonel David Crockett," *Hogg's Weekly Instructor*, III (June 20, 1846), 258–262.

Curtis, George William. Sir Nathaniel, "George William Curtis," *New Monthly Mag.*, XCVIII (Aug., 1853), 476–484.

See also under *General:* 1898.

Dana, Richard Henry. "Dana's Buccaneer," *Blackwood's*, XXXVII (Feb., 1835), 416–427.

Dana, Richard Henry, Jr. Sir Nathaniel, "Richard Henry Dana," *New Monthly Mag.*, XCVIII (May, 1853), 77–83.

See also under *Fiction:* 1856, 1884.

Deland, Margaret. F. W. Farrar, "John Ward, Preacher," *London Society*, XII (Sept., 1888), 473–488.

Deland, Margaret (continued)

D. Macmillan, "Recent Religious Novels and the Moral Theory of Another Life," *Scots Mag.*, New Ser., VI (Oct., 1890), 321–335.

Dickinson, Emily. "A Poet and Some Others," *Saturday Rev.*, LXXII (Sept. 5, 1891), 279–280.

Hamilton Aïde, "Noticeable Book—Emily Dickenson's [*sic*] Poems," *Nineteenth Century*, XXXI (April, 1892), 703–706.

See also under *Poetry: 1891.*

Downing, Jack. "Major Downing's Letters," *Quart Rev.*, LIII (April, 1835), 396–406.

Edwards, Jonathan. "Works of President Edwards," *Eclectic Rev.*, 3d Ser., XII (Sept., 1834), 181–198.

Leslie Stephen, "Jonathan Edwards," *Fraser's Mag.*, New Ser., VIII (Nov., 1873), 529–551.

Emerson, Ralph Waldo. R. M. Milnes, "American Philosophy.—Emerson," *Westminster Rev.*, XXXIII (March, 1840), 345–372.

"Emerson's Essays," *Eclectic Rev.*, 4th Ser., XII (Dec., 1842), 667–687.

"Emerson," *Blackwood's*, LXII (Dec., 1847), 643–657.

George Gilfillan, "Ralph Waldo Emerson; or, The 'Coming Man,'" *Tait's Edinburgh Mag.*, XV (Jan., 1848), 17–23.

"Lectures of R. Waldo Emerson, 'On Representative Men,'" *Reasoner*, IV (1848), 8–11, 17–19, 38–40, 45–48, 63–66, 80–82, 85–89, 117–120, 138–140.

"Emerson," *Dublin Rev.*, XXVI (March, 1849), 152–179.

"The Emerson Mania," *English Rev.*, XII (Sept., 1849), 139–152.

"Ralph Waldo Emerson," *British Quart. Rev.*, XI (May, 1850), 281–315.

Lucian Paul, "Ralph Waldo Emerson," *Critic*, X (Aug. 1, 1851), 347–348.

"Emerson on English Traits," *Westminster Rev.*, New Ser., X (Oct., 1856), 494–514.

"The Sceptic and the Infidel," *Oxford and Cambridge Mag.*, I (Oct. and Nov., 1856), 605–620, 645–663.

"Emerson's English Traits," *London Quart. Rev.*, VII (Jan., 1857), 381–406.

"Oxford, the English Church, and Mr. Emerson," *Dublin University Mag.*, L (Aug., 1857), 226–234.

"Emerson—The Conduct of Life," *Eclectic Rev.*, 8th Ser., III (Nov., 1862), 365–409.

Moncure D. Conway, "Recent Lectures and Writings of Emerson," *Fraser's Mag.*, LXXV (May, 1867), 586–600.

J. Nichol, "Ralph Waldo Emerson," *North British Rev.*, XLVII (Dec., 1867), 319–358.

"The Culture of Emerson," *Fraser's Mag.*, LXXVIII (July, 1868), 1–18.

Moncure D. Conway, "Emerson's *Society and Solitude*," *Fraser's Mag.*, New Ser., II (July, 1870), 1–18.

"Ralph Waldo Emerson," *Graphic*, X (Sept. 12, 1874), 261.

Moncure D. Conway, "Ralph Waldo Emerson," *Fortnightly Rev.*, New Ser., XXXI (June 1, 1882), 747–770.

Alex. H. Japp, "A Gift from Emerson," *Gentleman's Mag.*, CCLIII (Nov., 1882), 618–628.

"The Carlyle–Emerson Correspondence," *Westminster Rev.*, New Ser., LXIII (April, 1883), 451–493.

"The Correspondence of Carlyle and Emerson," *Modern Rev.*, IV (April, 1883), 318–340.

Richard H. Shepherd, "The Carlyle-Emerson Correspondence," *Gentleman's Mag.*, CCLIV (April, 1883), 415–427.

Henry Norman, "Ralph Waldo Emerson: an Ethnical Study," *Fortnightly Rev.*, New Ser., XXXIV (Sept. 1, 1883), 422–432.

"Emerson's Social Philosophy," *Scottish Rev.*, II (Sept., 1883), 222–234.

C. E. Tyrer, "Emerson as a Poet," *Manchester Quart.*, III (April, 1884), 105–128.

Matthew Arnold, "Emerson," *Macmillan's Mag.*, L (May, 1884), 1–13.

C. A. Ward, "Emerson," *Temple Bar,* LXXII (Oct., 1884), 236–248.

W. L. Courtney, "Ralph Waldo Emerson," *Fortnightly Rev.*, New Ser., XXXVIII (Sept. 1, 1885), 319–331.

Coulson Kernahan, "Some Aspects of Emerson," *Gentleman's Mag.*, CCLIX (Nov., 1885), 472–480.

W. L. Courtney, "Emerson's Philosophy," *Time,* New Ser., III (June, 1886), 653–661.

"Ralph Waldo Emerson," *Westminster Rev.*, CXXVIII (Nov., 1887), 985–997.

Henry James, "The Life of Emerson," *Macmillan's Mag.*, LVII (Dec., 1887), 86–98.

"Cabot's Life of Emerson," *Quart. Rev.*, CLXVI (Jan., 1888), 130–159.

George Stewart, Jun., "Emerson, the Thinker," *Scottish Rev.*, XI (April, 1888), 288–307.

"A Half-Made Poet," *London Quart. Rev.*, LXXIII (Oct., 1889), 25–35.

P. L., "Emerson's Meeting with De Quincey," *Blackwood's,* CLV (April, 1894), 480–491.

"M. Maeterlinck on the Mystics and on Emerson," *Bookman,* VI (June, 1894), 111–112.

Emerson, Ralph Waldo (continued)

Vernon Lee, "Emerson, Transcendentalist and Utilitarian," *Contemporary Rev.*, LXVII (March, 1895), 345–360.

James Nairn, "Emerson's Home in Concord," *Temple Bar*, CXV (Oct., 1898), 290–297.

Patrick Dillon, "The Non-Sequaciousness of Ralph Waldo Emerson," *Irish Month.*, XXVIII (July, 1900), 415–421.

Coulson Carnahan, "Is Emerson a Poet?" *National Rev.* [monthly], XXXVI (Dec., 1900), 523–536.

See also under *General:* 1857, 1864, 1882, 1887, 1899; *Poetry:* 1868; *Humor:* 1876.

Franklin, Benjamin. "Franklin's Familiar Letters," *Eclectic Rev.*, 3d Ser., X (July, 1833), 261–268.

"Franklin's Works," *Eclectic Rev.*, 4th Ser., XIV (July, 1843), 19–38.

"Benjamin Franklin," *Hogg's Weekly Instructor*, I (June 14, 1845), 242–244.

"American Diplomacy," *Fraser's Mag.*, XLVIII (Sept., 1853), 299–307.

"Benjamin Franklin," *London Quart. Rev.*, XXIII (Jan., 1865), 483–514.

Thomas Hughes, "Benjamin Franklin," *Contemporary Rev.*, XXXV (July, 1879), 581–595.

"Bigelow's Life of Benjamin Franklin," *Edinburgh Rev.*, CLI (April, 1880), 321–358.

Frederic, Harold. "Mr. Frederic Once More," *Rev. of Reviews*, V (March, 1892), 256–257.

" 'Illumination' and Its Author," *Bookman*, X (Aug., 1896), 136–138.

Robert H. Sherard, "Harold Frederic," *Idler*, XII (Nov., 1897), 531–540.

Gertrude Atherton, "The Reader. Harold Frederic," *Bookman*, XV (Nov., 1898), 37.

See also under *Fiction:* 1898.

Fuller, Margaret. "Margaret Fuller Ossoli," *Gentleman's Mag.*, New Ser., XXXVII (May, 1852), 453–460.

"Margaret Fuller Ossoli," *British Quart. Rev.*, XVI (Aug., 1852), 221–237.

S. Waddington, "Margaret Fuller Ossoli," *Tinsley's Mag.*, XVI (Feb., 1875), 172–179.

Mabel Collins, "Margaret Fuller," *University Mag.*, II (Nov. and Dec., 1878), 542–551, 686–704.

Elsie Rhodes, "The Personality of Margaret Fuller," *Temple Bar*, CVIII (June, 1896), 226–232.

See also under *General:* 1847.

Glasgow, Ellen. "Ellen Glasgow, the Author of 'The Voice of the People,' " *Bookman*, XVIII (Sept., 1900), 167–168.

Harland, Henry. Henry James, "The Story-Teller at Large: Mr. Henry Harland," *Fortnightly Rev.,* New Ser., LXVI (April 1, 1898), 650–654.

Harris, Thomas Lake. "The Literature of Spirit-Rapping," *National Rev.,* IV (Jan., 1857), 131–151.

Harte, Bret. "American Lights. Bret Harte," *Cope's Tobacco Plant,* I (Aug., 1871), 199.

"Bret Harte," *Temple Bar,* XXXIX (Sept., 1873), 257–265.

"Mr. Bret Harte," *Anthenæum,* No. 2675 (Feb. 1, 1879), pp. 152–153.

M. S. V. De V., "Francis Bret Harte," *Belgravia,* XLV (Aug., 1881), 232–236.

"The Works of Bret Harte," *Westminster Rev.,* New Ser., LXIX (Jan., 1886), 71–83.

G. M. Wallen, "The Writings of Bret Harte," *Westminster Rev.,* CXXV (Jan.–April, 1886), 71–83.

Luke Sharp and G. B. Burgin, "Francis Bret Harte. Two Interviews with Him on Somewhat Dissimilar Lines," *Idler,* I (April, 1892), 301–311.

Bret Harte, "My First Book," *Idler,* IV (Jan., 1894), 553–561.

See also under *General:* 1871, 1898; *Humor:* 1876.

Hawthorne, Julian. "Hawthorne in Saxony," *Cope's Tobacco Plant,* I (Aug., 1876), 929–930.

Mabel Collins, "The Son of Nathaniel Hawthorne," *Dublin University Mag.,* XC (Aug., 1877), 236–239.

"Biography, New Style. Mr. Julian Hawthorne," *University Mag.,* Quarterly Ser., I (Michaelmas, 1880), 53–57.

Hawthorne, Nathaniel. "Nathaniel Hawthorne," *New Monthly Mag.,* XCIV (Feb., 1852), 202–207.

Sir Nathaniel, "Nathaniel Hawthorne," *New Monthly Mag.,* XCVIII (June, 1853), 202–212.

"Modern Novelists—Great and Small," *Blackwood's,* LXXVII (May, 1855), 554–568.

"Nathaniel Hawthorne," *Dublin University Mag.,* XLVI (Oct., 1855), 463–469.

"Nathaniel Hawthorne," *Tait's Edinburgh Mag.,* New Ser., XXIII (Dec., 1856), 756–757.

"American Imaginings," *Dublin University Mag.,* LV (June, 1860), 679–688.

"Imaginative Literature. The Author of Adam Bede and Nathaniel Hawthorne," *North British Rev.,* XXXIII (Aug., 1860), 165–185.

"Nathaniel Hawthorne," *National Rev.,* XI (Oct., 1860), 453–481.

"Hawthorne on England," *Blackwood's,* XCIV (Nov., 1863), 610–623.

Hawthorne, Nathaniel (continued)

Edward Dicey, "Nathaniel Hawthorne," *Macmillan's Mag.,* X (July, 1864), 241–246.

"Nathaniel Hawthorne," *Once A Week,* XVIII (June 27, 1868), 562–563.

"Nathaniel Hawthorne," *North British Rev.,* XLIX (Sept., 1868), 173–208.

James T. Fields, "Nathaniel Hawthorne," *Cornhill Mag.,* XXIII (March–May, 1871), 321–336, 444–456, 566–575.

Matthew Browne, "Nathaniel Hawthorne," *St. Paul's Mag.,* VIII (May, 1871), 151–161.

"Nathaniel Hawthorne's Life and Writings," *London Quart. Rev.,* XXXVII (Oct., 1871), 48–78.

G. P. Lathrop, "Hawthorne's French and Italian Notebooks," *St. Paul's Mag.,* IX (Dec., 1871), 311–313.

H. A. P., "Nathaniel Hawthorne in Undress," *Argosy,* XIII (Feb. 1, 1872), 109–115.

"Nathaniel Hawthorne," *Graphic,* VI (Aug. 24, 1872), 168–170.

Keningale Cook, "Nathaniel Hawthorne," *Belgravia,* XIX (Nov., 1872), 72–79.

Leslie Stephen, "Nathaniel Hawthorne," *Cornhill Mag.,* XXVI (Dec., 1872), 717–734.

George Barnett Smith, "Nathaniel Hawthorne," *New Quart. Mag.,* III (Jan., 1875), 274–303.

Edward Markwick, "Hawthorne and His Wife," *Temple Bar,* LXXV (Dec., 1885), 523–538.

W. L. Courtney, "Hawthorne's Romances," *Fortnightly Rev.,* New Ser., XL (Oct., 1886), 511–522.

George Morley, "Hawthorne's Warwickshire Haunts," *Gentleman's Mag.,* CCLXXXVIII (April, 1900), 408–413.

Frances B. Embree, "Nathaniel Hawthorne," *New Century Rev.,* VIII (Aug., 1900), 122–128.

See also under *General:* 1847, 1864, 1887; *Fiction:* 1853, 1875.

Hay, John. "A New American Novelist," *Saturday Rev.,* LVII (Feb. 2, 1884), 155.

"The New United States Ambassador as Man of Letters," *Academy,* LI (Feb. 27, 1897), 259–260.

Holmes, Oliver Wendell. Sir Nathaniel, "Oliver Wendell Holmes," *New Monthly Mag.,* XCIX (Sept., 1853), 77–84.

J. M. Ludlow, "Elsie Venner and Silas Marner: a Few Words on Two Noteworthy Novels," *Macmillan's Mag.,* IV (Aug., 1861), 305–309.

"Dr. Oliver Wendell Holmes and Elsie Venner," *National Rev.,* XIII (Oct., 1861), 359–372.

"Holmes' Poems," *Eclectic Rev.,* II (April, 1862), 326–335.

"The Works of Oliver Wendell Holmes," *Dark Blue,* V (March, 1873), 103–104.

Keningale Cook, "Oliver Wendell Holmes," *Belgravia,* XX (April, 1873), 222–232.

R. E. Prothero, "Oliver Wendell Holmes," *London Society,* VIII (July, 1886), 300–306.

"Dr. Oliver Wendell Holmes," *Illustrated London News,* LXXXIX (July 3, 1886), 5–6.

Edward Delille, "Oliver Wendell Holmes," *Fortnightly Rev.,* New Ser., XL (Aug., 1886), 235–243.

"Oliver Wendell Holmes," *Blackwood's,* CLII (Aug., 1892), 194–207.

"Oliver Wendell Holmes," *Bookman,* II (Sept., 1892), 171–173.

James A. Noble, "Oliver Wendell Holmes," *Leisure Hour,* XLIV (Dec., 1894), 82–88.

"Oliver Wendell Holmes," *Quart. Rev.,* CLXXX (Jan., 1895), 189–206.

Leslie Stephen, "Oliver Wendell Holmes," *National Rev.,* [monthly], XXVII (July, 1896), 626–641.

"Life and Letters of Oliver Wendell Holmes," *London Quart. Rev.,* LXXXVII (Oct., 1896), 77–94.

See also under *General:* 1887; *Poetry:* 1876; *Fiction:* 1867; *Humor:* 1860.

Howe, Edgar Watson. "American Stories," *Saturday Rev.,* LIX (June 20, 1885), 835–836.

Howells, William Dean. Mrs. Sutherland Orr, "International Novelists and Mr. Howells," *Contemporary Rev.,* XXXVII (May, 1880), 741–766.

"Mr. Howells' Novels," *Westminster Rev.,* New Ser., LXVI (Oct., 1884), 347–375.

"Scott's Latest Critics," *Saturday Rev.,* LXVII (May 4, 1889), 521–522.

William Archer, "The Novelist as Critic," *Illustrated London News,* XCIX (Aug. 8, 1891), 175.

Andrew Lang, "The New Fiction," *Illustrated London News,* CVII (Aug. 3, 1895), 141.

"The Modern American Mood," *Speaker,* XVI (July 3, 1897), 13–14.

See also under *General:* 1883; *Poetry:* 1868; *Fiction:* 1884.

Irving, Washington. "Irving's Tour on the Prairies," *Dublin University Mag.,* V (May, 1835), 554–572.

William S. Somner, "The Writings of Washington Irving," *Parterre,* IV (March 26, 1836), 196–198.

J. A. R., "Astoria," *Westminster Rev.,* XXVI (Jan., 1837), 318–348.

"Astoria; or, Enterprise beyond the Rocky Mountains," *Dublin University Mag.,* IX (Feb., 1837), 167–176.

Irving, Washington (continued)

"Washington Irving," *Bentley's Miscellany*, XIX (1846), 622–623.

"Washington Irving," *Hogg's Weekly Instructor*, New Ser., I (Aug., 1848), 401–403.

"Mahomet and the Koran," *North British Rev.*, XIII (Feb., 1850), 189–224.

Sir Nathaniel, "Washington Irving," *New Monthly Mag.*, XCVII (April, 1853), 424–433.

"Residences of the Late Washington Irving," *Illustrated London News*, XXXV (Dec. 24, 1859), 624.

Cyrus Redding, "Washington Irving," *New Monthly Mag.*, CXVIII (Feb., 1860), 213–221.

"Washington Irving," *New Monthly Mag.*, CXXVII (Feb., 1863), 165–176.

"Washington Irving," *Quart. Rev.*, CXIV (July, 1863), 151–179.

"Washington Irving. A Third Volume," *New Monthly Mag.*, CXXIX (Sept., 1863), 49–63.

"Irving at Sunnyside," *New Monthly Mag.*, CXXXI (July, 1864), 297–309.

"Knickerbocker on Smoke," *Cope's Tobacco Plant*, I (Aug., 1870), 55.

A. H. W., "Washington Irving's Love Story," *London Society*, XLI (Feb., 1882), 200–207.

"Washington Irving," *Temple Bar*, XCVI (Nov., 1892), 321–341.

See also under *General:* 1838.

James, Henry. "Mr. Henry James," *Murray's Mag.*, X (Nov., 1891), 641–654.

Lena Milman, "A Few Notes upon Mr. James," *Yellow Book*, VII (Oct., 1895), 71–83.

"Living Critics. VII—Mr. Henry James," *Bookman*, X (June, 1896), 76–77.

See also under *General:* 1883, 1898; *Fiction:* 1884.

Johnston, Mary. "Miss Mary Johnston," *Bookman*, XVIII (April, 1900), 5.

Judd, Sylvester. "Sylvester Judd," *Fraser's Mag.*, LXXVI (July, 1867), 45–60.

Lanier, Sidney. Richard Le Gallienne, "Sidney Lanier," *Academy*, LVIII (Feb. 17, 1900), 147–148.

See also under *Poetry:* 1891.

Leland, Charles Godfrey. "Hans Breitmann's Party," *St. James's Mag.*, New Ser., II (March, 1869), 817–822.

"Hans Breitmann," *Cope's Tobacco Plant*, I (Oct., 1871), 223–225.

Alex. H. Japp, "The Gypsies as Seen by Friendly Eyes," *Gentleman's Mag.*, CCLV (Dec., 1883), 575–587.

"The Breitmann," *Academy*, LIII (June 4, 1898), 608–609.

See also under *General:* 1871; *Humor:* 1872.

Longfellow, Henry Wadsworth. "Longfellow's Poems," *Eclectic Rev.*, 4th Ser., XXVI (July, 1849), 78–84.

"Longfellow," *Dublin University Mag.*, XXXV (April, 1850), 461–473.

"Longfellow," *Ainsworth's Mag.*, XVIII (Aug., 1850), 146–154.

"Living Litterateurs: Longfellow," *Duffy's Fireside Mag.*, I (April, 1851), 173–178.

"Longfellow's Golden Legend," *Blackwood's*, LXXI (Feb., 1852), 212–225.

"Longfellow's Golden Legend," *Eclectic Rev.*, 5th Ser., III (April, 1852), 455–467.

"Longfellow," *Fraser's Mag.*, XLVII (April, 1853), 367–382.

"Longfellow's Works," *Dublin Rev.*, XXXIV (June, 1853), 359–407.

Sir Nathaniel, "Henry Wadsworth Longfellow," *New Monthly Mag.*, XCIX (Oct., 1853), 228–235.

"Modern Poetic Genius," *Illustrated London News*, XXVII (Nov. 10, 1855), 554–555.

"The Song of Hiawatha," *Oxford and Cambridge Magazine*, I (Jan., 1856), 45–49.

"Longfellow's 'Song of Hiawatha,' " *New Monthly Mag.*, CVI (Feb., 1856), 242–246.

"Poetry under a Cloud," *Irish Quart. Rev.*, VI (March, 1856), 1–30.

"Hiawatha," *London Quart. Rev.*, VI (July, 1856), 333–345.

"Longfellow," *National Rev.*, VIII (Jan., 1859), 198–209.

Eden Glen, "Longfellow," *National Mag.*, X (1861), 261–262.

"Longfellow's New Poems," *British Quart. Rev.*, XXXIX (Jan., 1864), 31–61.

W. Clark Russell, "Henry Wadsworth Longfellow," *Broadway*, I (Dec., 1867), 282–287.

"Dante," *British Quart. Rev.*, XLVII (April, 1868), 366–398.

"The Poet Longfellow," *Illustrated London News*, LV (July 17, 1869), 70.

"New Hiawatha Legends," *Once A Week*, XXI (Nov. 13, 1869), 315–317.

Alexander H. Japp, "The Puritan Element in Longfellow," *British Quart. Rev.*, LXXVI (July, 1882), 34–53.

Henry Norman, "A Study of Longfellow," *Fortnightly Rev.*, New Ser., XXXIII (Jan. 1, 1883), 100–115.

"Longfellow," *Macmillan's Mag.*, LIV (May, 1886), 28–38.

Richard H. Shepherd, "Longfellow and His Friends," *Gentleman's Mag.*, CCLXI (July, 1886), 71–83.

George Stewart, Jun., "Life and Times of Longfellow," *Scottish Rev.*, VIII (July, 1886), 101–126.

Longfellow, Henry Wadsworth (continued)

"Longfellow and His Friends," *London Quart. Rev.*, LXVII (Oct., 1886), 1–17.

Helen Atteridge, "Longfellow," *Dublin Rev.*, 3d Ser., XVI (Oct., 1886), 260–294.

Alice Longfellow, "Longfellow with His Children," *Strand Mag.*, XIV (Aug., 1897), 250–253.

"The Homes of Two Poets," *Scots Mag.*, New Ser., XXV (May, 1900), 460–470. [Longfellow and Tennyson.]

See also under *General:* 1887; *Poetry:* 1843, 1852, 1854, 1868; *Fiction:* 1853.

Lowell, James Russell. "A Fable for Critics," *Eclectic Rev.*, 4th Ser., XXVIII (Nov., 1850), 586–593.

Sir Nathaniel, "James Russell Lowell," *New Monthly Mag.*, CI (June, 1854), 222–231.

"An American Humourist," *Eliza Cook's Jour.*, XI (June 17, 1854), 114–117.

"The Author of 'Tom Brown's School-Days' on the 'Biglow Papers,' " *Saturday Rev.*, VIII (Nov. 5, 1859), 541–542.

F. T., "Mr. Lowell's Poems," *Cornhill Mag.*, XXXI (Jan., 1875), 65–78.

H. R. Haweis, "James Russell Lowell, Poet and Essayist," *Gentleman's Mag.*, CCXLIX (Oct. and Nov., 1880), 464–487, 544–562.

G. Barnett Smith, "James Russell Lowell," *Nineteenth Century*, XVII (June, 1885), 988–1008.

H. D. Traill, "Mr. J. R. Lowell," *Fortnightly Rev.*, New Ser., XXXVIII (July 1, 1885), 79–89.

"Littérateur, Ambassador, Patriot, Cosmopolite," *Academy*, LVII (July 29, 1889), 113–115.

H. D. Traill, "Mr. Lowell in London," *Illustrated London News*, XCIX (Aug. 22, 1891), 231.

Sidney Low, "Lowell in His Poetry," *Fortnightly Rev.*, New Ser., L (Sept., 1891), 310–324.

Bret Harte, "A Few Words about Mr. Lowell," *New Rev.*, V (Sept., 1891), 193–201.

Francis H. Underwood, "James Russell Lowell," *Contemporary Rev.*, LX (Oct., 1891), 477–498.

"The Writings of James Russell Lowell," *Edinburgh Rev.*, CLXXIV (Oct., 1891), 377–404.

"James Russell Lowell," *Temple Bar*, XCVI (Sept., 1892), 88–95.

"Lowell's Letters," *London Quart. Rev.*, LXXXI (Jan., 1894), 242–264.

"A Neglected 'Lowell,' " *Academy*, LVII (Aug. 5, 1899), 135–136.

"James Russell Lowell," *Edinburgh Rev.*, CXCI (Jan., 1900), 157–181.

See also under *General:* 1887, 1898; *Poetry:* 1853, 1854; *Humor:* 1860, 1872.

Mahan, Alfred Thayer. "The Influence of Sea Power upon History," *Blackwood's*, CXLVIII (Oct., 1890), 576–584.

"Captain Mahan on Maritime Power," *Edinburgh Rev.*, CLXXII (Oct., 1890), 420–453.

"The Literature of the Sea," *Macmillan's Mag.*, LXVIII (Aug., 1893), 279–285.

W. O. Morris, "Captain Mahan's 'Nelson,'" *Fortnightly Rev.*, New Ser., LXI (June, 1897), 895–910.

Mather, Cotton. Andrew Lang, "An American Pepys," *Illustrated London News*, CIV (May 5, 1894), 548.

Melville, Herman. "Melville's Marquesas Islands," *Eclectic Rev.*, 4th Ser., XIX (April, 1846), 448–459.

"Melville's Residence in the Marquesas," *New Quart. Rev.*, No. 15 (July, 1846), pp. 18–35.

"Adventures in the South Seas," *Dublin Rev.*, XXIII (Dec., 1847), 341–363.

"Polynesia," *English Rev.*, IX (Dec., 1848), 51–84.

"Mr. Melville and South-Sea Missions," *Eclectic Rev.*, 4th Ser., XXVIII (Oct., 1850), 425–436.

"Literary Novelties for the Winter Season," *Bentley's Miscellany*, XXXI (Jan., 1852), 101–106.

Sir Nathaniel, "Herman Melville," *New Monthly Mag.*, XCVIII (July, 1853), 300–308.

"Life in an American Man-O'-War," *National Miscellany*, III (1854), 100–109.

H. S. Salt, "Marquesan Melville," *Gentleman's Mag.*, CCLXXII (March, 1892), 248–257.

See also under *Fiction:* 1856, 1884.

Miller, Joaquin. George F. Armstrong, "Mr. Miller's 'Songs of the Sierras,'" *Dark Blue*, II (Sept., 1871), 120–128.

"Joaquin Miller's Songs of the Sierras," *Fraser's Mag.*, New Ser., IV (Sept., 1871), 346–355.

"Joaquin Miller's Poetry," *New Monthly Mag.*, New Ser., IV (July, 1873), 58–66.

"Joaquin Miller," *Dublin University Mag.*, LXXXVII (Jan., 1876), 90–95.

J. H. E. Partington, "Joaquin Miller at Home," *Black and White*, VI (July 1, 1893), 12–14.

"Joaquin Miller, the Poet of the Sierras," *Academy*, LI (June 26, 1897), 24.

Miller, Joaquin (continued)

"Joaquin Miller, Browning, and the Prince Imperial," *Academy,* LIII (Feb. 12, 1898), 181–182.

See also under *General:* 1871.

Mitchell, Donald Grant. Sir Nathaniel, "Donald G. Mitchell," *New Monthly Mag.,* C (Jan., 1854), 73–77.

See also under *Fiction:* 1867.

Mitchell, Silas Weir. "New Writers. Dr. Silas Weir Mitchell," *Bookman,* XIII (Dec., 1897), 60.

Motley, John Lothrop. "The Rise of the Dutch Republic," *Westminster Rev.,* New Ser., IX (April, 1856), 313–337.

"The Rise of the Dutch Republic," *Eclectic Rev.,* 6th Ser., IV (Aug., 1858), 125–138.

"Motley's Dutch Republic," *Blackwood's,* LXXXVI (Dec., 1859), 690–710.

"Motley's *History of the United Netherlands,*" *Edinburgh Rev.,* CXIII (Jan., 1861), 182–220.

"The United Netherlands," *Quart. Rev.,* CIX (Jan., 1861), 64–105.

"Motley's History of the United Netherlands," *Temple Bar,* I (March, 1861), 516–532.

"The History of the United Netherlands," *British Quart. Rev.,* XXXIII (April, 1861), 285–325.

"Motley's History of the Netherlands," *Blackwood's,* LXXXIX (May, 1861), 555–571.

"Motley's *United Netherlands,*" *North British Rev.,* XXXIV (May, 1861), 428–451.

"Motley's History of the Netherlands," *Blackwood's,* CIV (July, 1868), 83–97.

"Motley's Life and Death of Barnevelt," *Edinburgh Rev.,* CXL (July, 1874), 107–143.

"Mr. Motley's New Historical Work," *British Quart. Rev.,* LX (Oct., 1874), 392–425.

"Mr. Motley's Historical Works," *Dublin Rev.,* New Ser., XXX (April, 1878), 359–397; New Ser., XXXI (Oct., 1878), 349–380.

"Motley's Correspondence," *Quart. Rev.,* CLXVIII (April, 1889), 297–331.

"Motley's Correspondence," *Westminster Rev.,* CXXXII (July, 1889), 26–43.

"Motley's Letters," *London Quart. Rev.,* LXXII (July, 1889), 308–325.

See also under *General:* 1857.

Moulton, Louise Chandler. Coulson Kernahan, "The Poems of Louise Chandler Moulton," *Fortnightly Rev.,* New Ser., LIII (April, 1893), 499–504.

"A Singer from Over Seas," *London Quart. Rev.*, LXXX (July, 1893), 281–291.

"Mrs. Louise Chandler Moulton. An Interview," *Bookman*, IV (Aug., 1893), 143–144.

M. A. B., "Mrs. Louise Chandler Moulton," *Album*, II (July 22, 1895), 124–125.

Paine, Thomas. Moncure D. Conway, "Thomas Paine," *Fortnightly Rev.*, New Ser., XXV (March 1, 1879), 397–416.

J., "Thomas Paine," *Our Corner*, I (Jan., Feb., March, 1883), 58–62, 122–124, 185–188.

"Mr. Conway's Life of Thomas Paine," *Westminster Rev.*, CXXXVIII (Nov., 1892), 469–482.

Leslie Stephen, "Thomas Paine," *Fortnightly Rev.*, New Ser., LIV (Aug., 1893), 267–281.

Parkman, Francis. "The French in North America," *Edinburgh Rev.*, CLXII (July, 1885), 84–127.

Francis H. Underwood, "Francis Parkman," *Contemporary Rev.*, LIII (May, 1888), 642–661.

"The Historical Writings of Francis Parkman," *Quart. Rev.*, CLXXXV (April, 1897), 530–558.

Parley, Peter. F. B., "Literature of Childhood," *Westminster Rev.*, XXXIII (Oct., 1839), 137–162.

Poe, Edgar Allan. "Edgar Poe," *Tait's Edinburgh Mag.*, New Ser., XIX (April, 1852), 231–234.

"Edgar Allan Poe," *Eliza Cook's Jour.*, VII (May 15, 1852), 45–48.

Appolodorus, "Edgar Poe," *Critic*, XIII (March 1, 1854), 119–121.

K. P. I., "Edgar Allan Poe," *Fraser's Mag.*, LV (June, 1857), 684–700.

"Edgar Allan Poe," *Edinburgh Rev.*, CVII (April, 1858), 419–442.

"Edgar Allan Poe," *Once A Week*, XXV (Nov. 4 and 18, 1871), 404–410, 447–450.

John H. Ingram, "Edgar Allan Poe's Early Poems," *Gentleman's Mag.*, CCXXXIV (May, 1874), 580–588.

—— "Edgar Poe," *Temple Bar*, XLI (June, 1874), 375–387.

James Purves, "Edgar Allan Poe," *Dublin University Mag.*, LXXXV (March, 1875), 336–351.

"Edgar Allan Poe," *British Quart. Rev.*, LXII (July, 1875), 194–218.

James Purves, "Edgar Allan Poe's Works," *Dublin University Mag.*, LXXXVI (Sept., 1875), 296–306.

John H. Ingram, "The Unknown Poetry of Edgar Poe," *Belgravia*, XXIX (June, 1876), 502–513.

—— "The Bibliography of Edgar Poe," *Athenæum*, No. 2544 (July 29, 1876), pp. 145–146.

Poe, Edgar Allan (continued)

James A. Noble, "Edgar Allan Poe," *New Quart Mag.,* VIII (July, 1877), 410–427.

John H. Ingram, "Unknown Correspondence by Edgar Poe," *New Quart. Mag.,* X (April, 1878), 1–30.

William Minto, "Edgar Allan Poe," *Fortnightly Rev.,* New Ser., XXVIII (July 1, 1880), 69–82.

"Edgar Poe and New York," *Saturday Rev.,* LI (Jan. 29, 1881), 139–140.

G. Barnett Smith, "Poe: His Life and Work," *Tinsley's Mag.,* XXVIII (Jan., 1881), 15–32.

Esmé Stuart, "Charles Baudelaire and Edgar Poe: a Literary Affinity," *Nineteenth Century,* XXXIV (July, 1883), 65–80.

"Edgar Poe and His Biographers," *Temple Bar,* LXVIII (Aug., 1883), 530–539.

B. Montgomerie Ranking, "Edgar Allan Poe," *Time,* IX (Sept., 1883), 352–360.

John Robertson, "Edgar Allan Poe," *Our Corner,* VI (Sept.–Dec., 1885), 154–162, 204–213, 303–310, 346–357.

Charles Whibley, "Edgar Allan Poe," *New Rev.,* XIV (June, 1896), 612–625.

"Edgar Allan Poe," *Academy,* LVII (Aug. 5, 1899), 137.

Francis Howard, "On a Portrait of Edgar Allan Poe," *Anglo-Saxon Rev.,* IV (March, 1900), 95–96.

See also under *General:* 1847, 1898; *Poetry:* 1852, 1853, 1854.

Prescott, William Hickling. "Prescott's *History of Ferdinand and Isabella,*" *Quart. Rev.,* LXIX (June, 1839), 1–58.

"Prescott's Conquest of Mexico," *Dublin Rev.,* XVI (March, 1844), 45–65.

"History of the Reign of Ferdinand and Isabella," *British Quart. Rev.,* I (Feb., 1845), 232–276.

"Prescott's *Conquest of Mexico,*" *Edinburgh Rev.,* LXXXI (April, 1845), 434–473.

"Prescott's Peru," *Blackwood's,* LXII (July, 1847), 1–20.

"Prescott's Conquest of Peru," *Eclectic Rev.,* 4th Ser., XXII (July, 1847), 20–47.

Sir Nathaniel, "William H. Prescott," *New Monthly Mag.,* C (Feb., 1854), 173–179.

"History of the Reign of Philip II., King of Spain," *British Quart. Rev.,* XXIII (Jan., 1856), 3–35.

I. R. C., "Prescott's Philip the Second," *Fraser's Mag.,* LIII (Jan., 1856), 20–38.

"Prescott's Philip II," *Blackwood's,* LXXIX (April, 1856), 421–438.

"Prescott, the American Historian," *Leisure Hour,* VI (Aug. 6 and 13, 1857), 502–504, 524–526.

See also under *General:* 1857.

Ripley, George. William Henry Channing, "George Ripley," *Modern Rev.,* IV (July, 1883), 520–557.

Sedgwick, Catharine. H. M., "Miss Sedgwick's Works," *Westminster Rev.,* XXVIII (Oct., 1837), 42–65.

"Lady Travellers," *British and Foreign Rev.,* XIII (1842), 486–508.

Smith, John. "The True Founder of Virginia," *St. James's Mag.,* IV (May, 1862), 199–216.

Story, William Wetmore. "Roba di Roma," *National Rev.,* XVI (April, 1863), 426–442.

"Miss Smedley and Mr. Story," *Tinsley's Mag.,* V (Dec., 1869), 514–524.

Stowe, Harriet Beecher. A. H., "Uncle Tom's Cabin," *Fraser's Mag.,* XLVI (Aug., 1852), 237–244.

"American Slavery and 'Uncle Tom's Cabin,'" *North British Rev.,* XVIII (Nov., 1852), 235–258.

An Alabama Man, "Some Account of Mrs. Beecher Stowe and Her Family," *Fraser's Mag.,* XLVI (Nov., 1852), 518–525.

"Uncle Tom's Cabin and Its Opponents," *Eclectic Rev.,* 5th Ser., IV (Dec., 1852), 717–744.

"American Slavery," *Westminster Rev.,* New Ser., III (Jan., 1853), 125–167.

"Key to Uncle Tom's Cabin," *Eclectic Rev.,* 5th Ser., V (May, 1853), 600–617.

"Uncle Tom's Cabin," *Blackwood's,* LXXIV (Oct., 1853), 393–423.

"Mrs. Stowe's Sunny Memories of Foreign Lands," *Eclectic Rev.,* 5th Ser., VIII (Sept., 1854), 327–341.

"Mrs. Stowe's Sunny Memories," *Blackwood's,* LXXVI (Sept., 1854), 301–317.

"Slavery in the United States," *Edinburgh Rev.,* CI (April, 1855), 294–331.

"Mrs. Stowe's 'Dred,'" *Eclectic Rev.,* 5th Ser., XII (Oct., 1856), 323–332.

"Dred," *Blackwood's,* LXXX (Dec., 1856), 693–714.

"Dred—American Slavery," *Quart. Rev.,* CI (April, 1857), 324–352.

"Two New Novels," *Scottish Rev.: A Quart. Jour.,* Jan., 1860, pp. 53–61. [Mrs. Stowe and Thackeray.]

"The Minister's Wooing," *Dublin Rev.,* XLVIII (May, 1860), 190–228.

"The Pearl of Orr's Island," *Eclectic Rev.,* 7th Ser., V (June, 1861), 625–630.

Stowe, Harriet Beecher (continued)

An American, "The Rev. Henry Ward Beecher and Mrs. Beecher Stowe," *Cassell's Mag.*, New Ser., I (1869), 282–284.

"The Byron Scandal," *Athenæum*, No. 2185 (Sept. 11, 1869), p. 337.

"Lord and Lady Byron," *Argosy*, VIII (Oct. 1, 1869), 274–289.

"Lady Noel Byron and Mrs. Beecher Stowe. A Short Chapter of 'Ifs,' " *New Monthly Mag.*, CXLV (Oct., 1869), 447–449.

"Stowe versus Byron," *St. James's Mag.*, New Ser., IV (Oct., 1869), 58–68.

"Lord Byron Vindicated," *Fraser's Mag.*, LXXX (Nov., 1869), 599–617.

"Some Thoughts in Connexion with Byron's Name," *New Monthly Mag.*, CXLV (Nov., 1869), 558–562.

Cyrus Redding, "Lord Byron," *New Monthly Mag.*, CXLV (Nov., 1869), 497–504.

"Mrs. Stowe's *Vindication,*" *Quart. Rev.*, CXXVIII (Jan., 1870), 218–250.

"The Byron Mystery and Mrs. Stowe," *Saturday Rev.*, XXIX (Jan. 29, 1870), 140–144.

"Lady Byron and Mrs. Beecher Stowe," *New Monthly Mag.*, CXLVI (Feb., 1870), 217–219.

Cyrus Redding, "Mrs. Stowe's Second 'True' Story," *New Monthly Mag.*, CXLVI (March, 1870), 352–366.

"Mrs. Stowe's 'Vindication,' " *Argosy*, IX (April 1, 1870), 269–287.

"The Author of 'Uncle Tom's Cabin,' " *Leisure Hour*, XXXIX (March, 1890), 307–309.

"Harriet Beecher Stowe," *London Quart. Rev.*, LXXIV (April, 1890), 28–42.

"Mrs. Stowe's 'Life and Letters,' " *London Quart. Rev.*, XC (July, 1898), 326–335.

See also under *Poetry:* 1868; *Fiction:* 1853.

Street, Alfred Billings. "Memoir of Alfred B. Street," *Bentley's Miscellany*, XXV (1849), 563–566.

Taylor, Bayard. "Recent American Poetry," *Athenæum*, No. 2045 (Jan. 5, 1867), pp. 11–12.

"Books of the Season," *Broadway*, 3d Ser., IV (Feb., 1872), 159–167.

See also under *Fiction:* 1867.

Thoreau, Henry. "Henry Thoreau, the Poet-Naturalist," *British Quart. Rev.*, LIX (Jan., 1874), 181–194.

Mabel Collins, "Thoreau: Hermit and Thinker," *Dublin University Mag.*, XC (Nov., 1877), 610–621.

R. L. Stevenson, "Henry David Thoreau: His Character and Opinions," *Cornhill Mag.*, XLI (June, 1880), 665–682.

H. S. Salt, "Henry D. Thoreau," *Temple Bar*, LXXVIII (Nov., 1886), 369–383.

Grant Allen, "Sunday at Concord," *Fortnightly Rev.*, New Ser., XLIII (May 1, 1888), 675–690.

"Thoreau," *Belgravia*, LXXXI (Aug., 1893), 375–383.

See also under *General:* 1899.

Ticknor, George. "Ticknor's History of Spanish Literature," *British Quart. Rev.*, XI (Feb., 1850), 200–229.

"Ticknor's History of Spanish Literature," *Quart. Rev.*, LXXXVII (Sept., 1850), 289–330.

A. Hayward, "Ticknor's Memoirs," *Quart. Rev.*, CXLII (July, 1876), 160–201.

Twain, Mark. "Modern Comic Literature," *Saturday Rev.*, LIX (March 7, 1885), 301–302.

"Mark Twain's New Book," *Rev. of Reviews*, I (Feb., 1890), 144–156.

Andrew Lang, "The Art of Mark Twain," *Illustrated London News*, XCVIII (Feb. 14, 1891), 222.

Luke Sharp, "Mark Twain: a Conglomerate Interview," *Idler*, I (Feb., 1892), 79–92.

D. F. Hannigan, "Mark Twain as a Critic," *Free Rev.*, V (Oct. 1, 1895), 39–43.

"Mark Twain Up-To-Date," *Idler*, IX (July, 1896), 901–906.

"Mark Twain, Benefactor," *Academy*, LI (June 26, 1897), 653–655.

"Mark Twain," *Rev. of Reviews*, XVI (Aug., 1897), 123–133.

Robert Barr, "Samuel L. Clemens, 'Mark Twain,' " *Idler*, XIII (Feb., 1898), 22–29.

Charles W. Dilke, "The Real Mark Twain," *Pall Mall Mag.*, XVI (Sept., 1898), 29–38.

Anne E. Keeling, "American Humour: Mark Twain," *London Quart. Rev.*, XCII (July, 1899), 147–162.

"Mr. Kipling and Mark Twain," *Academy*, LVIII (March 17, 1900), 237.

J. E. Hodder Williams, "Mark Twain," *Bookman*, XVIII (Sept., 1900), 169–174.

See also under *Humor:* 1876.

Ward, Artemus. "Mister Artemus Ward, His Book," *Eclectic Rev.*, 8th Ser., VIII (April, 1865), 348–356.

"Artemus Ward," *Chambers's Jour. of Popular Literature*, 4th Ser., II (June 10, 1865), 357–361.

G. J. H. Northcroft, "Artemus Ward, the Baldinsville Showman," *Time*, New Ser., VII (April, 1888), 452–457.

See also under *Humor:* 1876.

Ware, William. S., "Letters from Palmyra," *Westminster Rev.*, XXVIII (Jan., 1838), 436–470.

Warner, Charles Dudley. W. Davenport Adams, "A New American Humorist," *London Society*, XXVI (Dec., 1874), 487–495. See also under *General:* 1883.

Westcott, Edward Noyes. E. A. B., "'David Harum.' An Enquiry," *Academy*, LVII (Sept. 16, 1899), 289–290.

White, Richard Grant. Sir Nathaniel, "Richard Grant White," *New Monthly Mag.*, CII (Nov., 1854), 283–294.

Whitman, Walt. Moncure D. Conway, "Walt Whitman," *Fortnightly Rev.*, VI (Oct. 15, 1866), 538–548.

    Robert Buchanan, "Walt Whitman," *Broadway*, I (Nov., 1867), 188–195.

    Edward Dowden, "The Poetry of Democracy: Walt Whitman," *Westminster Rev.*, New Ser., XL (July, 1871), 33–68.

    Roden Noel, "A Study of Walt Whitman, the Poet of Modern Democracy," *Dark Blue*, II (Oct. and Nov., 1871), 241–253, 336–349.

    "Walt Whitman," *Once A Week*, XXVI (June 1, 1872), 501–505.

    T. S. Omond, "Is Verse a Trammel?" *Gentleman's Mag.*, CCXXXVI (March, 1875), 344–354.

    Arthur Clive, "Walt Whitman, the Poet of Joy," *Gentleman's Mag.*, CCXXXVII (Nov., 1875), 704–716.

    "Walt Whitman," *Cope's Tobacco Plant*, I (Dec., 1875), 834.

    Peter Bayne, "Walt Whitman's Poems," *Contemporary Rev.*, XXVII (Dec., 1875), 49–69.

    "Walt Whitman," *Saturday Rev.*, XLI (March 18, 1876), 360–361.

    R. L. Stevenson, "The Gospel According to Walt Whitman," *New Quart. Mag.*, X (Oct., 1878), 461–481.

    James Thomson, "Walt Whitman," *Cope's Tobacco Plant*, II (May, June, Aug., Sept., Dec., 1880), 471–473, 483–485, 508–510, 522–524, 558–559.

    G. C. Macaulay, "Walt Whitman," *Nineteenth Century*, XII (Dec., 1882), 903–918.

    "Walt Whitman," *Scottish Rev.*, II (Sept., 1883), 281–300.

    A. C. Swinburne, "Whitmania," *Fortnightly Rev.*, New Ser., XLII (Aug., 1887), 170–176.

    Walter Lewin, "Leaves of Grass," *Murray's Mag.*, II (Sept., 1887), 327–339.

    Gabriel Sarrazin, "Walt Whitman," *Universal Rev.*, VI (Feb., 1890), 247–269.

    "Walt Whitman," *Black and White*, III (April 2, 1892), 424–426.

    R., "Recollections of Walt Whitman," *Illustrated London News*, C (April 2, 1892), 418.

Pauline W. Roose, "A Child-Poet: Walt Whitman," *Gentleman's Mag.*, CCLXXII (May, 1892), 464–480.

"Walt Whitman," *Temple Bar*, XCIX (Oct., 1893), 252–259.

Edmund Gosse, "A Note on Walt Whitman," *New Rev.*, X (April, 1894), 447–457.

Grace Gilchrist, "Chats with Walt Whitman," *Temple Bar*, CXIII (Feb., 1898), 200–212.

R. Corlett Cowell, "The Wound-Dresser," *London Quart. Rev.*, XCI (Jan., 1899), 87–97.

J. A. MacCulloch, "Walt Whitman: the Poet of Brotherhood," *Westminster Rev.*, CLII (Nov., 1899), 548–564.

See also under *General:* 1857, 1899.

Whitney, Adeline. Keningale Cook, "Adeline Whitney," *Belgravia*, XVIII (Oct., 1872), 506–516.

Whittier, John Greenleaf. "Home Ballads and Poems," *North British Rev.*, XXXIV (Nov., 1860), 210–217.

"Whittier's Poems," *Eclectic Rev.*, 8th Ser., I (Sept., 1861), 351–362.

H. Savile Clarke, "The American Poet Whittier," *Cassell's Mag.*, 1885, pp. 696–698.

R. E. Prothero, "John Greenleaf Whittier," *London Society*, IX (Dec., 1886), 182–189.

"John Greenleaf Whittier," *London Quart. Rev.*, LXXXIX (Oct., 1892), 224–244.

T. Cuthbert Hadden, "The Quaker Poet," *Gentleman's Mag.*, CCLXXIII (Oct., 1892), 408–417.

Mary Negreponte, "John Greenleaf Whittier," *Westminster Rev.*, CXXXIX (Jan., 1893), 7–11.

Isabella F. Mayo, "Whittier, the Quaker Poet," *Leisure Hour*, XLII (Jan., 1893), 164–170.

"Whittier's 'Barbara Frietchie,'" *Leisure Hour*, XLII (May, 1893), 485–486.

C. E. Tyrer, "Whittier's Poem on the Rose," *Manchester Quart.*, XIII (July, 1894), 287–292.

See also under *General:* 1887.

Wigglesworth, Michael. "New England Puritan Literature: Michael Wigglesworth," *London Quart. Rev.*, XXXIX (Oct., 1872), 118–131.

Wilkins, Mary Eleanor. "Mary E. Wilkins," *Bookman*, I (Dec., 1891), 102–103.

See also under *Fiction:* 1898.

Williams, Roger. Tal-a-Hen, "Roger Williams," *Red Dragon*, V (Jan., 1884), 1–18.

Willis, Nathaniel Parker. "Willis's Poems," *Blackwood's*, XXXVIII (Aug., 1835), 257–268.

Willis, Nathaniel Parker (continued)

"Willis's *Pencillings by the Way*," *Quart. Rev.*, LIV (Sept., 1835), 455–469.

"Willis's Pencillings," *British and Foreign Rev.*, II (Jan., 1836), 145–156.

"Willis's *Pencillings by the Way*," *Edinburgh Rev.*, LXII (Jan., 1836), 346–358.

"Willis' Pencillings by the Way," *Dublin University Mag.*, VII (March, 1836), 314–327.

C. A. H., "Willis's Sketches," *Westminster Rev.*, XXV (July, 1836), 466–485.

"Willis's *Dashes of Life*," *Edinburgh Rev.*, LXXXII (Oct., 1845), 470–480.

Sir Nathaniel, "N. P. Willis," *New Monthly Mag.*, XCIX (Dec., 1853), 425–429.

Winthrop, John. "Life and Letters of Governor Winthrop," *Blackwood's*, CII (Aug., 1867), 170–187.

Winthrop, Theodore. "American Novelists: Theodore Winthrop," *Westminster Rev.*, New Ser., XXVIII (July, 1865), 163–185.

Woolman, John. "Saint John Woolman," *Eclectic Rev.*, 7th Ser., V (June, 1861), 559–578.

INDEX

Abbott, Jacob, 26, 27
Academy, and *Literature,* 62
Academy of Letters, proposed, 141
Adams, Charles Francis, 8; letter from Leslie Stephen, 9
Adams, Henry, *re* American influence on European politics, 5; contributions to British reviews, 56; *Democracy,* 141
Ainsworth's, on Longfellow, 111
Alcott, Louisa May, 23, 26, 28, 71, 149
Aldrich, Thomas Bailey, 28, 36, 90, 97
Allen, Grant, on American humor, 98
Allen, James Lane, *A Kentucky Cardinal,* 129
Allen, John Barrow, 98n
All the Year Round, quoted, on American humor, 92
Amberley, Lord, quoted, on Longfellow, 100
American authors, *see* Authors
American Humourists, 96
American literature, reception conditioned by political and social views, 10, 136, 149; the product of the middle class, 11 f.; publication of first editions abroad, 14 ff., 34 ff.; criticism of early works, 14n; in English series publications, 20 ff.; humorists in English series, 23; sentimental school, 23, 26, 71; price of books first published in England, 32; importations, 39 ff.; English bibliographical guides to, 41 ff.; popularity, 46; dealers in, 64 f.; critical opinion of, 127-50; charges of imitation, 128 f., 131; demand for native background, 128 f., 131; new school in, 130; chief devotees in England, 132; introductions written by English men of letters, 134; English works on individual authors, 134; English works on history and criticism of, 137; absorbed into the body of English literature, 137, 140; influence in England, 143
American Miscellany, 53

American Revolution, effect on foreign interest in America, 14 f.
Americans, sensitivity to European opinion, 2
American Settler, 61n
American Traveller, 61n
Andersen, Hans, 27n
Anderson, Charles, "Melville's English Debut," 34n
Anglo-American Association, 7
Anglo-American News, 61n
Anglo-American relations, animosities, 2 ff.; new era in, 6 f.
Anglo-American Times, 61n
Annual Register, 107 f.
Anthologies, of American humor, 78 f., 86 f.; Griswold's, 134; of American poetry, 136 f.; of British and American works, list of, 137n
Anthon, Charles, 45
Anti-Philistine, 64
Appleton, Daniel, branch in England, 37
Archer, William, 6; on *Huckleberry Finn,* 129
Aristocracy, English, attitude toward America, 2 f., 6, 9
Arnold, Matthew, 148n; *re* American influence on England, 5n; quoted, 6; *re* American literature, 129; influence of American literature on, 143 f.; and Emerson, 146
"Art for art's sake," 130 f.
Athenæum, 18; and Longfellow, 104; on "America and American Writers," 127
Atherton, Gertrude, 18, 36, 56, 63, 64, 94; *Adventures of a Novelist,* 94n
Atlantic Monthly, Fun quoted on, 68; Dent quoted on, 69
Austin, Alfred, "A Voice from the West," quoted, 8
Authors, American, residence abroad and copyright, 17, 18, 33; in English series, 20 ff.; as contributors to English periodicals, 50 ff.; charges of unoriginality, 51n, 128; in English "libraries" of humor, 90; in cheap reprints, 94;

Authors, American (*Continued*)
English works on individual, 134; chief subjects of critical articles, 138 f.; effect of British approval on American reputation, 142 ff.
Authors, English, attitude toward and friendships with American authors, 132 f.

Balfe, Michael W., 103
Ball, James, *Dr. Oliver Wendell Holmes and His Works*, 135
Ballot Act of 1872, 5
Bancroft, George, 22
Bangs, John Kendrick, editor of *Literature*, 62
Barlow, Joel, scant English interest in, 71
Barnum, P. T., article on, in *Tait's Edinburgh Magazine*, 81 f.
Barr, Robert, 59
Bartram, William, influence of, 144
Bay Psalm Book, British editions, 14
"Beadle's American Library," 22
Beeton, Samuel O., 29; "Beeton's Humorous Books," 24, 95
Bell and Daldy, "Elzevir Series of Standard Authors," 23
Bennett, William Cox, 125
Bennoch, Francis, 125
Benson, A. C., 146
Bentley, Richard, "Standard Novels and Romances," 21; publication of American works, 35; *Bentley's Miscellany*, Longfellow in, 105
Bent's Monthly Literary Advertiser, 41
Besant, Sir Walter, 8; *Autobiography*, 70n
Best sellers, 22
Bibliographical guides to American literature, in England, 41 ff.
Bierce, Ambrose, 64, 94
Billings, Josh, 23, 86, 87, 90; *Spectator* on, 93
Blackwood's, articles on American writers, 54; comment on the *Century*, 69; quoted, on the influence of American works, 91 f.; on Longfellow, 112
Blessington, Lady, 55
Blodgett, Harold, *Walt Whitman in England*, 43n
Bogue, David, 29; "Miniature Classical Library," 22
Bohn, Henry G., 20, 35; "Bohn's Standard Library," 136

Bookman (London), on the New York *Nation*, 69
Bookseller, announcements of American books, 90
Booksellers' Association, in England, 20
Bookstores, 39 ff.
Booktrade, Anglo-American, 14-46, 48; transatlantic branch houses, 36 ff.; predominance of American works in, 46; Longfellow and, 106; quantity of books sold, 141
Braye, Lord, 125
Bright, Henry, 101n
Bright, John, quoted, *re* Anglo-American relations, 3
British musicians, settings for Longfellow's poems, 103
Broadway, 60 f.
Brock, Thomas, bust of Longfellow, 126
Brown, Charles Brockden, 21; English reprints, 15
Browning, Elizabeth Barrett, 120
Browning, Robert, and Longfellow, 119
Brownson, Orestes, 45n
Brussel, Isadore R., *Anglo-American First Editions*, 33n
Bryant, William Cullen, 26, 46, 51, 52, 61n, 139; "Lectures on Poetry," 11; "To a Waterfowl," 50
Bryce, James, *American Commonwealth*, 7, 9
Bulwer-Lytton, Edward, 1st Baron, *The Crisis*, 31; quoted, on newspapers in America and England, 47n; *Personal and Literary Letters*, 96n
Bunner, H. C., humor of, 97
Burgess, Gelett, 94
Burns, Robert, 32n
Burroughs, John, 36, 58, 129, 143
Byron, Lord, price paid for *Don Juan*, 34

Cable, George W., 25, 36, 56; and Barrie, 134
Cairns, William B., "British Republication of American Writings, 1783–1833," 15n; *British Criticisms of American Writings, 1815–1833*, 50n
California, popularity of tales of, 93 f.
Cambridge University, proposed lectureship on American institutions, 4
Cameron and Ferguson, publications of Negro humor, 76
"Canadian copyright," 17, 25, 33

Carlson, C. Lennart, "Richard Lewis and the Reception of His Work in England," 50n

Carlyle, Thomas, 1, 12; literary friendships, 133

Carroll, Lewis, 28

Cary, Phoebe, 52, 61

Cassell and American reprints, 24; branch in America, 37

Century, *Blackwood's* comment on, 69

Chambers, W. and R., 19; *Hand-Book of American Literature,* 137

Chambers' Edinburgh Journal, American contributors to, 51

Channing, William Ellery, 16, 22, 26, 51, 52, 100, 132, 146, 148; English critics *re,* 127; critical estimate of, 138

Chap-Book (Chicago), 64

Chapman, John, 147n; publication of American works, 34, 35; importer of American books, 42 f.; *re* English tax on imported books, 44n; and the *Dial,* 60

Chatto and Windus, 36; and American reprints, 24; Twain and, 25; books of American humor, 95 f.

Cheap book, 18; works on history of, 19n; in the English series, 20 ff.; American humor, 82 ff., 90, 95; American reprints, 82 ff., 94

"Cheap Series," 22

Child, Lydia M., 50, 51

Children's books, *see* Juvenile literature

Civil War, English reaction, 3, 4n, 91, 148

Clarke, H. G., 29, 106

Clavel, Marcel, *Fenimore Cooper and His Critics,* 129n

Clements, J., 21

Clough, Arthur, 115n; *Bothie,* 99n

Cole, Henry, quoted, *re* children's books, 27

Coleridge-Taylor, Samuel, musical settings for Longfellow's poems, 103

Colvin, Sidney, on Hawthorne, 139

Commonwealth Fellows, 93

Connecticut Wits, *see* Hartford Wits

Constable & Co., 19

Contemporary Review, American contributors to, 56

Conway, Moncure, 33, 35, 61, contributions to English reviews, 55 f.; and Carlyle, 133

Cook, Keningale, 139n

"Coon song," 74 f.

Cooper, James Fenimore, 16, 21, 22, 23, 26, 33, 46, 51, 53, 128, 129n, 148, 149; price paid for earlier novels, 35; *Gleanings in Europe,* 72n; critical discussion of, 127, 138, 141, 142, 143

Cooper, Thomas, on Emerson, 132

Copyright, history of, 16 ff.; legislation, 16n; and first publication, 16 f., 33 ff., 39, 95; and residence, 17, 18, 33, 42; effect on English criticism of American works, 18; Act of 1891, 25n, 36, 38, 63, 95

Cornhill Magazine, 69n, 122; American contributors to, 56; *Fun* quoted on, 68

Cosmopolis, 62

Crane, Stephen, 18, 59, 63; contributions to English periodicals, 58; *Red Badge of Courage,* 36, 57, 98n

Crawford, Francis Marion, 33, 57, 59

Critic (New York), 69

Critics, English, on American literature, 127-50; demand for native materials, 128; characteristics of devotees of American literature, 132; friendships with American authors, 133; estimate of individual American authors, 138 ff.; influence of, in America, 142; *see also* Periodicals

Crockett, Davy, 76 f.

Cruse, Amy, *The Victorians and Their Reading,* 102n

Cummins, Maria, 22, 23, 24, 26; Kingsley vs., 143

Cunningham, *see* Elliott

Curtis, George W., 36

Damon, S., Foster, 11n

Dante, Longfellow's translation, 102

Dark Blue, 58

Darley, George, on American poets, 117

Darwin, Charles, *The Origin of Species,* 70

Darwin, Erasmus, on Timothy Dwight, 72

Davis, Charles A., 76n

Deland, Margaret, *John Ward, Preacher,* 59

Delf, Thomas, 40

De luxe editions, 32

Democracy, American, influence on England, 10-12

Dent, John C., *re* American magazines, 69

Dial, 59 f.

Dickens, Charles, 32*n*; *Pickwick Papers,* quoted, 5-6; and Bret Harte, 65; influence of Irving on, 72 f.; as editor of *The Pic-Nic Papers,* 81; Longfellow's friendship with, 116 f.; *Household Words,* 117; attitude toward America, 132

Dickinson, Emily, 139

Dime novels, 22; Beadle, 77*n*

Disraeli, Benjamin, Act of 1867, 5

Dobson, Austin, 84*n*

Dodge, Mary Mapes, 23; *Hans Brinker,* 26*n*

Douglas, David, 26, 36

Downing, Jack, 23, 86; stock character, 76 f.

Doyle, Conan, 144; dedication of *The White Company,* 8

Dublin University Magazine on Longfellow, 111

Duffy's Fireside Magazine, on Longfellow, 112

Dunne, Peter Finley, "Mr. Dooley," 97

Duyckinck, Evert, 61

Dwight, Timothy, reputation in England, 71 f.

Eclectic Review, on Longfellow, 111

Edwards, Jonathan, 14

Eliot, George, 31*n*, 68*n*, 139*n*, 143, 144; on *Hiawatha* and *The Scarlet Letter,* 120; and Emerson, 147

Elliott, Ebenezer, on Longfellow, 118

Elliott and Cunningham, "Novel Newspaper," 53

Emerson, Ralph Waldo, 11, 12, 22, 24, 26, 35, 46, 52, 59, 100, 128; quoted, 7; circulation of *Nature,* 60*n*; as humorist, 97; critical opinion of, 132, 138, 139, 142, 143; and Carlyle, 133, 134; introduction writers, 134; works on, by English authors, 134 f.; influence of, 145 ff.

England, causes of change in attitude, c. 1870, toward America, 6; population, 6*n*; ignorance of America, 7, 9; literature for the masses, 18 ff.; popularity of American works in, 46; expansion of the reading public, 104

English authors, *see* Authors

English Catalogue, The, 22 f., 45

English Illustrated Magazine, American contributors to, 59

English literature, influence on America, 10-11; published in America, 43

English-speaking Unions, 7, 61

Essays, collections, 140

Evangeline, 99*n*, 106, 107, 117, 120; critical opinion of, 109, 110 f., 113, 114, 118

Farrah, Frederick, 91*n*

Faust, Bertha, *Hawthorne's Contemporaneous Reputation,* 129*n*

Field, Eugene, 64

Fields, James T., 56*n*; *Yesterdays with Authors,* 102*n*

Firebaugh, Joseph J., "Samuel Rogers and American Men of Letters," 133*n*

Fiske, John, 4*n*

First editions, of American works abroad, 14 ff.

First publication, and copyright, 16 f., 33 ff., 39, 95; price of American works abroad, 32

Fisher's River Scenes and Characters, 82*n*

Fiske, John, lectures on the United States, 4*n*

Fleming, Canon, on Longfellow, 124

Flint, Timothy, 53, 78; contributions to the *Athenæum,* 54

Follen, Eliza, 21

Fortnightly, on Longfellow, 113 f.

Forster, John, correspondence with Longfellow, 116*n*

Franklin, Benjamin, 26, 50, 72*n*, 80, 131

Fraser's Magazine, on Longfellow, 112 f.; quoted, 109

Frederic, Harold, 36, 59, 63

Freeland, Humphry W., 101*n*

Freeman, Mary Wilkins, 58, 59

Freneau, Philip, 11, 72

Frontier, in "native" American humor, 78 f.; English interest in tales of, 93

Froude, James H., 145

Fuller, Margaret, 37, 115, 139*n*, 143

Fun, "Some magazines for June" (1875), 68

Fun for the Million, American humor in, 73

Gandhi, Mohandas K., influence of Thoreau, 149

Garfield, James A., resolutions on the death of, 8n
Garnett, Richard, study on Emerson, 134 f.
Germany, threat of ascendancy, 6, 8
Gilfillan, George, on Longfellow, 102
Gladstone, William E., 132; re new books published in England, 19
Goodrich, Samuel, 51; "Peter Pauley" Series, 27
Gosse, Edmund, on Holmes, 85
Gostwick, Joseph, 136n; *Hand-Book of American Literature*, 137
Granville, Lord, 125
Gray, Thomas, 126
Great Thoughts from Master Minds, 52
"Great Writers Series," 135
Green, John, "Standard American Literature," 21
Griswold, Rufus, anthologies, 134; on Poe, 135n
Growell, Adolph, *Book-Trade Bibliography in the United States in the XIXth Century*, 40n
Guiney, Louise I., 59

Habberton, John, 90; *Helen's Babies*, 90n
Haliburton, Thomas Chandler, reception of Sam Slick in England, 76 f.; anthologies of humor, 78, 80
Hans Breitmann, 36; success in England, 87 ff.
Hardy, Thomas, on Twain, 129; reception in America 130n
Harlan, Lee, 20n, 116n
Harland, Henry, 59
Harmsworth, Alfred, *see* Northcliffe
Harper, J. Henry, *The House of Harper*, 38n
Harpers, 37 f.
Harper's, circulation in England, 66 ff.
Harris, Joel Chandler, 26, 28n, 36, 58, 59, *Uncle Remus*, 28; *Punch* on Uncle Remus, 76
Harris, Julia Collier, "Uncle Remus at Home and Abroad," 28n
Harrison, Frederic, on *Uncle Tom's Cabin*, quoted, 30; on Longfellow, 123
Harrow, vote for Longfellow, 100
Harte, Bret, 10, 18, 23, 24, 33, 58, 59, 64, 87, 89, 90, 91, 92, 94, 96, 128,

139, 141, 148, 149; in the cheap series, 26; reputation in England, 65; anthology of western poets, 93; re American humor, 98n; and Tom Hood, 134; effect of British approval, 143; influence on Kipling, 144
Hartford Wits, 71 f.
Harvard University, 4
Hatton, John L., 103
Haweis, Hugh R., 134; lectures on American humor, 96
Hawthorne, Julian, 24, 33, 57, 59
Hawthorne, Nathaniel, 10, 11, 23, 26, 33, 37, 46, 52, 80, 135, 139, 141, 143; "The Celestial Railroad," 97; re Longfellow's vogue, 100; popularity, 128; *The Scarlet Letter*, 138; critical estimate of, 139; *Transformation (The Marble Faun)*, 18, 128
Hay, John, humorous verses of, 92n
Hazlitt, William, comparison of Irving and Lamb, 12n
Heindel, Richard H., 61n; *The American Impact on Great Britain 1898–1914*, 8n, 49n
Heinemann, William, 36
Herald (New York), 47; influence in England, 49
Hiawatha, 106, 107, 109, 111, 114, 118; parodies, 103 f.
Hildreth, Richard, 22
Hingston, Edward P., *The Genial Showman*, 135
Historians, American, 131
Hodgson, "Parlour Library," 22
Hogg's Instructor, American contributors to, 51 f.
Holland, J. G., 52
Holmes, Oliver Wendell, 22, 23, 26, 33, 36, 40n, 46, 86, 90, 91, 96, 134n, 139; *Poems*, 40n; reputation in England, 83 ff.; *The Autocrat*, 84, 87, 89; Ball's study on, 135; and realism, 130n
Home Circle, 51
Hotten, John C., 24, 36, 43; edition of *The Biglow Papers*, 82 f.; chief distributor of American humor, 86; reprints of Ward, 86; cheap American reprints, 94; first English publisher of Whitman, 94
Houghton, Lord, and Longfellow, 102; literary friendships, 133

Howells, William Dean, 25 f., 35, 36, 46, 61, 63, 129*n*, 139, 143; *Criticism and Fiction*, 12; copyright, 25 f.; *Venetian Life*, 35; quoted, on English periodicals, 49; quoted, on simultaneous publication, 57; articles for *Literature*, 62 f.; as humorist, 97

Hows, John W. S., 136*n*

Hubbard, Elbert, *Philistine*, 64

Hughes, Hugh Price, 8

Hughes, Thomas, 5; and the Anglo-American Association, 7, 134; and Lowell, 83

Humor, American, 35; reception in England, 71-98; stock characters in, 73 f., 76; importations into England, 77; anthologies, 78 f., 86 f.; English reviewers on the character of, 81 f.; causes for phenomenal success in England, 91; reprints, 82 ff., 90, 95; superior quality of, 92; authorized editions, 95 f.; English critics *re*, 129; influence in England, 149 f.

Humphreys, David, 72; *The Yankey in England*, 74

Hunt, William Holman, on Longfellow, 103*n*

Hutton, R. H., on Longfellow, 124

Illustrated London News, 30, 109*n*; quoted, *re* American humor, 80; quoted, on Longfellow, 101

Illustration, superiority of American methods, 67 f.

Ingraham, J. H., 26

Ingram, John H., *Edgar Allan Poe*, 135

Introduction for English reprints, 107, 134

Irish Penny Journal, 51

Irish Penny Magazine, 51

Irving, Washington, 16, 18, 22, 23, 24, 26, 33, 46, 51, 56, 80, 96, 132, 143, 149; "English Writers on America" 2 f.; Hazlitt on, 12*n*; and Murray, 34; biography of Goldsmith, 35*n*; proposed editorship of a British magazine, 54; reputation in England and influence on Dickens, 72 f.; English critics *re*, 127, 138; influence of, 144 f.

James, Henry, 18, 23, 24, 33, 36, 57, 58, 59, 63, 139, 141, 143; contributions to English periodicals, 57, 62, 63; articles for *Literature*, 62; *re Helen's Babies*, 90*n*; as humorist, 97; *Transatlantic Sketches*, 128; Howells *re* the art of, 130; influence of, 144

Jerrold, Walter, 135

Jewett, Sarah Orne, 57, 58; *The King of Folly Island*, 130 f.

Johnson, Merle, 89

Johnson, Samuel, 142*n*

Jonathan, stock character in American humor, 73 f.

Jonathan Slick, 80

Jordan, William, *Yankee Humour*, 79

Jowett, Benjamin, 139*n*

Juvenile literature, 26 ff., 44; popularity in England, 28; magazines, 69

Kerr, Orpheus C., 85, 86, 98

Kingsley, Charles, 93; course on American history, 4 f; influence of American authors on, 143

Kipling, Rudyard, *re* influence of Harte, 144*n*

Klingberg, F. S., "Harriet Beecher Stowe and Social Reform in England," 30*n*

Knight, Charles, 19; quoted, *re* series publications, 21*n*; quoted, on the cheap periodical, 51

Lamb, Charles, Hazlitt on, 12*n*

Lane, John, branch in America, 37

Lang, Andrew, 134*n*; on Longfellow, 124

Lanier, Sidney, *The Boy's Froissart*, 67*n*, 70*n*

Lathrop, George Parsons, 59

Le Gallienne, Richard, *re* Lanier's poems, 70*n*

Leland, Charles Godfrey, 33, 36, 58, 91, 92, 94; success in England, 87 ff.; *Pidgin English Sing-Song*, 89

Lewin, Walter, 134*n*

"Libraries," *see* Series

Lilly, William S., lecture on "The Theory of the Ludicrous," 96; *Studies in Religion and Literature*, 96*n*

Lincoln, Abraham, 4; enjoyment of tall tales, 91

Linton, W. J., *Poetry of America*, 136

Literary piracy, *see* Piracy, literary

Literature, 62

Local color, 76, 95, 97, 128 f.

Locker, Frederick, on Holmes, 85

Lockhart, John G., on Longfellow, 109

London University, 4*n*

Longfellow, Henry, 11, 23, 24, 26, 33, 52, 56, 59, 97, 145*n*; verses composed in his honor, 101; translations, 102, 114; British visitors, 102 f.; musical settings for his poems, 103; parodies of his verse, 103 f.; reprints of favorite poems, 104 f.; British imprints, 32, 105 ff.; piracy of his works, 106 f.; collections, 106; prices of British editions, 107; introduction for his works, 107; quoted, on reviews of Hiawatha, 109; journalistic reviewers on, 108 ff.; critical articles analyzed, 110 ff.; shorter lyrics, 111 ff.; critical opinion of British men of letters, 115 ff.; and the Rossettis, 118*n*; American critics, 115; visits to and friendships in England, 115 ff.; correspondence with European authors, 116; bust in Westminster Abbey, 124 ff.; popularity, 128, 148; critical estimate of, 28, 138, 139, 142 f.

—— Works: *Evangeline*, 106, 107, 109, 110 f., 113, 114, 117, 118, 120; *The Golden Legend*, 112 f., 121; *Hiawatha*, 106, 107, 109, 111, 114, 118; parodies, 103 f.; *Kavanagh*, 112, 113; *Hyperion*, 106, 107, 111, 113, 122; *The Masque of Pandora*, 110; *Miles Standish*, 110; *Outre-Mer*, 40*n*, 105; *Paul Revere's Ride*, 114; *The Spanish Student*, 112; *Voices of the Night*, 113

Longmans, branch in America, 35, 36

Longman's Magazine, American contributors to, 58 f.

Low, Sampson, 45, 82*n*; "Copyright Editions of American Authors," 22 f.; "Rose Library," 26; and *Uncle Tom's Cabin*, 29; and the American booktrade, 36, 42; *The American Catalogue of Books*, 42

Lowell, James Russell, 10, 26, 33, 46, 52, 85, 90, 91, 94, 96, 132, 134*n*, 139, 142, 149*n*; "On a Certain Condescension in Foreigners," 3; *A Fable for Critics*, quoted, 7; *re* a true lyric, 12; *Among My Books*, 39; *The Biglow Papers*, 82 f., 86, 87, 89, 92, 104*n*; Lilly on, 96; *re* Thoreau's humor, 97; speech on Longfellow, in Westminster Abbey, 126; and Fitzgerald, 133; critical estimate of, 140; and Leslie Stephen, 144

Macaulay, Thomas B., quoted, on English vs. American publication of his works, 43 f.

McCarthy, Justin, on Longfellow, 124

McCrie, George, quoted, on Longfellow, 108

Macmillan, Alexander, 37*n*

Macmillan (London), 36, 38*n*; branch in America, 37

Magazines, *see* Periodicals

Mahan, Alfred T., 141

Major Jack Downing, 76*n*

Marston, Edward, 43*n*; *re* new books and reprints, 25*n*

Martineau, James, 147*n*

Marvel, Ik, 97

Masses, the, American works written for, 12; publication of books for, in England, 18 ff.; works preferred by, 31 f.; reading habits, 47; periodicals for, 50 ff.; effect of American literature on, 149 f.

Mather, Increase, publication abroad, 14, 22

Mathews, Charles, *Trip to America*, 73 f.; adaptation of Humphrey's, *The Yankee in England*, 74

Matthews, Brander, 58, 59; on literary piracy, 24

Meiklejohn, J. M. D., quoted, on Longfellow, 108

Melville, Herman, 22, 26, 35, 36, 46, 139; *Typee* and *Omoo*, 34

Meredith, George, 139*n*; reception in America, 130*n*

Mesick, Jane L., *The English Traveller in America 1785–1835*, 47n

Mill, John S., 4*n*, 5

Miller, Joaquin, 33, 93, 94, 132, 139; contributions to English journals, 58, 64; critical estimate of, 141

"Miller of Black Friars," 40

Minstrel Show, 75

Mitford, Mary Russell, anthologies of American stories, 78 f.; on Holmes, 84; on Longfellow, 120 f., quoted, 121

Moncrieff, William T., *Tarnation Strange*, 75*n*

Morley, John, 70*n*; introduction for Emerson's works, 134; influence of Emerson on, 145 f.

Motley, John L., 10, 56, 88, 131; *History of the United Netherlands*, 34

Moulton, Louise Chandler, 139; contributions to English journals, 58, 59
Moxon, Edward, edition of Longfellow, 105 f.
Mudie's Select Library, 32, 46*n*, 60*n*, 93; circulation of American magazines, 68
Muirhead, James F., quoted, on American humor, 97; *American Shrines on English Soil*, 126*n*
Müller, Max, 69*n*; on Emerson, 146
Murdoch, Frank, *Davy Crockett*, 77*n*
Murray, John, publication of American works, 34 f.

Nasby, Petroleum V., 86
Nast, Thomas, 92*n*
Nation (New York), Leslie Stephen *re*, 69
National Observer, quoted, on American humor, 93
National Review, on Longfellow, 105, 113
Neal, John, 33, 40, 54
Neal, Joseph C., *Charcoal Sketches*, 81*n*
Negro humor, 75 f.
Nelson, T., branch in America, 37
Nevins, Allan, *American Social History as Recorded by British Travellers*, 6*n*
New books, 25*n*; English publication of, 19 f.
New Monthly Magazine, on Longfellow, 113
Newspapers, American, production, 47; and spread of American humor, 91 f.; influence of, 49, 149
Nichol, John, on Twain's influence, 92*n*; work on American literature, 137 f.
Noble, James Ashcroft, review of *The King of Folly Island*, 130 f.
Norman, Henry, essay on Longfellow, 113 f.
Northcliffe, Lord, *Daily Mail*, 49
Norton, Charles Eliot, and Carlyle, 133
Noyes, Alfred, 132*n*; "The Undiscovered Longfellow," 115*n*
Nutt, David, 40
Nye, Bill, 25, 95

Osgood, James R., McIlvaine and Co., 38
Oxford University Press, branch in America, 37

Palgrave, Francis Turner, on Longfellow, 116*n*
Paper, English tax on, 19, 47*n*, 50
Parker, Theodore, 52, 146, 147*n*
Parley, Peter, 26, 27
"Parlour Library," 21*n*; American works in, 22
Patmore, Coventry, on Longfellow, 118*n*
Paul, Henry Howard, *Dashes of American Humor*, 79
Payne, J. B., plan for a series of English poets, 108*n*
Peabody, George, 124 f.
Penny Magazine, American contributors to, 50
People's Journal, 60*n*
Periodicals, 47-70; cheap, 50 ff.; intellectual, piracy in, 53 ff.; international, 59 ff.; American and English compared, 67 ff.
—— American, British contributions to, 48; effect on English periodicals, 49 ff.; success in Great Britain, 64 ff.; British agents, 65 ff.; superiority of illustrations, 67; estimated number of, 67*n*; quantity imported into Great Britain, 67 f.; quality of, 68 ff.; introduced American authors in England, 70
—— English, American editions, 48 f.; original transatlantic contributions to, 53 f.; Howells *re*, quoted, 49; American contributors to, 50 ff.; increase in, after 1870, 57; special departments devoted to American works, 133; quantity of articles on American literature, 138
"Peter Parley" Series, 27
Phelps, Elizabeth Stuart, 23, 26, 71
Phillips, George Searle, study on Emerson, 135
Pic-Nic Papers, The, 81
Pickwick Papers (Dickens), quoted, 5-6
Piracy, literary, 15, 16, 17, 24, 25, 29, 127, 142; in English cheap-book series, 25; of British critical journals in America, 48; in British intellectual periodicals, 53 ff.; *see also* Copyright
Plagiarism, Putnam *re*, 45*n*; *see also* Piracy, literary
Poe, Edgar Allan, 24, 26, 46, 51*n*, 134*n*, 139, 142; quoted, *re* the democratic appeal of the Short Story, 12; in the English series, 32; "The Raven," 41*n*; "The Gold Beetle," 51; charges of unoriginal-

ity, 51n; Ingram's biography of, 135; Griswold's study on, 135n; Saintsbury on, 140; influence of, 143 f.

Poetry, American, imitation in, 129; anthologies, 136

Pollard, Percival, 64

Porter, T. O., and the *Corsair,* 48

Porter, William T., 80

Prefaces, 134

Pre-Raphaelites, 117

Prescott, William H., 22, 51, 131, 143

Publishers, American, English works brought out by, 43; British, and books for the masses, 19 ff.; controlled market, 19 f.; transatlantic branch houses, 36 ff.; bookstores, 39 f.

Publishers' Circular, 18, 25n, 30, 42, 45; Longfellow items in, 106 f.

Publishing, simultaneous, 56 f.

Punch, 150n; "Americanism for Italy," 75; quoted, on *Uncle Remus,* 76; verse on Lowell, 83; verse on Holmes, 85

Putnam, George P., quoted, on plagiarism, 45n; on American works pirated in English journals, 53

Quarterly Journal of Education, piracy of American works, 53

Quarterly Review, Irving and, 54

Quinn, Arthur H., 135n

"Railway Libraries," 21; Holmes in, 84

Read, Opie, 64

Reade, Charles, asks more money of Harpers, 48

Realism, 130

Religious books, 45

Religious journals, 65, 67

Reprints, of American works in England, 11, 15, 21n, 33 ff., 53; and copyright, 17; and "cheap" books, 18; frequently not reviewed, 18; vs. new books, 19 f.; summary of history of, 20; of American works in England, classified, 45; introduction for, 134

Review of Reviews, career of, 63

Reviews, *see* Critics; Periodicals

Rhys, Ernest, "Camelot Series," 134

Rich, Obadiah, 40; editions of Murdoch's *David Crockett,* 76 f.; publisher of Holmes, 84

Richards, Irving T., "The Life and Works

of John Neal," 54n; "Longfellow in England," 115n

Riley, James Whitcomb, 64

Ripley, George, 43

Robertson, Eric S., *Life of Henry Wadsworth Longfellow,* 103n; on Longfellow, 112n

Robinson, Henry Crabb, 120n

"Robinson Crusoe," 32n

Roe, E. P., 23, 26

Rogers, Samuel, on Longfellow, 117; literary friendships, 133

Roosevelt, Franklin D., quotation from Longfellow, 99

Roscoe, William, *Specimens of the American Poets,* 136

Rosebery, Lord, and Longfellow, 102 f.

Rossetti, Dante, 117; quoted, on Longfellow, and Whitman, 118; Poe's influence on, 144

Rossetti, William M., 1868 edition of *Leaves of Grass,* 43; on Longfellow, 101, 108; on Whitman, 108; re Longfellow's bust in Westminster Abbey, 126; *American Poems,* 136

Routledge, George, 20, 77n; "Railway Libraries," 21; "Cheap Series," 22; American reprints, 23, 31; "Excelsior Series of Standard Authors," 23 f.; branch in America, 37; *Broadway,* 60 f.; series of American humor, 90; and Longfellow, 106, 110; price paid to Longfellow, 120

Ruskin, John, 132, 148; quoted, re Americans, 3; quoted, on Longfellow, 122

Russell, T. Baron, *Current Americanisms,* 95n

Russell, W. Clark, 44, 61n

St. Nicholas, 28

Saintsbury, George, *Selected Poems of Longfellow,* 115n; on Poe, 140

Salmon, Edward G., "What Girls Read," 28n

Saltus, Edgar, 64

Saltus, Francis, 64

Sam Slick, reception in England, 76 f.

Scarlet Letter, The, 79, 139n

Schiller, Friederich, 123

Scott, Walter, 32n; "Canterbury Poets," 24

Scott, William Bell, 43

Scribner's, English edition, 67

Sentimental school, 23, 26, 71
Series publication, 20 ff., 32; importance to sale of American books, 26; children's books in, 26 f.; "libraries" of humor, 90; *see also* Reprints
Shakespeare, William, 32n
Sharp, William, 24; *American Sonnets,* 136
Shaw, Albert, and *Review of Reviews,* 63
Shelta, 88
Shorthouse, J. H., quoted, on Longfellow, 123
Short Story, Poe on, 12; Mitford anthologies, 78 f.; tall tales, 78 f., 91
Simms, William G., 53
Simultaneous publication, 56 f.
Smalley, George W., *Studies of Men,* 84n
Smeaton, Oliphant, *Longfellow & His Poetry,* 115n
Smith, Alexander, 136n
Smith, J. R., "Library of Old Authors," 22
Smith, Sydney, 131
Smith, W. H., railway bookstalls, 21
Smith and Elder, 18
Society for the Diffusion of Useful Knowledge, 19
Socinianism, 4
Southworth, Mrs. E. D. E. N., contributions to English journals, 55
Spectator, quoted, on American humor, 92; quoted, on Josh Billings, 93
Spencer, Herbert, and Emerson, 146
Spenser, Edmund, 144
Spirit of the Times (New York), 78
Stead, W. T., 49; and *Review of Reviews,* 63; *James Russell Lowell,* 149
Stephen, Leslie, attitude toward America, 4; letter to Charles Francis Adams, quoted, 9
Stevenson, Morley, *The Spiritual Teaching of Longfellow,* 103n
Stockton, Frank R., 25, 26, 28, 36, 58, 59, 95, 97
Stoddard, Charles Warren, 94
Stoddard, R. H., 61
Stowe, Harriet Beecher, 22, 23, 24, 26, 28, 71, 134n, 139, 144, 148; *Uncle Tom's Cabin,* 29 ff., 75, 79, 100, 128, 132, 144; critical discussion of, 30, 138 f.; *Dred,* 39; attack on Lord Byron, 57; and George Eliot, 133
Sullivan, Sir Arthur, 103

Swinburne, Algernon Charles, *Poems and Ballads,* 43; on Longfellow, 123
Symonds, John A., study of Emerson, 134

Taine, Hippolyte, 128
Tait's Edinburgh Magazine, article on Barnum, quoted, 81 f.
Tall Tales, 78 f., 91
Tax, English, on paper, 19, 47n, 50; on imported books, 44n
Tegg, Thomas, 20
Temple Bar, quoted, on American humor, 92
Tennyson, Hallam, 118 f.
Tennyson, Alfred, Lord, and Longfellow, 116, 118 f.
Textbooks, American, in England, 44 f.
Thackeray, William M., 126n; on *The Autocrat,* 84; and Longfellow, 122 f
Theatre, English, popularity of American plays and actors, 75
Thomas, W. Moy, 136n
Thoreau, Henry D., 26, 36, 46, 97, 134n, 139, 145; English studies on, 135; influence on Gandhi, 149
Ticknor, George, 3n; on the American reading public, 12; and Wordsworth, 133
Times (London), 47; attitude toward the Civil War, 5; quoted, on *Uncle Tom's Cabin,* 30; on Longfellow, 100 f., 124n
Tinsley, William, 88
Tinsley's, 93
Traill, H. D., "The Future of Humour," 96 f.
Translations, of German and French works, 43
Trollope, Anthony, 31n
Trübner, Nicholas, 36; publication of American works, 35; importation of American books, 40; *re* the Anglo-American booktrade, 41n; *American and Oriental Library Record,* 41, 44, 65; *Bibliographical Guide to American Literature,* 41, 42; editions of *Hans Breitmann,* 86
Trumbull, John, *M'Fingal,* 72, 80
Tupper, Martin, and Longfellow, 108 f.
Twain, Mark, 11, 23, 24, 25, 28, 46, 87, 90, 91, 93 f., 96, 139, 141, 142, 149; quoted, *re* his appeal to the masses, 12; and Chatto and Windus, 25; in the cheap series, 26; "Cannibalism in the

Cars," 61; *A Connecticut Yankee,* 63; "The Tramp Abroad Again," 58; and *Harper's,* 70; English editions, 89 f.; *Screamers,* 92; and Hotten, 94; *Library of Humor,* 95; English reputation, 97; Hardy and Archer on, 129; effect of British reputation upon, 142

Tyler, Royall, English reprints, 15

Uncle Remus, 28
Uncle Tom's Cabin, 29 ff., 75, 79, 100, 128, 132, 144
United States, dominance of British blood and culture, 1; influence on English franchise and education, 5 f.; population, 6n; increasingly Anglophile attitude, 7; intellectual dependence on England, 15; interest in British authors, 33 f.; reading habit of the masses, 47

Victoria, queen of England, 125; on Longfellow, 101 f.
Vizetelly, Henry, 29
Voss, Johan H., *Louise,* 120

Waddington, Samuel, on American humor, 93; on Longfellow, 101
Wales, Prince of, 125
Wallace, Lew, 25
Ward, Artemus, 23, 79n, 85, 87, 89, 91, 93, 94, 97, 149; Hotten's reprints, 86; Hingston's study on, 135
Ward and Lock, series publications, 23
Ward, Lock and Tyler, "Home Treasury Library," 24
Warne and Co., "Star Series" and "Select Books," 24; branch in America, 37; and Longfellow, 106
Warner, Charles D., 23

Warner, Susan, 22, 23, 24, 26, 71; popularity in England, 28, 32; *The Wide Wide World,* 29, 31, 32; Kingsley vs., 143
Waterloo, Stanley, 64
Watson, Robert A., and Elizabeth S., *George Gilfillan,* 102n
Westminster Abbey, Longfellow's bust in, 124 ff.
Westminster Review, 61n, 62n; quoted, on Irving and Dickens, 73; quoted, on American humor, 80 f.
Whewell, William, quoted, on Longfellow, 109
Whitman, Walt, 11, 26, 46, 61, 94, 139, 145; in Scott's "Canterbury Poets," 24; *Leaves of Grass,* 43, 118, 134; "Whispers of Heavenly Death," 61; and Rossetti, 108, 126, 134; and Tennyson, 133; Nichol on, 138; works on, by English authors, 134; English appreciation of, 140 f.; Kingsley vs., 143; influence of, 144
Whittier, John Greenleaf, 26, 46, 52, 135, 139
Wilcox, Ella Wheeler, 59
Wiley and Putnam, 40; branch in England, 37
Willis, N. P., 33, 51; quoted on the *Corsair,* 48; contributions to English journals, 54 f.; and Barry Cornwall, 134; critical discussion of, 138
Woolson, Constance Fenimore, 58
Wordsworth, William, and Longfellow, 119 f.; *re* his income, 120n; and Ticknor, 133
Wright, Carroll D., 38n

Yankee, the, a stock character, 73 ff.
Yankee Drolleries, 86

Date Due